a voice arises that dares to resist such distortion, finding the courage to forge anew the link between faith and truth, love and the thirst for justice.

In this way, *Beatitudes and Terror* resists the triumphalist posture of modern Christianity, which often betrays fissures within its own values. Instead it points toward a Christianity that, while vulnerable and threatened, is nevertheless unbroken, marked by genuine vitality and the authenticity of lived experience. By placing the Beatitudes within the Ukrainian context, the authors contribute to the rich polyphony of biblical interpretation. For it is crucial to recognize that true worship and also the proclamation of the word of God are not confined to "here" or "there," but are possible in every place. This act itself enriches us with genuine polyphony and beauty.

I therefore warmly commend this book. Without a doubt, it will be of benefit to all: scholars, students, church leaders, and the wider public. Yet it is not a work for comfortable or casual reading; rather, it is a genuine journey, capable of deepening our encounter with the word of God.

Valeriy Sekisov, PhD
Academic Dean,
Ukrainian Evangelical Theological Seminary, Kyiv

What emerges when Scripture is read not in comfort but under fire? Nine Ukrainian evangelical theologians have allowed their hermeneutics to be refined by missiles and martyrdom, demonstrating courage in wrestling with Christ's most challenging teachings while war rages around them.

This work transcends academic exercise – it is living theology born from trauma, exile, and faith forged by fire. What strikes me most is their refusal to retreat into pietistic abstraction. Instead, they engage Scripture with the urgency of those for whom "blessed are the persecuted" represents not metaphor but lived reality. This book offers the global church both sobering witness and surprising hope, revealing how the Beatitudes retain their subversive power even in humanity's darkest hours.

Tatiana Kopaleishvili, PhD
Guest Assistant Professor,
Department Religious Studies and Missiology,
Evangelische Theologische Faculteit, Leuven, Belgium

The full-scale military aggression Russia foisted upon Ukraine in early 2022 shocked the world and has continued to decimate Ukraine's people, industry, infrastructure, churches, and countryside. In the face of such profligate evil and a bitter cauldron of conflict, the authors attempt to answer important questions such as: how can Christ's call for peace and love towards the enemy be reconciled with the necessity to defend your land and your neighbor? How can humanity and mercy be preserved when faced with inhuman cruelty? How can hope be found amid despair and destruction? This project seeks answers in Christ's Beatitudes, the high point of Jesus's kingdom ethics. With solid exegesis, insightful interaction with worldwide interpreters throughout the centuries, and contextual interpreters in the Ukrainian theological tradition, *Beatitudes and Terror* does its work in the context of the Russian-Ukrainian war, but the wisdom and applications that emerge will encourage and fortify followers of Jesus in challenges and conflicts worldwide.

Kirk Mackie, DMin
Mission Lead and CEO,
Aspire Network

This book speaks through our silence challenged by the violence of the present moment. Nine evangelical pastors, theologians, and devoted believers from Ukraine raise their voices with theological depth, hearts full of grief, love for Christ, and passion, asking how can one be Jesus-like amid terror.

Structured around the Beatitudes, the chapters offer a profound theological reflection on suffering – drawn not only from biblical explorations but also with many academic sources and from personal experience. They testify to God's presence; witnesses to the divine in the midst of war. This book is a must-read for everyone. It provides a powerful example of how to remain fervent in deep biblical exploration while engaging critically with political reality and its theological implications.

Julijana Mladenovska-Tešija, MTh
Lecturer,
Evangelical Theological Seminary, Osijek, Croatia

This book will leave you feeling enriched, inspired, enlightened, and challenged. In their meticulous exegesis and profound theological reflection, the editors and contributors demonstrate the highest standards of scholarship. However, the power of these chapters far transcends mere academic thinking; it derives from the contributors' raw personal experiences of encountering divine truth amidst their collective trauma, grief, and indignation in the face of the barbaric Russian invasion of Ukraine. The whole volume bristles with a prophetic pathos that lends a depth and integrity that I have rarely encountered in any other commentary on the Beatitudes. I wholeheartedly endorse this remarkable and compelling collection as a profound witness to the power of faith amidst suffering, and a reminder of the transformative hope at the heart of the gospel.

Joshua Searle, PhD
Co-Founder and Trustee,
Dnipro Hope Mission

This timely and profound book provokes reflection on realities that seem, at first glance, almost opposed and difficult to reconcile within ordinary experience. After all, the false dichotomy between the heavenly and the earthly, so deeply inherited by much of contemporary theological thought, only intensifies in times of crisis and upheaval. It is therefore of great significance when

Beatitudes and Terror

GLOBAL LIBRARY

Beatitudes and Terror

A Ukrainian Theological Response to Russian Aggression

Edited by
Oleksandr Geychenko, Roman Soloviy, and Yevgeny Ustinovich

© 2025 Eastern European Institute of Theology

First published in 2025 in Ukrainian by Дух і літера (Spirit and Letter) in collaboration with the Eastern European Institute of Theology, Ukraine. ISBN: 978-617-8445-40-9

Published 2025 by Langham Global Library
An imprint of Langham Publishing
www.langhampublishing.org

Langham Publishing and its imprints are a ministry of Langham Partnership

Langham Partnership
PO Box 296, Carlisle, Cumbria, CA3 9WZ, UK
www.langham.org

ISBNs:
978-1-78641-191-4 Print
978-1-78641-283-6 ePub
978-1-78641-284-3 PDF

All rights reserved. No part of this publication may be reproduced, stored in a retrieval system or transmitted, in any form or by any means, electronic, mechanical, photocopying, recording or otherwise, without the prior written permission of the publisher or the Copyright Licensing Agency.

Requests to reuse content from Langham Publishing are processed through PLSclear. Please visit www.plsclear.com to complete your request.

All Scripture quotations, unless otherwise indicated, are taken from the Holy Bible, New International Version®, NIV®. Copyright ©1973, 1978, 1984, 2011 by Biblica, Inc.™ Used by permission of Zondervan.

Scripture quotations marked (ESV) are taken from The Holy Bible, English Standard Version® (ESV®), copyright © 2001 by Crossway, a publishing ministry of Good News Publishers. Used by permission. All rights reserved.

Scripture quotations marked (NASB) are taken from the New American Standard Bible®, Copyright © 1960, 1962, 1963, 1968, 1971, 1972, 1973, 1975, 1977, 1995, 2020 by The Lockman Foundation. Used by permission.

Scripture quotations marked (NKJV) are taken from the New King James Version (NKJV). Copyright © 1982 by Thomas Nelson, Inc. Used by permission. All rights reserved.

British Library Cataloguing-in-Publication Data
A catalogue record for this book is available from the British Library

ISBN: 978-1-78641-191-4

Cover & Book Design: projectluz.com
Translated by Mykola Leliovskyi
Cover Illustration © Katerina Sad / full name SADOVSHCHUK KATERYNA

Langham Partnership actively supports theological dialogue and an author's right to publish but does not necessarily endorse the views and opinions set forth here or in works referenced within this publication, nor can we guarantee technical and grammatical correctness. Langham Partnership does not accept any responsibility or liability to persons or property as a consequence of the reading, use or interpretation of its published content.

Contents

Abstract xi

Foreword xiii

Introduction 1
Yevgeny Ustinovich

1 "Blessed are the poor in spirit, for theirs is the kingdom of heaven" (Matthew 5:3) 17
Eduard Borysov, Oleksandr Geychenko

2 "Blessed are those who mourn, for they will be comforted" (Matthew 5:4) 41
Sergiy Bermas

3 "Blessed are the meek, for they will inherit the earth" (Matthew 5:5) 71
Stanislav Stepanchenko

4 "Blessed are those who hunger and thirst for righteousness, for they will be filled" (Matthew 5:6) 91
Ivan Rusyn

5 "Blessed are the merciful, for they will be shown mercy" (Matthew 5:7) 121
Vitalii Stankevych

6 "Blessed are the pure in heart, for they will see God" (Matthew 5:8) 139
Fyodor Raichynets

7 "Blessed are the peacemakers, for they will be called children of God" (Matthew 5:9) 155
Taras Dyatlik

8 "Blessed are those who are persecuted because of righteousness" (Matthew 5:10–11) 185
Yevgeny Ustinovich

References 211

Contributors 223

Abstract

Throughout history, Scripture has demonstrated its enduring significance by addressing humanity's varied historical situations and social contexts. During times of significant struggle, believers request guidance in God's word, seeking prophetic answers for life's pressing questions. Moments of existential crisis – triggered by conflicts, shifts in cultural paradigms, or sociopolitical changes – necessitate fresh interpretations of established theological concepts and biblical exegesis. This volume unites Ukrainian evangelical theologians who explore Christ's Beatitudes as a source of spiritual and ethical guidance for Christians facing major upheavals, including revolutions, wars, and natural disasters. Why emphasize the Beatitudes? These teachings have been pivotal to Christian doctrine and practice for two thousand years, embodying a concentrated summary of Jesus's entire message. Historically, Christians have regarded the Beatitudes as a key to understanding Scripture, an ideal model for those spiritually rejuvenated through faith in Christ's life, death, and resurrection, and as essential virtues for nurturing personal spirituality and pursuing social engagement and justice.

Foreword

In the darkest hour of human history, the light of God's word shines the brightest. When established core values crumble, when war not only obliterates buildings, but also destroys human lives, both literally and figuratively, Christians turn to the timeless wisdom of the Scriptures in search of answers to burning questions.

Russia's full-scale military aggression against Ukraine, ongoing since February 2022, has been a horrific crucible for millions of Ukrainians and people around the world. It had raised many complex theological questions, each demanding serious consideration and deliberation. How can Christ's call for peace and love towards the enemy be reconciled with the necessity to defend your land and your neighbor? How can humanity and mercy be preserved when faced with inhuman cruelty? How can hope be found amid despair and destruction?

The book you're holding right now is an endeavor by eight Ukrainian evangelical theologians to revisit Jesus's Sermon on the Mount, particularly the Beatitudes, in light of present-day Ukrainian experience of Russia's military aggression. This book is more than academic research, although these authors follow the highest standard of biblical exegesis. It is a vibrant dialogue between the text written two millennia ago and realities in Ukraine in the twenty-first century.

Here, the authors don't offer oversimplified answers but rather invite the reader to join in the reflection, to come along on a spiritual journey through the pages of the Gospel, to rethink one's own understanding of Christian faith and its practical manifestation amid war, hardships, and trials. The authors lean into the exegetical tradition of interpreting the Beatitudes throughout various historical periods of the church. They also bring in Ukrainian literature, art, and heritage while highlighting reflections of the Gospel truth.

The authors devote significant consideration to the challenging aspects of understanding the Beatitudes in wartime. How to be a "peacemaker" if the enemy does not seek peace? What does it mean to "hunger and thirst for righteousness" if the propaganda distorts understanding of right and wrong? How to remain "pure in heart" amid gore and death? What does "meekness" look like when faced with the need to protect your homeland? These – and other questions are considered here in light of the Scriptures, theological traditions, and lived experience.

The editors would like to express their heartfelt appreciation to all who made this book possible. We would first like to thank Langham Publishing for supporting the editors' initiative. We are grateful to the authors – despite the enormous challenges of ministry in the context of war, they still found a way to undertake substantive theological research and present their findings in this book. Our literary editor and consultant, Lina Borodynska, deserves special thanks for her invaluable efforts to help the authors identify reflections of the Beatitudes in Ukrainian cultural works.

This book is dedicated to all Ukrainian Christians, who, at a time when hatred and violence threaten to destroy the very foundations of humanity, continue to remind us all about God's values that transcend all human considerations. Through their lives, testimony, and following Christ, each day they point to the Kingdom that "is not of this world" but is now springing up in our midst.

Oleksandr Geychenko
Roman Soloviy
Yevgeny Ustinovich

Introduction

Yevgeny Ustinovich

The majority of Ukrainians holding this book have experienced traumatic events. The authors of this collection also draw upon their own experiences of lives shattered by war, pandemic, and other disasters. The devastation endured by Ukraine – the worst since World War II – is frequently termed a "humanitarian crisis." One in four Ukrainians has been forced to leave their homes and become a refugee (or an internally displaced person). The violence inflicted upon Ukrainians in occupied territories largely goes unreported in the media, but when information about the abuse of civilians reaches journalists, these accounts are truly shocking.

Christians of all denominations (except the Russian Orthodox Church in Ukraine) often become targets of particularly brutal attacks, as the gospel fundamentally contradicts the ideology of the "Russian world," which, according to Timothy Snyder, is based on the false idea of a "chosen people" who supposedly purify the world through violence.[1]

In a series of academic and popular science publications, the authors attempt to draw attention to the suffering of Ukrainian Christians, but overall, what is currently occurring is persecution eclipse[2] – a situation where the persecution of the church takes place against the backdrop of a massive "humanitarian crisis."[3]

---

1. Timothy Snyder, "We Should Say it. Russia is Fascist," *New York Times*, May 19, 2022. https://www.nytimes.com/2022/05/19/opinion/russia-fascism-ukraine-putin.html?auth=login-google1tap&login=google1tap (accessed 11 February 2024).

2. Thomas Müller, Frans Veerman, and Matthew D. Rees, "Highlighting the Dark Corners of Persecution Using the Open Doors World Watch List as a basis," *IJRF* Vol 12:1/2 2019 (17–28).

3. A striking example is the latest report from an international organization that researches the persecution of Christians. According to the 2023 report, Ukraine was not even included in the list of countries where Christians are persecuted. The interactive map accompanying this list contributes to the impression that the situation with religious freedom in Ukraine (and even Russia) is better than in Mexico: https://www.opendoors.org/en-US/theadvocacyreport/ (accessed 11 February 2024). The war in Ukraine is mentioned only as a factor worsening the economic situation in some Third World countries.

For many evangelical Christians in Ukraine, an additional factor exacerbating their situation is the lack of a clear stance from Western church leaders. Some of them almost openly echo Russian propaganda slogans, allowing Russian narratives that blur the lines between aggressor and victim to gain a significant foothold even in conservative religious circles. Consequently, Western Christians are often inclined to perceive Ukraine as one of the "sides in the conflict," bearing its share of blame. We are deeply saddened to hear naive calls for concessions to the aggressor, but it is also worth noting that such an unrealistic position is based on a peculiar interpretation of biblical texts, particularly the Sermon on the Mount.

War and mass displacement are not the best times for "armchair theology," but it is precisely in such times that our theology begins to strive for maturity and a comprehensive worldview (if it survives at all). We begin to critically re-evaluate certain interpretations of Scripture that, until recently, seemed irrefutable and inviolable. The Sermon on the Mount (often cited by proponents of Ukraine's capitulation) concludes with the parable of the two builders. The house built by the wise person withstood the crisis, although the house did not escape it. We begin to compare different interpretations of well-known biblical passages and see that not all these interpretations are of equal value. Some of these interpretations help us endure our trials, while others only hinder us, becoming a real burden (Matt 23:4) – sand on which there is no sense to build.

In our interpretation, we are not limited to such pragmatic criteria alone; we also strive to find biblical foundations for the correct interpretation of the Sermon on the Mount and, in particular, the promises of the Beatitudes. Among all criteria, two are most important to us: correspondence to the historical context (the events against the backdrop of which Matthew wrote his Gospel) and correspondence to the literary context (that is, the rest of the Gospels, the rest of the New Testament, and the entire Holy Scripture as a unified text).

The Labyrinth of Reception

The history of the reception (perception and interpretation) of the Beatitudes contains numerous contradictions and attempts (not always successful) to overcome the conflict between popular but mutually incompatible interpretations. Rebekah Eklund, in her monograph, describes some of the main factors that have influenced the perception of these promises primarily in the Western world.[4]

While aiming to maintain an academic approach, Eklund herself largely refrains from judgments regarding the correctness or incorrectness of one interpretation or another. However, such impartiality is not always possible because the logic of the biblical context itself requires the reader to discern the difference between helpful and harmful examples of using Scripture.

Shortly before the Sermon on the Mount, Jesus overcomes temptations in the wilderness. One of these temptations is accompanied by a quotation from Scripture ("for it is written . . ." Matt 4:6). Matthew, the evangelist, demonstrates that biblical quotations taken out of context can be a tool of manipulation – a point confirmed in many subsequent chapters where Jesus's enemies attack him using Scripture (for example, 19:7).

Almost every religious community has its own history of misusing the Bible and, as a result, a set of the most popular biblical texts are used to justify certain pathological tendencies in church life. For example, among Russian Christians, one of the most beloved passages is Romans 13:1: "for there is no authority except that which God has established" – a quotation that supposedly demands absolute obedience to all the whims of secular authorities.

For Ukrainian churches, problematic passages often come from the Sermon on the Mount, particularly the commands to not resist evil and to love enemies (Matt 5:39–44). The problem lies not in the passages but in their unfounded interpretations, which can lead to irrational behavior. One of the best ways to prevent such errors is to strengthen the exegetical foundation. Then we can reject false interpretations not because we "dislike" them but because they contradict the teaching of Christ himself, which is revealed in other passages of Matthew's Gospel. We hope that the results of our research will have not only practical, pastoral value, but also a certain academic significance. We will attempt to show which interpretations of the Beatitudes have the greatest potential within the context of Matthew's Gospel itself.

The irony is that now, when Ukrainian churches have very limited opportunities for "armchair theology" (many church buildings and seminaries have effectively become refugee camps or humanitarian aid centers), we find ourselves in conditions that allow us to focus on the primary context of Matthew's Gospel because our lives are increasingly beginning to resemble the situation familiar to Matthew and his first readers.

---

4. Rebekah Eklund, *The Beatitudes through the Ages* (Grand Rapids: Eerdmans, 2021), Introduction (electronic book, no page numbers).

Matthew's Original Audience and Contemporary Ukraine

The disciples to whom Jesus speaks in the Gospel of Matthew will later experience persecution, torture, and psychological violence. "You will be handed over to the local councils and be flogged in the synagogues. . . . You will be hated by everyone because of me" (Matt 10:17–18, 22). "Then you will be handed over to be persecuted and put to death, and you will be hated by all nations because of me" (Matt 24:9). But Jesus is confident that all of them (except Judas Iscariot) will be able to endure these sufferings and even rejoice amidst all trials (Acts 5:40–41).

The first readers of this Gospel were also a persecuted, marginalized community, and their homeland was plunging into chaos that eventually led to a war of apocalyptic proportions (AD 66–70). As a result, Jerusalem and the Temple – the spiritual center of Israelite life – were completely destroyed, and most of the surviving Jews were scattered throughout the provinces of the Roman Empire. Matthew is not writing for some abstract audience but primarily for specific people traumatized by conflicts and persecutions. He does not offer advice for a successful religious life but describes the ministry and suffering of Jesus who left an example for his disciples.

Already, in one of the first episodes of this Gospel, the mass killing of children in Bethlehem is described. "A voice is heard in Ramah, weeping and great mourning, Rachel weeping for her children; and refusing to be comforted [παρακληθῆναι], because they are no more" (Matt 2:18). The attentive reader will remember, will continue to "hear" this weeping when they reach Jesus's words: "Blessed are those who mourn, for they shall be comforted [παρακληθήσονται]" (Matt 5:4). They will notice the tension, the conflict between this promise and the reality present in passages such as Matthew 9:24. This conflict will only be resolved in the final chapter, which describes the resurrection of Jesus.

What we hear and see during this war traumatizes us even more than we realize. Our lives will never be the same as before the war. But this traumatic experience also changes our perception of the Gospel, prompting us to reject superficial religious formulas and seek a deeper resolution to the conflict between God's promises and contemporary reality. Such a resolution is impossible without the suffering and resurrection of Christ.

Matthew also describes Joseph and Mary's flight with Jesus to Egypt. They do not even have time to prepare for this escape, everything happens suddenly, in the middle of the night (2:14). The evangelist mentions this to prepare his first readers for fleeing Jerusalem or other cities, which they will be forced to leave due to persecution or the threat of Roman legions. Similarly, thousands of Ukrainian parents have recapitulated this experience, leaving their homes in the middle of the night under shelling. Now they know what a mother feels when she sets off with her child to an unknown country without a return ticket.

Matthew describes many other kinds of suffering without which it is impossible to follow Christ. Like Jesus himself, the disciples will be rejected by the religious leaders of society. Such rejection can even occur within the family: "Brother will betray brother to death, and a father his child; children will rebel against their parents and have them put to death. You will be hated by everyone because of me, but the one who stands firm to the end will be saved" (Matt 10:21–22). "Do not suppose that I have come to bring peace to the earth. I did not come to bring peace, but a sword. For I have come to turn a man against his father, a daughter against her mother, a daughter-in-law against her mother-in-law – a man's enemies will be the members of his own household" (Matt 10:34–36).

Contemporary Ukrainians are discovering some of these aspects of biblical theology for themselves. Unfortunately, in many cases, relatives and colleagues poisoned by Russian propaganda provoke conflicts of an almost religious nature because the ideology of the "Russian world" is indeed a quasi-religious myth. Even when there are no internal conflicts in families and churches, division often occurs due to emigration or death.

Soldiers defending their country are separated from their loved ones not only physically. When soldiers return home to society, their traumatic experiences of war have created a wall of alienation between them and other people who cannot even cope with their own problems.

The alienation between those who have fought abroad and those who have stayed behind is also gradually increasing, and one of the main reasons for this alienation is summarized in Matthew 24:12 ESV, "And because lawlessness will be increased, the love of many will grow cold."

Matthew knows that some of his readers will be demoralized by persecution and conflict, and he knows how to help them survive this crisis. Like Jesus himself, the evangelist uses a paradoxical approach to teaching: to become victors, disciples must not avoid suffering but prepare for it in union with Jesus. All our exegetical studies offered in this collection have a practical purpose – to help contemporary readers navigate this time of trial.

Methodology

The authors have attempted to make this collection accessible to a relatively broad readership; therefore, the book contains almost no specialized discussions around the "technical" aspects of the text and its interpretation. Individual chapters employ different methods that best correspond to the intentions of the respective authors, their experiences, and church traditions. However, all these methods are, in one way or another, subordinate to a holistic approach to the Bible.

We explored answers to the question: "What does the Bible say about the Beatitudes?" We understood that different biblical authors and figures gave different answers to this question: in the era of king Solomon, when God's people enjoyed peace and tranquility, blessedness might have been perceived differently than in the time of John, who endured severe persecution for his faithfulness to the great descendant of Solomon (cf. 1 Kgs 10:8 and Rev 14:13). But within the context of the unified canon of Holy Scripture, all contradictions find resolution.

This approach, employed in biblical theology, differs from systematic theology. Our task was not to summarize everything said in the Bible on the topic of blessedness (such a task would have made the book dozens, if not hundreds, of times thicker). Instead, we focused on how the idea of blessedness was perceived by biblical authors and figures who lived in specific historical eras and under specific life circumstances.

Authors and their Chapters

Each of the eight chapters in this collection is dedicated to a separate beatitude. The authors have tried to interpret the biblical context of these promises objectively, but we all recognize that our own context cannot help but influence our perception of the text. Therefore, the interpretation of each beatitude is shaped by the interpreter's prior academic and ecclesiastical experience. In each chapter, one can trace a characteristic individual emphasis on certain aspects of the text that the author has sought to illuminate in the context of the challenges they have encountered in their own lives and in their own faith community amidst the physical and spiritual devastation of war.

In the first chapter ("Blessed are the poor in spirit"), the co-authors examine the history of the interpretation of the word "poor" in ancient texts, with a digression into the exegesis of the church fathers, and draw attention to the fact that some modern meanings of this word are in no way related to the biblical sense revealed by Matthew. They emphasize that the evangelist did not mean "poor" to be understood as "fainthearted and timid." On the contrary, true spiritual poverty cannot be separated from firm faith which gives strength even when it becomes obvious how futile hopes in anything other than God have been. And paradoxically, it is precisely the destruction of such illusions that prompts Ukrainian Christians to seek hope in God. "Hope in international institutions, which were supposed to prevent this war from starting, died first. Doubts about the ability to restore just peace through the efforts of political leaders are melting like dew in the sun. We very quickly realized that in these conditions, we have neither external nor internal resources to endure the horrors of war and overcome the catastrophic consequences to which it has already led," chapter authors Eduard Borysov and Oleksandr Geychenko write.

In the second chapter ("Blessed are those who mourn"), author Sergiy Bermas considers mourning within the context of the broader biblical narrative. He writes, "Thus, mourning not only becomes the state of the church but calls for mourning as a tradition and practice of prayer, calls for the practice of help and comfort." This call to mourning as a normal church practice is accompanied by a realistic assessment of the current situation. Ukrainian Christian communities generally have the necessary spiritual resources but some are only taking the first steps toward accepting our brokenness, toward an honest discussion on this topic. But it is precisely in this acceptance that the path to true peace lies.

The third chapter ("Blessed are the meek") examines the paradoxical nature of the promise to the meek. Jesus promises that the meek will inherit the earth. Over the past eleven years, we have seen a seemingly opposite pattern: the land is seized by aggressors who have no concept of what meekness is. This conflict – between what we see and what Jesus promises – has an eschatological dimension. It is a conflict between what is and what will be. The author draws upon a range of studies on the semantics of the Greek word translated as "meek." The study also has practical value in that it shows that the true "meekness" referred to in Matthew differs from the caricatured interpretations that are widespread in modern post-Christian society. Meekness is a spiritual strength that does not contradict justice but, on the contrary, contributes to its ultimate victory.

This theme continues in the fourth chapter ("Blessed are those who hunger"). As author Ivan Rusyn states, "We do not need to choose between righteousness and justice . . . we cannot separate righteousness from justice." Renouncing justice (something often expected of Ukrainian Christians in the context of war) does not make us righteous. It is precisely the pursuit of justice that is one of the signs of a Christ-centered life.

The fifth chapter ("Blessed are the merciful") contains an investigation into the topic of mercy – a concept around which much speculation occurs in religious and even secular circles. Is it appropriate to speak of justice during wartime? Yes, if there are clearly defined biblical concepts related to mercy. This chapter argues that mercy is one of the attributes of God himself, and Jesus's teaching on mercy develops this theme within the context of the entire Holy Scripture as a unified text. In other words, Jesus's words in the Sermon on the Mount cannot be understood without the Old Testament context. These observations are particularly significant at a time when appeals to "mercy" without a clear explanation of the meaning of this word are often used for manipulation.

The sixth chapter ("Blessed are the pure in heart") reveals the paradoxical connection between the heart and the ability to see – to see the suffering of God amidst the destruction that has become an almost daily backdrop to our lives. Author Fyodor Raichynets writes, "To see the invisible God in the visible world, in the visible person amidst evil, violence, and suffering . . . It is precisely in such times that there is a great need for people who can minister to those who have suffered, who have experienced loss and unspeakable pain. People of *pure heart*, by their presence and actions in the lives of the afflicted, make their suffering bearable and God's presence palpable" (emphasis original).

Taras Dyatlik, the author of the seventh chapter ("Blessed are the peacemakers") accompanies his research with personal memories and observations that contribute to the development of one of the main theses: the greatest obstacle to true peace is the imitation of peace. Superficial formulas are often used as tools of "appeasement." The author contrasts this simplistic and flawed notion with the concept of true biblical shalom which is not limited to religious clichés. "War has exposed the spiritual nature of conflicts. Confronting ideologies of dehumanization requires the church not only to engage in social ministry but also to have a prophetic voice and engage in spiritual warfare. The church must be a space where truth is not sacrificed for the sake of hasty 'reconciliation,' and where justice leads to true reconciliation."

The final chapter ("Blessed are those who are persecuted for righteousness' sake") attempts to place the religious persecutions in the occupied territories of Ukraine in the context of global trends of violence against Christians. This global context also has a diachronic dimension: the theme of the suffering of the righteous is revealed in all the books of Holy Scripture. Almost all periods of church history also contain testimonies of Christians who suffered persecution for their faithfulness to Jesus. It is to be expected that this trend will continue in our time.

The sufferings endured by Ukrainian Christians prompt us to critically re-evaluate our liturgical emphases. To summarize these changes in one phrase: we have begun to discover the Psalms and other lament texts that were previously on the periphery of "normal" church life. But the more we can identify with the biblical authors in their cries, the more the joy that is available even amidst suffering is revealed to us.

Persecution also becomes a challenge for contemporary ecclesiology: what can the church do to identify with Christians who are being persecuted? This topic has many practical, applied aspects but ultimately it is a question of identity.

These eight chapters reflect both the diversity of the authors, their ecclesiastical and academic traditions, and the unity we seek amidst all the chaos of recent years. We hope that readers will also find in this collection ideas and observations that will be helpful during their crisis. The next part of this introduction will describe the most promising direction for further independent study of the Beatitudes. Such a direction opens up when these promises are interpreted in the context of biblical wisdom literature. Next, we will briefly summarize some of the main features of this genre, to which the Sermon on the Mount also belongs to some extent.

The Beatitudes and Wisdom Literature

All of Holy Scripture – from the first page to the last – reveals God's wisdom to the attentive reader. But biblical scholars often distinguish certain texts (for example, Proverbs, Ecclesiastes, Job, as well as Psalms 1 and 37 among others) as wisdom literature – a separate part of the canon. This wisdom is often associated with king Solomon – one of its main and most successful representatives (1 Kgs 4:29–30). It is inextricably linked to God the Creator, who chose Israel and revealed his will to them. Such wisdom is based on God's law, and its precepts help one live according to God's will in a world where there is much sin and chaos. It promises blessedness to those who constantly meditate on God's law (Ps 1:1–3); this blessedness has both a physical, material dimension (the blessings of the covenant listed, for example, in Deut 28:1–14) and a psychological, spiritual one. Wisdom gives peace, a sense of security; it frees one from anxiety and other burdens associated with the consequences of sin.

Reading Old Testament wisdom literature provides an opportunity to imagine a life filled with truth, beauty, and justice: we live in a universe that has a clear moral structure. God rewards faithfulness and punishes lawlessness. But some readers (not only modern but also ancient) may perceive such a worldview as somewhat simplistic and naive. Do not the biblical wise men pay attention to cases where the righteous suffer and the wicked prosper?

Before answering this question, it is worth noting that a large part of the material contained in wisdom literature is didactic and educational in nature.

Most of Solomon's proverbs are addressed to his "son" (Prov 1:8). Wise parents and teachers practice the principle of "from simple to complex." They begin with rules and only when these rules are firmly learned do they move on to exceptions. In the context of the entire Bible, evil is considered not as an independent ontological category but rather as an exception – a corruption or absence of good. But it is precisely good that is a key concept in a world where God observes human behavior and rewards the righteous and the wicked. Such retribution is not always immediate, but patience, the ability to wait and observe, is also one of the virtues that the wise man tries to convey to the "son," and the author to his audience.

When the reader is sufficiently rooted in the precepts of the book of Proverbs, they can move on to Ecclesiastes. This book, of course, can also be studied as a separate text, but its modern criticism often leads to a superficial perception caused by insufficient attention to the problem of continuity and discontinuity. Those who see "cynicism" or "despair" in Ecclesiastes do not take into account that it is actually the "second volume" of Solomon's reflections. In the "first volume" (Proverbs), the wise man reveals the secret of blessedness (Prov 8:34) and shows how this blessedness extends to all spheres of life. In the "second volume," he draws attention to so-called liminal situations[5] associated with death and other factors of chaos, including injustice as a consequence of sin.

True wisdom recognizes its potential and its limitations. Solomon calmly considers situations where he does not have specific answers. Before the coming of Christ, who conquered death and broke the power of sin, the wise man can only give a few general pieces of advice, although these pieces of advice point in the right – eschatological – direction (Eccl 12:13–14). They give hope, although this hope is not yet as concrete and tangible (1 John 1:1) as in the New Testament.

The content of the book of Proverbs can be called "wisdom of the instructional level." The problem of the suffering of the righteous is mentioned (for example, in Proverbs 24:16) but does not become the subject of in-depth study. The transition to the "second level" – the level where the author deeply reflects on suffering and death – is characterized by both continuity and discontinuity.

---

5. Brant interprets liminality as a set of "psychological and social events characterized by ambiguity or indeterminacy. In these liminal states, individuals or groups no longer fit into the categories that define normalcy or social status" (Jo-Ann Brant, *John* [Grand Rapids: Baker Academics, 2011], 171). War, death, migration – all these events can be called liminal (from the Latin word *limen* – "threshold").

In the book of Job, this discontinuity appears as a real break. If Proverbs shows us a world of blessedness and harmony, Job opens the door for us to a world of catastrophe. From the first chapter of the book of Job, we know that the main character is righteous, and there can be no doubt about his righteousness, because it is confirmed by God himself (Job 1:8). But righteousness does not exempt Job from suffering: on the contrary, he is chosen by God for a terrible trial precisely because of his righteousness. His friends do not know this, so they constantly try to apply the rules of the "first level" of wisdom to this "second," catastrophic level. The gap between these two levels becomes obvious.

The Suffering and Blessedness of the Righteous

These observations may be relevant to the contemporary Ukrainian reality, where many people suffer precisely because of their righteousness, if righteousness is understood in a broad sense. This is how this word was understood outside of religious, cultic contexts in ancient societies. A soldier or a police officer who remained faithful to their oath could be called "righteous," for example. A doctor who, risking their life, continues to operate even when the windows in their office are shattered by artillery fire could be called "righteous." A conscript who decided to fulfill their duty instead of taking advantage of an effective but corrupt scheme to evade service could be called "righteous." A citizen who, remaining in the occupied territory, refuses to cooperate with the enemy could be called "righteous."[6]

All these manifestations of "righteousness" are associated with suffering. As the experience of Job's friends reveals, the application of "first level" wisdom in such situations must be very careful and measured. The friends provided Job with support when they simply sat with him and remained silent, but when they began to speak, their speeches only worsened the psychological state of the afflicted man. When we encounter manifestations of truly terrible suffering, our words have a very limited ability to help and a very great destructive power. In many cases, "second level wisdom" consists precisely in recognizing one's own limitations.

---

6. Such an interpretation of "righteousness" may not have purely religious, Protestant connotations ("righteousness through faith in Christ") but helps to illuminate certain applied aspects of biblical righteousness, which manifests itself in concrete deeds. Of course, we do not assert that good deeds can give a person the "righteousness" that leads to salvation; such imputed righteousness comes only by God's grace through faith. But neither should we narrow the meaning of the word "righteousness," that is, limit it only to soteriological aspects.

Job's catastrophe signifies a break with the wisdom of the level of Proverbs, but this break is not complete and final. Even in this terrible darkness, Job expresses hope in God:

> I know that my redeemer lives,
>   and that in the end he will stand on the earth.
> And after my skin has been destroyed,
>   yet in my flesh I will see God;
> I myself will see him
>   with my own eyes – I, and not another.
> How my heart yearns within me! (Job 19:25–27)

Long before the coming of Christ, Job understands that wisdom has an eschatological dimension. His hope in the Redeemer does not yet have the clear manifestations it has in the apostles, who saw the Redeemer with their own eyes. But even here we see manifestations of "third level" wisdom – the level at which the power of the resurrection operates. This level is impossible without the personal intervention of God. In the book of Job itself, the conflict between the "wisdom of order" and the "wisdom amidst chaos" is resolved through a theophany: God appears in the storm. The judgment that the righteous man so desired took place, although not at all as he expected.

God's judgment stops chaos and restores physical and moral order. It is through theophany and judgment that the transition from the "level of catastrophe" to the "level of restoration" occurs. This is a very important feature of Old Testament wisdom: the "first level" wisdom, the level of Proverbs, can order chaos. But when chaos reaches catastrophic proportions, it can no longer be overcome through gradual improvement. Higher wisdom is needed, which comes with the personal presence of God. This is the wisdom of the New Testament.

In the Gospel of Matthew, Jesus acts as a wise King "greater than Solomon" (Matt 12:42). His wisdom is associated with perfect righteousness, and, like the Old Testament Job, it is precisely through his righteousness that he finds himself in a catastrophic situation. Jesus endures terrible suffering, and to many of his contemporaries, even the disciples, it seemed that after the crucifixion his wisdom and righteousness were no longer relevant – the gap between the level of harmony and the level of chaos was too great (Luke 24:21).

They were partly right. The situation in which they found themselves after Jesus's death could not be significantly changed by human efforts. When we face a person who has lost their home, loved ones, and health, we cannot restore their shattered life with our words. On Good Friday, the disciples could have quoted Jesus's words to each other: "Blessed are those who mourn, for they will be comforted" (Matt 5:4). To some extent, they were already blessed, although, of course, they did not feel that blessedness. They would only be "comforted" on Easter Sunday. Jesus's promise was fulfilled through a special act of God – the resurrection from the dead. Through the resurrection of Jesus, the gap between the "first" and "second" levels of wisdom was eliminated, and now it is possible to speak of a holistic perception of blessedness in the context of the Bible. Blessedness helps us endure the catastrophic events of the current war and even experience (yes, this is an oxymoron) death itself, because true blessedness is inseparable from the resurrection of Christ and our own promised resurrection. As the apostle Paul reminds us, "If Christ has not been raised, your faith is futile . . . If only for this life we have hope in Christ, we are of all people most to be pitied" (1 Cor 15:17, 19). The promises of blessedness are absurd if a person does not have faith in the resurrection of Christ.

The paradox of Holy Scripture and the Christian life is that we cannot fully enjoy the triumph expressed in many Psalms and other biblical texts if there is no place in our liturgy for the psalms of lament and other biblical forms of expressing sorrow, despair, and anxiety. We cannot rejoice with James (Jas 1:2) if we do not know how to weep with David (Pss 6, 10, 38) and Job.

The promises of the Beatitudes can also belong to such texts: in a very concise form, they highlight the brokenness of this world and the painful experience of Christ's disciples: poverty, weeping, persecution – all this will be part of the path they follow Jesus on. Those who are not ready to accept such conditions cannot be his true followers, and the sooner they understand this, the better for themselves.

Defining Blessedness

Before moving on to the next question, let us briefly consider the problem of definition. How can blessedness be characterized? What specific signs of a blessed state can we observe or expect?

Biblical revelation does not contain a clear definition of "blessedness," but biblical teaching on this topic includes many specific aspects. Blessedness is the state of the heirs of the kingdom of heaven. To understand what Matthew and other biblical authors mean, it is best to begin with the eschatological aspect of the Beatitudes and then move on to the realization of this eschatology in history.

In the last book of the New Testament, where it is shown how all the ancient prophecies are fulfilled, the representatives of God's people celebrate the final victory over the forces of sin and death. They are already completely freed from all suffering and from their own darkness. "They will be his people, and God himself will be with them and be their God. 'He will wipe every tear from their eyes. There will be no more death' or mourning or crying or pain, for the old order of things has passed away" (Rev 21:3–4).

The absence of suffering, anxiety, the fullness of joy, and perfect freedom – blessedness includes all these components but is not limited to them. The saints receive all these gifts from God himself, and for them, what is important is not only that they, for example, will never again suffer from thirst (Rev 7:16), but that the Lord himself leads them to the springs of living water (Rev 7:17). They rejoice not only because they have eternal life but also because they have eternal life in the presence of God. These are people who have realized their purpose – to glorify God and eternally dwell in his presence (Ps 16:11).

In the context of the entire Holy Scripture, this eschatological picture is connected with the initial state of humanity described in Genesis 1:28: "God blessed them and said to them, 'Be fruitful and increase in number; fill the earth and subdue it. Rule over [it].'" Although Adam, because of his sin, lost dominion over the world, Christ, the New Adam, proclaims, "All authority in heaven and on earth has been given to me" (Matt 28:18).

Blessedness is possessing the world according to God's will. It is the ability to see how God finally establishes justice, and this divine judgment will also bring perfect comfort to those who mourn. They will finally inherit the earth, although now, in times of persecution, they are losing property, homeland, social status, and security.

From this perspective, blessedness is connected not so much with "life after death" as with what N. T. Wright called "life after life after death" – the eschatological reality of the resurrection of the body. In this state, the blessed will be able to see what Moses desired but could not see (Exod 33:20; Matt 5:8).

The anticipation of those eternal blessings can become a joyful experience even "here and now" as we draw closer to them. We learn to live according to our identity in Christ. The process of learning, of discipleship, is often called "spiritual growth." This term in itself is not problematic, but it can have false associations. Usually, "growth" means a gradual increase in specific indicators, and this applies to many of the skills needed for Christian life in peacetime. But in a period of liminality (war, grief, emigration, etc.), it is difficult to observe such gradual growth.

Some readers may confirm that they currently feel less peace and love in their lives than, for example, before the start of the full-scale invasion of the aggressors (24 February 2022), and more anger, despair, and doubt. Compared to the pre-war (or "pre-COVID-19") state, we seem to have lost many of God's blessings, and this gap is obvious. In this state, it is difficult to talk about "growth" compared to what was before. But we realize the continuity of our experience when we begin to perceive the "previous" life as a time of preparation for this crisis.

Following Christ means not only the gradual restoration of the disciple and their surroundings but also overcoming the crisis. To some extent, our entire life of faith can be seen as a series of different crisis situations, the last of which will be our physical death – a crisis that will also be overcome by new life in Jesus.

For Whom Are the Promises of Blessedness Intended?

The last question to address in this introduction concerns the original audience of the Beatitudes. Are they meant only for Jesus's disciples, or also for other people? A satisfactory answer to this question cannot be static: the Sermon on the Mount envisions several different groups of readers, between whom there is a complex, dynamic relationship. Jesus addresses the disciples, but he does so in the presence of a huge crowd, which consists of representatives from various strata of society – people who came "from Galilee and the Decapolis and Jerusalem and Judea and from beyond the Jordan" (Matt 4:25). Some of them (for example, the inhabitants of the Gentile Decapolis) had very primitive and erroneous ideas about the God of Israel, while others had a relatively deep knowledge of the Old Testament. Later, some of these people will also become followers of the Messiah. The disciples are situated between Christ and the world, and this position reflects the direction of their mission. They perform a priestly function when they pray for this world, and a prophetic function when they bring the words of Christ to this world.

The contemporary Ukrainian church, together with those of its members who are scattered far abroad, finds itself in just such a situation. We share the brokenness of this world with other people, we weep with those who weep (Rom 12:15), but we can also rejoice in our paradoxical faith. We have hope that our brokenness will be healed and the injustice of the current Russian aggression will be punished. This joy and hope, which come from Christ's resurrection, are an important element of our witness and ministry in this world.

Working on this interpretation has helped us to realize our own brokenness, which is actually greater than we expected. But we are also beginning to realize our own blessedness, although we may still be far from any striking manifestations of this state.

Our old life has already been destroyed, and no one even knows when the time of post-war reconstruction of the country will begin. We are going through a period of deep darkness, and most likely this darkness will only intensify for some time – we do not know how long, only that it is not forever. We reflect on the words of Jesus, as much as possible in our liminal state, and find a source of strength to worthily endure all the trials with him today, "here and now" – and he asks for nothing more (Matt 6:34).

1

"Blessed are the poor in spirit, for theirs is the kingdom of heaven"

(Matthew 5:3)

Eduard Borysov, Oleksandr Geychenko

Jesus's Sermon on the Mount has long captivated readers with its moral idealism while also instilling a sense of awe and challenge due to the seemingly unattainable demands it places upon the Lord's followers. The Beatitudes, often seen as the quintessence of the ethics of the kingdom of God, have astounded both religious leaders and secular philosophers. Yet, how do we understand the blessedness of the "poor in spirit" during times of war? Is this concept a utopian luxury, a spiritual resource neglected by Christians, a misunderstood virtue, a divine promise, a command of Christ, or a defining characteristic of the heirs to God's kingdom? In this chapter, we will attempt to address these questions from the perspective of an evangelical Christian and as a Ukrainian enduring the military aggression of the Russian Federation against Ukraine. We will begin with a hermeneutical analysis of the first beatitude, examining the Matthean account in comparison with the shorter Lukan version. This exploration will be followed by a historical survey of how Jesus's teaching on spiritual poverty has been received and interpreted over the centuries. Moreover, Ukrainian writers have engaged with this significant theme, offering contextualized interpretations that reflect the national experience. Finally, we will consider the relevance of the beatitude of the "poor in spirit" in the context of the current Russian-Ukrainian war, drawing on both biblical insights and historical precedents. We hope that this reevaluation will not only provide a fresh reading but also serve as an encouragement for believers in the Global South, who face similar challenges. Additionally, we hope our perspective will offer a thought-provoking challenge to those in the Global North, whose socio-cultural contexts may lead to different interpretations of the Gospel.

The Blessedness of the Poor in Spirit: A Biblical Perspective

Some biblical scholars draw parallels between the Gospel of Matthew and the Pentateuch of Moses, noting numerous similarities between these two texts. In particular, they argue that the Sermon on the Mount serves as a legal and ethical framework akin to the laws found in the Pentateuch. However, a key difference emerges when comparing the two: while Moses begins with decrees and laws, Jesus opens with the Beatitudes, offering blessings rather than commandments. Another significant distinction is found in the emphasis on blessings versus curses. In Deuteronomy 28, the list of curses significantly outnumbers the blessings.[1] Jesus, by contrast, does not include curses in his articulation of the new covenant with God's people. The "woes" that can be seen as parallels to the curses of the Mosaic covenant are directed at a different audience, specifically, the scribes and Pharisees (Matt 23:13–36). Despite the appeal of this comparison, it is important to recognize a key feature of the Mosaic law: the giving of the law follows an act of divine salvation. God rescues the Israelites from Egypt, enters into a covenantal relationship with them, and only then provides the laws that will govern their lives and serve as a testimony to the surrounding nations. In a similar way, the Beatitudes reflect the character of Jesus Christ as Savior, embodying the very qualities they describe: the poor in spirit, the meek, those who hunger for righteousness, the mourners, and others.[2] As Paul writes to the Corinthians, "For you know the grace of our Lord Jesus Christ, that though he was rich, yet for your sake he became poor, so that you by his poverty might become rich" (2 Cor 8:9). This highlights the Lord's gracious approach, that is, he blesses and helps before issuing any commands.[3] It is also important to clarify that the Beatitudes

---

1. Jack R. Lundbom, *Jesus' Sermon on the Mount: Mandating a Better Righteousness* (Minneapolis: Fortress, 2015), 94.

2. Joachim Jeremias, *The Sermon on the Mount* (Philadelphia: Fortress, 1963), 24.

3. Frederick Dale Bruner, *Matthew: A Commentary. Vol. 1: The Christbook. Matthew 1–12*, rev. and exp. ed. (Grand Rapids: Eerdmans, 2004), 157.

are not commandments or ethical requirements for salvation. Rather, they describe the blessedness of those who reflect the character of Christ and live in the reality of God's kingdom.[4]

Μακάριοι. Jesus begins his sermon with the Beatitudes, just as the first Psalm begins: "Blessed is the one who does not . . . sit in the company of mockers." The Greek term μακάριοι, which is most often translated as "blessed" or "happy,"[5] is a translation of the Hebrew אשרי (e.g. Ps 1:1; 2:12). This word in biblical texts refers to the state of a person in a relationship with God, despite negative feelings or lack of blissful emotions.[6]

Οἱ πτωχοὶ τῷ πνεύματι.[7] Jesus begins his teaching with a phrase that is both unexpected and countercultural. While modern readers may be more accustomed to the glorification of the "strong in spirit" or the "courageous in spirit," the notion of being "poor in spirit" stands in stark contrast. It can be reasonably assumed that even for a first-century Galilean, Jesus's proclamation of the blessedness of the "poor in spirit" would have been surprising. In that cultural context, blessedness was often associated with faithfulness to the Law of Moses, liberation from foreign occupation, and material prosperity. The term "poor" (עָנִי) in Hebrew, much like the Greek equivalent (πτωχός), refers not only to those who are materially destitute but also to those subjected to exploitation and oppression by the wealthy and powerful.[8] The term conveys a sense of humility and submissiveness, often brought about by social degradation.[9] The economically oppressed, especially the "poor in spirit," attract the

---

4. Michael J. Wilkins, *Matthew*, The NIV Application Commentary (Grand Rapids: Zondervan, 2004), 211.

5. Samuel Tobias Lachs, *A Rabbinic Commentary on the New Testament: The Gospels of Matthew, Mark, and Luke* (Hoboken: KTAV Publishing House, 1987), 70. Lahs insists on the translation "happy." Gerald Friedlander calculated that 37 sentences in the Old Testament begin with the word "blessed." The term ʾašrê is used 45 times, 27 of which appear in the Psalms. Unlike Jesus, David affirms a different reality: "Blessed is the one who cares for the poor" (Ps 41:2). Gerald Friedlander, *The Jewish Sources of the Sermon on the Mount* (London: Routledge, 1911), 17–18.

6. Wilkins, *Matthew*, 199.

7. According to Lachs, Luke simplified the Semitic idiom in his usual way, shortening the phrase "poor in spirit" to "poor" (Luke 6:20). Lachs, *A Rabbinic Commentary on the New Testament*, 70.

8. T. Muraoka, "Πτωχός," in *A Greek-English Lexicon of the Septuagint* (Louvain: Peeters, 2009), 607.

9. Francis Brown, S. R. Driver, and Charles A. Briggs, "עָנָה," in *The Enhanced Brown-Driver-Briggs Hebrew and English Lexicon: With an Appendix Containing the Biblical Aramaic* (Oxford: Clarendon, 1951), 1867–69. Gordon Zerbe notes that the hymns of thanksgiving of the Qumranites (*Hadayot*) trace the idea of the psalms that the oppressed in spirit are purified by suffering, and that God will raise those trampled in the mud from the ruins (1QHa 13.21–22).

special attention of God, who is depicted as a divine protector and advocate for the disadvantaged. As seen in 1 Samuel 2:8: "He raises the poor from the dust and lifts the needy from the ash heap; He seats them with princes and has them inherit a throne of honor." Similarly, in Psalm 12:5, God responds to the plight of the oppressed: "Because of the oppression of the weak and the groaning of the needy, I will now arise," says the Lord. "I will protect them from those who malign them" (see also Ps 9:19; 40:18; 72:2). God's promise to care for and defend the rights of the poor serves as a foundational source of hope and security for the marginalized. This divine commitment is underscored in texts like Psalm 14:6 ESV, which declares, "You would shame the plans of the poor, but the LORD is his refuge," as well as in Psalms 72:12 and 109:31, and Isaiah 25:4.

Poverty, in itself, is not a virtue, nor is being poor a desirable condition in Jewish or any other society. Poverty is typically associated with various forms of suffering and social marginalization. It limits individuals, pushing them to the fringes of society. Moreover, asceticism was not upheld as the ideal of righteousness in the Old Testament. Traditional Jewish wisdom linked happiness with prosperity – health, wealth, and success were seen as signs of divine favor. Therefore, Jesus's proclamation that the "poor in spirit" are blessed challenges the common Jewish understanding of God's blessing, and his words would have shocked his audience by questioning the established norms. In the biblical tradition, the material impoverishment of certain groups was viewed as symptomatic of broader systemic issues within society, such as a lack of generosity toward the needy, the denial of fair wages and justice, contempt for the poor and weak, extortion, treachery, and even the murder of the defenseless (Deut 15:7-8; Ps 82:3-4; Amos 2:6-8; Jer 2:34; Ezek 22:29). In Ezekiel, the sin of Sodom is explicitly connected to its indifference to the poor and its cultivation of attitudes antithetical to the "poverty of spirit," such as pride and excess (Ezek 16:49).

Isaiah foretold that when the Messiah comes, he will judge the poor with righteousness (Isa 11:4). Furthermore, the Servant of the Lord is anointed to "bring good news to the poor . . . to bind up the brokenhearted . . . to comfort all who mourn . . . to bestow on those who mourn in Zion a crown of beauty instead of ashes, the oil of joy instead of mourning, and a garment of praise

---

The author writes: ". . . the elect person or group as 'poor' in its textual context refers concretely to the experience of persecution or oppression, not merely to spiritual poverty." Gordon M. Zerbe, "Economic Justice and Nonretaliation in the Dead Sea Scrolls: Implications for the New Testament Interpretation," in *The Bible and the Dead Sea Scrolls: The Scrolls and Christian Origins*, ed. James H. Charlesworth, vol. 3 (Waco: Baylor University Press, 2006), 335–36.

instead of a spirit of despair" (Isa 61:1–3).[10] The evangelist Luke records that Jesus applied these messianic words to himself in the synagogue of Nazareth (Luke 4:18). Those whose lives were marked by tears, misery, and suffering were now hearing "good news" from the mouth of the Lord's Servant. This message was about the restoration of justice and retribution for the oppressed. Matthew, on the other hand, places these themes within the context of Jesus's response to the disciples of the imprisoned John the Baptist, who inquired whether the expected Messiah had indeed come, or if they should wait for another (Matt 11:5).[11] Jesus points to his works as the signs of the dawning messianic age, subtly indicating that he himself is the fulfillment of these prophecies. Thus, Jesus Christ's concern for the poor mirrors the care and protection extended by the Lord to the marginalized in the Old Testament.

Mark Powell observes that, in the context of Jesus's mission to reach all nations (Matt 12:18, 21) and not exclusively Israel, the term "the poor" should be understood not merely as a social class within Israel, but as encompassing "the dispossessed and abandoned people of the world in general."[12] This perspective indicates that the Lord does not bless those who are self-sufficient and spiritually affluent, even if they are economically impoverished, but rather those who are spiritually impoverished due to their economic circumstances. According to Powell, this beatitude represents a joyous reversal for individuals who find themselves without hope and on the brink of admitting defeat and despair. The imminent reign of heaven promises a transformative change for their hopeless situation.[13] Conversely, this approaching kingdom necessitates that the powerful and wealthy reassess their priorities in favor of "one of these little ones" (Matt 18:10). Such a reevaluation requires a genuine repentance, a

---

10. A similar activity of God's "servant" is described in a hymn from the Essene collection: ("to proclaim to the poor (לבשרענוים) the abundance of your compassion," leading to deliverance "[the bro]ken of spirit, and the mourning to everlasting joy" (1QHª 23 [top] 1.10, 14–15, see also 4Q521 frag. 2 2.6, 12). Zerbe, "Economic Justice and Nonretaliation in the Dead Sea Scrolls," 336. Schubert believes that the Essene community called themselves "the poor" (*ebionim*) because they had common property and contempt for money was their main principle. That is why Jesus's listeners in the first beatitude could hear the familiar call of the essays to poverty. Kurt Schubert, "The Sermon on the Mount and the Qumran Texts," in *The Scrolls and the New Testament*, ed. Krister Stendahl (New York: Harper & Brothers, 1957), 122. See also D. Flusser, "Blessed Are the Poor in Spirit . . .," *Israel Exploration Journal* 10, no. 1 (1960): 5.

11. It is worth noting that in the following verse 6 Jesus uses the word μακάριος, although it characterizes a person who is not tempted on account of him, which is not one of the beatitudes in the Sermon on the Mount.

12. Mark Allan Powell, "Matthew's Beatitudes: Reversals and Rewards of the Kingdom," *The Catholic Biblical Quarterly* 58, no. 3 (July 1996): 464.

13. Powell, "Matthew's Beatitudes," 465.

profound turnaround in light of the impending eschatological reign of God. This shift is critical, as it underscores the biblical principle that "where your treasure is, there your heart will be also" (Matt 6:21).

In contrast to Luke, Matthew's version of this beatitude emphasizes spiritual poverty (τῷ πνεύματι)[14] rather than material poverty. While Matthew does not dismiss the material aspect, he introduces an essential distinction: spiritual poverty. This raises the question of how these elements relate to one another. For example, Clement of Alexandria says this, "And 'blessed are the poor,' whether 'in spirit' or in circumstances – that is, if for righteousness' sake. It is not the poor simply, but those who have been willing to become poor for righteousness' sake, that he proclaims blessed – those who have despised the honors of this world in order to attain 'the good.'"[15] Therefore, the pursuit of poverty is not an end in itself. One can easily envision a materially poor individual who is also proud and embittered, blaming both people and God for their circumstances. Thus, material poverty alone cannot be the foundation for the blessedness that Jesus proclaims. Instead, poverty of spirit fosters an acknowledgment of one's own shortcomings and a recognition of the need for others.[16] John Stott argues that this recognition leads to a dependence on God, which he refers to as spiritual poverty or "spiritual bankruptcy."[17] Spiritual self-sufficiency and this beatitude are fundamentally incompatible since true blessedness emerges from the orientation toward God and a complete trust in him. If a person is spiritually self-sufficient, they find no need for others – whether for fellow humans or for God.

The feeling of absolute satisfaction does not directly stem from the state of spiritual poverty; thus, it encompasses more than mere emotions. The phrase "poor in spirit" is notably absent in the Old Testament, rabbinic literature, and the New Testament itself.[18] The closest parallels can be found in Psalm 34:18:

---

14. In this case, the dative of the sphere ("in the sphere of the spirit") conveys the idea of the adverb "spiritually poor." Daniel B. Wallace, *Greek Grammar beyond the Basics: An Exegetical Syntax of the New Testament* (Grand Rapids: Zondervan, 2012), 155.

15. Clement of Alexandria, "Stromata," 4.6 in *Writings of Clement of Alexandria*, vol. 1 (ANF, 2:413).

16. Lachs adds that poverty prompts a Jew to repentance and "can be instructive, challenging, and sobering as a test of character." Lachs, *A Rabbinic Commentary on the New Testament*, 71.

17. John R. W. Stott, *Christian Counter-Culture: The Message of the Sermon on the Mount (Matthew 5–7)*, The Bible Speaks Today (Downers Grove: InterVarsity Press, 1978), 39.

18. Hans Dieter Betz, *The Sermon on the Mount: A Commentary on the Sermon on the Mount, Including the Sermon on the Plain (Matthew 5:3–7:27 and Luke 6:20–49)*, ed. Adela Yarbro Collins, Hermeneia – A Critical and Historical Commentary on the Bible (Minneapolis: Fortress, 1995), 111–12. Researchers of the Dead Sea Scrolls find references to "humble spirits" or "poor spirits" in 1QM 14:7 (the "Scroll of War"). Jean Duhaime, "War Scroll," in *The Dead*

"The LORD is close to the brokenhearted and saves those who are crushed in spirit," and Psalm 51:17: "My sacrifice, O God, is a broken spirit; a broken and contrite heart you, God, will not despise." Additionally, king David declares, "But as for me, I am poor and needy; may the LORD think of me. You are my help and my deliverer; you are my God, do not delay" (Ps 40:17). In the concluding chapter of Isaiah, the Lord proclaims, "These are the ones I look on with favor: those who are humble and contrite in spirit, and who tremble at my word" (Isa 66:2).[19] It is this state of spiritual poverty – where a person relies solely on God's mercy and is open to receiving help – that serves as a prerequisite for the subsequent aspects of blessedness.

The phrase ὅτι αὐτῶν ἐστιν ἡ βασιλεία τῶν οὐρανῶν reflects the great reversal within the heavenly kingdom: the brokenhearted find happiness, the hungry are satisfied, the weak are strengthened, the poor become rich, the lowly are exalted, and the childless are given descendants (1 Sam 2:4–8; cf. Luke 1:51–53). The term "kingdom of heaven" is a Semitic expression used as a reverent substitute for "kingdom of God." By using "heaven," Jews sought to protect the sanctity of God's name, ensuring it was not taken in vain (Exod 20:7).[20] For Luke, this concern is less pressing, as he freely uses the phrase "kingdom of God" (ἡ 3βασιλεία τοῦ θεοῦ) (Luke 6:20), addressing a Greek-speaking audience that would not share the same sensitivity regarding the divine name. Despite this difference in terminology, both Matthew and Luke refer to the same reality, the kingdom of God. In this context, Jesus likely emphasizes the meaning of God's "rule" or "reign" rather than a geographical territory with defined borders. As Psalm 103:19 states, "The LORD has established his throne in heaven, and his kingdom rules over all." Although this text introduces a spatial dimension, "in the heavens" and "over all," the focus remains on dominion, not territory. The spatial metaphors underscore the vast scope of God's authority. In the Gospel of Matthew, the theme of the kingdom of God is central, recurring throughout

---

Sea Scrolls: Hebrew, Aramaic, and Greek Texts with English Translations. Vol. 2, *Damascus Document, War Scroll, and Related Documents*, ed. James H. Charlesworth and James H. Baumgarten, Princeton Theological Seminary Dead Sea Scrolls Project (Tübingen: Mohr Siebeck, 1995), 124–25. Similarly, 1QS 3.7–9 states that a Qumranite can receive atonement for sin in the water of purification provided he has "an upright and humble spirit." James H. Charlesworth, ed., *The Bible and the Dead Sea Scrolls: The Scrolls and Christian Origins*, vol. 3 (Waco: Baylor University Press, 2006), 8.

19. Gerald Friedlander also points out Isa 11:4 and 57:15 in connection with a "broken spirit." Friedlander, *The Jewish Sources of the Sermon on the Mount*, 19.

20. Joachim Jeremias, *New Testament Theology: The Proclamation of Jesus* (New York: Charles Scribner's Sons, 1971), 9.

Jesus's ministry and frequently mentioned in his teachings and parables (Matt 4:23; 9:35; 13:11; 24:14).

The blessedness of the poor in spirit is that the kingdom of heaven belongs to them, emphasizing its eschatological dimension. However, God's rule is not confined to heaven alone. The prophet Zechariah expressed this hope of the Lord's reign: "And the LORD will be king over all the earth. On that day the LORD will be one and his name one" (Zech 14:9 ESV). Similarly, Daniel highlights that the "Son of Man" and God's people will be entrusted with the eternal power of the Almighty (Dan 2:44; 7:13–14, 18). Jesus offers comfort to the poor in spirit by pointing to the hope of their blessed reign in God's kingdom, as foretold in Daniel's prophecy. However, this does not imply that their blessedness is deferred to an indefinite future, when "the kingdom of the world has become the kingdom of our Lord and of his Christ" (Rev 11:15 ESV). Rather, the kingdom of heaven is at hand – it is present here and now – and those who are open to its message have already entered into it. The significance of this proclamation is so profound that it demands an immediate response; it is not something one can hear and remain passive. The kingdom of God is manifested in this urgent call to decision. Yet, while both John the Baptist and Jesus proclaimed the imminent arrival of the kingdom of God, its full manifestation remains a future hope (Matt 3:2; 4:17). Therefore, the blessedness of the poor in spirit, as heirs of this kingdom, possesses both a present reality and a future eschatological fulfillment. John Stott aptly summarizes this idea, noting that it was not the Pharisees or Zealots – relying on their own piety or military strength – who entered the kingdom, but tax collectors and prostitutes who had nothing to offer: "The kingdom is given to the poor, not the rich; to the feeble, not the mighty; to little children humble enough to accept it, not to soldiers who boast that they can obtain it by their own might."[21] In the kingdom of God, those who are last shall be first.

Thus, the blessedness of the poor in spirit encompasses several central themes of the biblical tradition: God's concern for the disadvantaged and those denied social justice, the perilous relationship between material wealth and pride, the importance of complete dependence on God, and, ultimately, the anticipation of the restoration of a just order with the coming of the kingdom of God. These themes form the core of this beatitude. How has the blessedness

---

21. Stott, *Christian Counter-Culture*, 40. The church in Laodicea became an illustrative example of true spiritual poverty, when, despite moral degradation, it considered itself exemplary and self-sufficient (Rev 3:17).

of the poor in spirit been understood throughout the history of Christian scriptural interpretation? This question will be explored in the following section.

The Beatitudes of the Poor in Spirit: A History of Interpretation

French bishop Jacques-Bénigne Bossuet (1627–1704) famously remarked, "If the Sermon on the Mount is the précis of all Christian doctrine, the eight beatitudes are the précis of the whole of the Sermon on the Mount."[22] It is therefore unsurprising that this text has garnered extensive attention from theologians and clergy, sparking intense debate among interpreters throughout the history of the church. Interpretive approaches to the Beatitudes have undoubtedly been shaped by the distinct developments within church tradition at various stages of its history, the dominant philosophical frameworks, and the specific theological questions arising from particular historical and cultural contexts. While certain motifs have remained constant, they have been understood and emphasized in distinct ways depending on the period.

Among the church fathers, a symbolic interpretation of the blessedness of the "poor in spirit" predominated, since they understood it primarily as a spiritual virtue. This interpretation was rooted in their Christological perspectives and held significant practical relevance for personal formation and character development. Most associated this virtue with humility and meekness (cf. Isa 66:2). Jerome (347–420), for instance, understood this phrase as referring to "humility in the spirit" (Ps 34:19), rather than material poverty. He saw it as a voluntary state brought about under the influence of the Holy Spirit.[23] Similarly, Gregory of Nyssa (c. 335–394), Augustine of Hippo (354–430), and much later Charles Spurgeon (1834–1892) regarded the Beatitudes as steps leading toward this condition.[24] Augustine contrasted the poor in spirit – those who are God-fearing and not arrogant – with the proud, who seek earthly kingdoms.[25] For him, the state of spiritual poverty marked the starting point on the path to true blessedness.[26]

---

22. Ian Boxall, *Matthew Through the Centuries* (Oxford: Wiley-Blackwell, 2018), 111.

23. St. Jerome, *Commentary on Matthew*, The Fathers of the Church, 117 (Washington, DC: Catholic University of America Press, 2008), 75.

24. Boxall, *Matthew Through the Centuries*, 111–12. Cf. St. Nicholas of Serbia, *Interpretation of the Beatitudes* (Christian Life, 2011), 3–6.

25. St. Augustine, *Commentary on the Lord's Sermon on the Mount with Seventeen Related Sermons*, The Fathers of the Church, 11 (Washington, DC: Catholic University of America Press, 2001), 21–22.

26. Boxall, *Matthew Through the Centuries*, 112.

A perspective similar to Augustine's is found in the writings of Orthodox Bishop Nicholas of Serbia (1880–1956), who viewed the Beatitudes as ascending levels in a pyramid of spiritual growth. He considered the blessedness of the poor in spirit to be the foundational and primary step on the path to perfection.[27] For Nicholas, spiritual poverty is a condition inherent in humans due to their frail nature: "The realization of one's weakness and the understanding of one's complete insignificance is called poverty of spirit."[28] The challenge, he argued, is that not everyone recognizes this limitation, and only such awareness marks the beginning of the journey toward complete trust in God. Spiritual poverty is opposed by spiritual pride, which Nicholas refers to as "the mother of all follies and all evil deeds of men."[29] In contrast, spiritual brokenness and humility form "the foundation of all good deeds, the basis of the spiritual life of every Christian, the foundation of the pyramid of heaven."[30] It is in this humble state that a person becomes a vessel for the Holy Spirit's transformative work, building what Nicholas calls the "pyramid of heaven."[31]

John Chrysostom (c. 344–407), in his sermon on the Gospel of Matthew, interpreted the phrase "poor in spirit" as referring to those who are "The humble and contrite in mind."[32] This humility is not a condition imposed by external circumstances but a voluntary act of submission. It is not a moderate form of humility but the profound humility of a person broken before God (Ps 51:19). Chrysostom contrasted the prideful ambitions of figures such as the devil, Adam, the Pharisee, and even well-meaning believers who sought to ascend to heaven in their own eyes, with the true blessedness found in the humble posture of a beggar, a stranger, or an ignoramus.

Gregory of Nyssa, reflecting on this beatitude, argued that it signifies voluntary poverty in relation to all forms of wickedness and the devilish treasures of the heart, especially pride. The blessed person, according to Gregory, possesses a fervent desire to imitate God's nature as much as possible within human limitations, becoming poor in their own will, just as Jesus Christ did (2 Cor 8:9). Gregory asks, what greater impoverishment could there be for the king of creation than to take on the form of a servant in human nature? (Phil 2:5–7). The Lord begins the Sermon on the Mount with this beatitude,

---

27. Nicholas of Serbia, *The Interpretation of the Beatitudes*, 7–11.
28. Nicholas of Serbia, *The Interpretation of the Beatitudes*, 9.
29. Nicholas of Serbia, *The Interpretation of the Beatitudes*, 9.
30. Nicholas of Serbia, *The Interpretation of the Beatitudes*, 10.
31. Nicholas of Serbia, *Interpretation of the the Beatitudes*, 10–11.
32. John Chrysostom, *Homilies on the Gospel of St. Matthew* (*NPNF* 10:211–12).

Gregory suggests, because it strikes at the root of evil: pride. He also sees a material dimension to this "impoverishment for the sake of the spirit,"[33] where one leaves behind material burdens to gain a lightness of virtue that elevates the soul.[34]

The motif of spiritual poverty as a virtue reaches its logical conclusion in the thought of Martin Luther (1483–1546). Luther understood spiritual poverty primarily as an individual characteristic, largely independent of external circumstances. This perspective aligns with his conceptual framework of the two kingdoms – the secular and the spiritual. In Luther's view, even an individual of considerable wealth could embody a state of spiritual poverty.[35] In contrast, contemporary scholars increasingly emphasize the inseparable connection between the material and eschatological dimensions of the kingdom of God. They argue that this connection significantly influences existential choices and socially responsible decision-making.

In his interpretation of the Gospel of Matthew, Edward Schweitzer (1913–2006) explains that in Jesus's time the word "poor" was never used figuratively, in isolation from social class.[36] In Judaism of the time, it was an honorific title that characterized the righteous, "because it was an important mark of righteousness and devotion to accept in faith the difficult way of God and not resist."[37] Therefore, according to Schweitzer, by "poor in spirit" Matthew "has in mind people whose outward circumstances force them to look to God for everything, but who also receive from God the gift of the spirit (faith) to look to him for everything."[38] Thus, we see that the image of the "poor in spirit" is interpreted holistically, combining the social status, the inner attitude of a person, and a person's attitude toward God.

An additional significant aspect that remained somewhat obscured during the era of the church fathers is the rule of God and his actions aimed at restoring justice. As Albert Schweitzer notes, "Jesus's original promise is addressed simply to the 'poor.' Any suggestion that a man must first do something is avoided. Salvation is promised to all the poor, not just to those who are aware of their condition or accept it humbly. God is on the side of all of them, taking

---

33. St. Gregory of Nyssa, *The Lord's Prayer. The Beatitudes*, Ancient Christian Writers, 18 (Westminster: The Newman Press, 1954), 89.

34. St. Gregory of Nyssa, 95.

35. Boxall, *Matthew Through the Centuries*, 114.

36. Eduard Schweizer, *The Good News According to Matthew* (Atlanta: John Knox, 1975), 86.

37. Schweizer, *The Good News According to Matthew*, 87.

38. Schweizer, *The Good News According to Matthew*, 87.

the part of the wretched just as the judges of the Old Testament did. They are all under the king's protection and are the objects of his mercy because it is God's royal prerogative to uphold the powerless."[39] This assertion is crucial, as it recontextualizes the Beatitudes within the framework of the prophetic hope of the Old Testament – a hope for God's intervention in the existing order and its transformation according to divine truth. Moreover, it underscores the imperative of social justice, which has often been marginalized in discussions of early Christian thought. In this interpretation, the Beatitudes are directed toward those who have embraced the message of the kingdom of God and, consequently, have received the promise of the transformative changes that the kingdom entails.

Another notable figure is Catholic theologian and social activist Michael Crosby (1940–2017), who seeks to transcend the dualistic notion that material wealth and spiritual poverty can coexist within a single individual.[40] In his work on spirituality, Crosby addresses Western Christians, emphasizing that the values promoted by modern consumer culture are in stark contrast to the teachings of Jesus in the Sermon on the Mount and the Gospel of Matthew. For instance, Matthew recounts the story of a rich young man who sought perfection but ultimately hesitated to part with his possessions, leaving Jesus's presence in sorrow (Matt 19:16–22). Jesus further astounds his disciples by stating, "It is easier for a camel to go through the eye of a needle than for a rich person to enter the kingdom of God" (Matt 19:24 ESV). In this context, Crosby warns of the peril of serving mammon and becoming ensnared by the spirit of consumerism.

At the same time, Crosby critiques the prevailing notion that earthly poverty is compensated by bliss in the age to come.[41] He contends that such assertions legitimize social injustice and encourage materially impoverished individuals to accept their circumstances, despite this being contrary to Jesus's teachings. He argues, "poverty is a curse and a scandal if it remains unrelated to a way of bringing about the plan of God and submitting the whole world to this new authority."[42] According to Crosby, poverty is acceptable only when it results from a voluntary renunciation of material goods aimed at advancing

---

39. Schweizer, *The Good News According to Matthew*, 87.

40. Michael Crosby, *Spirituality of the Beatitudes: Matthew's Challenge for First World Christians* (Maryknoll: Orbis, 1981), 49–52.

41. Crosby, *Spirituality of the Beatitudes*, 49.

42. Crosby, *Spirituality of the Beatitudes*, 56.

the kingdom of God, as exemplified by Jesus.[43] In all other instances, the existence of material poverty signifies a reality that contradicts the will of God.[44] He emphasizes that "Matthew presents at the core of his spirituality a God who lacks nothing. Every person has been made to portray this divine nature. Thus, to lack anything essential to life denies that image of God. Poverty is simply not good. It is ungodly."[45] In the earlier section examining the Beatitudes within the biblical tradition, it was noted that God actively opposes social injustice and the usurpation of power by the affluent, which often drives the vulnerable into poverty. Through the prophets, God pronounced judgment upon those who deprive individuals of their livelihoods. The Gospel of Matthew adheres to this tradition and maintains a strong emphasis on the social dimension of the good news.

However, the emphasis on the material component is not always persuasive. For instance, Catholic scholar Jerome Neyrey, in his effort to interpret the Beatitudes through the lens of the cultural code of honor and shame, goes so far as to completely overlook Matthew's reference to the "poor in spirit."[46] Neyrey focuses solely on Luke's version of this beatitude: "Blessed are you who are poor, for yours is the kingdom of God" (Luke 6:20).[47] While his interpretation is informative and provides valuable insight into the socio-cultural context of the first century, it ignores Matthew's unique emphasis on the blessedness of the poor in spirit. This seems like a notable oversight.

The church's interpretation of the Beatitudes unfolded within the framework of the biblical tradition, maintaining a focus on the central themes associated with the beatitude of the poor in spirit. Interpreting the Beatitudes through the lens of virtue introduced a new dimension that the biblical authors did not emphasize. In the twentieth century, themes of social justice, the eschatological dimensions of the kingdom of God, and the ethical and existential decisions arising from these themes emerged with renewed significance. Consequently, the Beatitudes transitioned from the realm of personal spirituality to that of community and social life. Unsurprisingly, the Beatitudes became not only the essence of church tradition and Christian spirituality but also an integral part of culture, particularly within the Ukrainian context. In the following sections

---

43. Crosby, *Spirituality of the Beatitudes*, 56.
44. Crosby, *Spirituality of the Beatitudes*, 49.
45. Crosby, *Spirituality of the Beatitudes*, 52.
46. See Jerome H. Neyrey and Eric Clark Stewart, eds. *The Social World of the New Testament: Insights and Models* (Peabody: Hendrickson, 2008).
47. Jerome H. Neyrey, *Honor and Shame in the Gospel of Matthew* (Louisville: Westminster John Knox, 1998), 164–73.

we will explore how the themes of bliss and poverty have been reflected in Ukrainian literary tradition.

Poverty and Blessedness in the Ukrainian Literary Tradition

The beginning of Ukrainian writing and literary tradition, in particular, is closely linked to the Christianization of Kievan Rus (tenth to eleventh centuries) and the subsequent development of Christian culture in the Galician-Volyn principality (twelfth to fourteenth centuries) and the later Hetmanate (seventeenth to eighteenth centuries). It is not surprising then that biblical themes have always been on the minds of Ukrainian writers and thinkers. It is noteworthy, however, that through the processes of interaction, reception, and comprehension, the biblical motifs were not retained in their original form, but rather acquired new emphases and nuances.

In his article "Poverty as a Cynic Gesture: The Ukrainian Version," literary scholar Leonid Ushkalov provides an insightful overview of attitudes toward material wealth and voluntary poverty in the works of Ukrainian writers, poets, and philosophers.[48] Ushkalov emphasizes that both in ancient times and today, there are those who glorify wealth and denigrate poverty, as well as those who aspire to the virtue of poverty. An example of the former is the monk Klymentii Zynoviyiv (eighteenth century, ca. 1717), who wrote the following in *On Poor People*, "O woe to the poor people of the world, / for they cannot have the fullness of joy." This statement reflects a harsh reality: it is challenging to experience complete happiness when one lacks the most essential necessities.

A little later, the writer Ivan Karpenko-Karyi (1845–1907), in his comedy *One Hundred Thousand*, praises wealth through the character Herasym Kalytka: "Oh, land, holy land, you are the daughter of God! It's a joy to pile you up into one heap . . . I would buy you without counting. How much better is it to walk on one's own land. You look around – everything is yours: there are herds grazing, there are plowing for fallow land, and here the wheat is already green and the rye is spiking; and all this is money, money, money. . . ." It is clear that Karpenko-Karyi ridicules the greedy attitude toward property embodied by Herasym Kalytka. Ushkalov mimics the stereotype that equates this worldview with the "Protestant work ethic," suggesting that wealth is a

---

48. Леонід Ушкалов, "Бідність як кінічний жест: українська версія", в *Сковорода, Шевченко, фемінізм . . .: Статті 2010–2013 років* [Leonid Ushkalov, "Poverty as a Cynic Gesture: A Ukrainian Version," in *Skovoroda, Shevchenko, Feminism . . .: Articles of the years of 2010–2013*] (Харків: Майдан, 2014), 259–69.

blessing. Indeed, parallels to the idea that abundance signifies God's favor can be found in the Old Testament tradition (for example, Gen 27:27–29; Deut 28). However, it is not the mere presence of wealth that is problematic, but rather a person's attachment to it (cf. 1 Sam 25). This motif is also emphasized in Pochaev's 1772 book *Seeds of God's Word*, where the author reflects on the apostle Paul's view of the Cynic philosopher Crates, who threw away the wealth that was tempting him into the sea.

Another important voice is that of the Ukrainian philosopher Hryhory Skovoroda (1722–1794), who spoke highly of "voluntary poverty, of poverty as a virtue, which, after all, has nothing to do with 'full purses.'"[49] Thus, in Song 24 in his *Garden of Songs* the author gladly accepts his difficult fate: "God blessed you with lands, yet it may vanish in a flash, / While my lot's with the poor, but He gave me wisdom's cache."[50] Skovoroda speaks of possessing treasures that "neither moth nor rust destroys, and where thieves do not break in and steal" (Matt 6:20). Disdain and pity for the rich can be seen in Skovoroda's other works. For example, in the dialog "The Struggle of the Archangel Michael with Satan," the author says that he is "the poorest in the eyes of the world, but the richest in God's estimation."[51] In the song "Blessed are the poor in spirit," the author chooses to live in the fields rather than in a rich city: "I don't want seaside trips or clothes of red, For underneath lies sorrow, deep and wide. / There's fear and chaos, tears that must be shed . . . No luxuries for me – I cast aside. I only wish for water and for bread, With poverty I've long been satisfied. / It is my friend, my partner – so I've said, We're bound together, walking side by side."[52] The reader can easily see the contempt for material wealth, power, aggression, and worldly wisdom, apart from the wisdom of Christ. Instead, the simplicity of everyday life, common Christian sense, peace, freedom, heavenly eternity, and victory over sin are held up. In this sense, Skovoroda's ideas reflect the patristic tradition, in which the Beatitudes were viewed as a pathway to perfection and development of virtue.

On the other hand, Skovoroda was well aware that it is not the absence of possessions that makes one truly blessed, but rather poverty of the soul. This is what he praises in his poem "Praise of Poverty," which ends with these words:

---

49. Ушкалов, "Бідність як кінічний жест" [Ushkalov, "Poverty as a Cynic Gesture"], 262.

50. Hryhory Skovoroda, *The Garden of Divine Songs and Collected Poetry of Hryhory Skovoroda* (London: Glagoslav Publications, 2016), 84.

51. Cited in Ушкалов, "Бідність як кінічний жест" [Ushkalov, "Poverty as a Cynic Gesture"], 262.

52. Skovoroda, *The Garden of Divine Songs*, 61, 62.

> How can I praise those beggars, tell me how?
> Their hearts still yearn for gold's alluring gleam,
> These greedy elders, to earthly wealth they bow,
> For treasures worldly, how their eyes do beam.
>
> No, while your gaze with greed still burns so bright,
> Like wretched Irus, gold your sole desire,
> Without gold chests, you'll never reach the height
> Of poverty true, to which the just aspire.
>
> Christ was poor indeed, for He scorned all wealth,
> Paul lived in need, for pleasures he denied,
> True poverty dwells not in beggar's stealth,
> But in pure hearts, where righteousness resides.[53]

According to Ushkalov, Skovoroda's view of poverty is in line with the Cynics and Stoics, such as Seneca with his statement that "the poor is not the one who has little, but the one who wants more."[54] But in the poem itself, the author refers to Christ and Paul rather than Diogenes or Seneca. Therefore, it is likely that the bliss of the poor in spirit had a more significant influence on the poet than Greco-Roman philosophy.

In the parable *The Poor Lark*, written by Skovoroda in 1787, the unreasonable grouse Friedrich mockingly connects the expression "The one who desires not the wealth of the earth? / Is the one who is closest to heaven" to Socrates.[55] Again, Ushkalov sees here the teachings of Greek philosophers about the closeness to the gods of a perfect man who has renounced his needs.[56] At the same time, Skovoroda could also have been under the influence of the Orthodox doctrine of deification, according to which the renunciation of passions and lusts leads a Christian to being conformed to the likeness of God. Later, when the meaning of the "poor in spirit" beatitude is discussed at the meeting of the birds, the following explanation is offered:

> Not he is poor who has not, but he who is rich up to his eyeballs, but does not set his heart on it, or rather does not set his hope in it; he is always ready to be deprived of it, if it pleases the Lord . . .

---

53. Cited in Ушкалов, "Бідність як кінічний жест" [Ushkalov, "Poverty as a Cynic Gesture"], 262–63.

54. Ushkalov quotes Seneca's *Moral Letters to Lucilius*, 263.

55. Сковорода, *Повна академічна збірка творів*, під ред. Леоніда Ушкалова [Skovoroda, *Complete Academic Works*, edited by Leonid Ushkalov] (Харків: Майдан, 2011), 923.

56. Ушкалов, "Бідність як кінічний жест" [Ushkalov, "Poverty as a Cynic Gesture"], 263.

> Poverty, which has acquired what it needs and despises what it does not, is true wealth and bliss, as it is a bridge between scarcity and excess.[57]

Thus, according to the author, being poor in spirit does not depend on the presence or absence of material wealth. Spiritual poverty is contentment with God's provision and dependence on his providence. It is as if the poor man holds his property in God's hands, not his own. The story later includes a song about the humble birth of Christ, in which not only the surroundings of the King's Son are poor, but Jesus himself is identified with poverty: "O Poverty! Blessed and Holy One! Open to us the door of your Paradise... O Poverty! Heaven's gift under the sun! Every Saint and Honest Man holds you in high price... Behold the Humble Cave! It hides the Blessed God In a Heart that's brave... This is holy Poverty indeed! Outwardly stark, inwardly of gold's breed, In the Soul of Peace it does reside."[58] The gospel motif of the incarnation of God and the renunciation of royal privileges by God the Son inspired Skovoroda to glorify spiritual and material poverty as opposed to "worldly grandeur."

The Ukrainian poet and thinker Taras Shevchenko (1814–1861) noted material poverty against the background of the spiritual wealth of the Ukrainian people in his novel *A Walk....* The narrator puts it this way,

> O my sweet, pure countrymen! If you were as rich in material wealth as you are in moral beauty, you would be the happiest people in the world! But no! Your land is like a paradise, like a garden planted by the hand of God, the man-loving God. And you are just free laborers in that fertile, luxurious garden. You are poor Lazarus, feeding on the crumbs that fall from the sumptuous meals of your greedy, insatiable brothers.[59]

Here we can see Shevchenko's attitude about the Ukrainian idea of freedom, independence and prosperity of the common people. The common people were constantly oppressed by the indifferent rich who abused their position and deprived the oppressed of the most necessary material goods, including freedom. At the same time, the impenetrable poverty of the poor serfs allowed

---

57. Сковорода, *Повна академічна збірка творів* [Skovoroda, *Complete Academic Works*], 928.

58. Сковорода *Повна академічна збірка творів* [Skovoroda, *Complete Academic Works*], 932–33.

59. Леонід Ушкалов, "Богатство," у *Моя шевченківська енциклопедія із досвіду самопізнання* [Leonid Ushkalov, "Wealth," in *My Shevchenko Encyclopaedia on the Experience of Self-Discovery*] (Харків: Майдан, 2014), 38.

them only to dream of the happy fate of their children, as in Shevchenko's poem "Dream," in which a serf woman sees the blissful life of her son:

She dreamed about her boy Ivan:

> Grown-up and handsome, well-to-do,
> And married, a fair maid he'd wooed –
> A maiden free, she saw – and he himself
> No longer a servant, but free,
> And on their own sunny and happy field
> Together harvesting the wheat they'd sown,
> Their youngsters bringing lunch from home.[60]

However, a just future in a woman's imagination is not about swapping places with the masters in order to oppress them in return. Her paradise is freedom and free labor in her own field with happy and well-fed children. This picture of abundance and freedom echoes the biblical motif of each Israelite sitting under his own vine and fig tree (Mic 4:4). The spiritual poverty of ordinary serfs recognizes everyone as free and worthy of the right to independent existence, honest work, property, and family happiness.

In another poem, "Imitation of Psalm 11" (1859), Taras Shevchenko alludes to the theme of God's protection for the oppressed, who are reduced to the status of silent slaves. He wrote this poem when he was under gendarme surveillance in St. Petersburg, where he returned after being exiled to Mangyshlak on the eastern coast of the Caspian Sea. In his poetry, Shevchenko illustrates how God confronts the proud and deceitful, who exploit the disadvantaged without remorse:

> "I shall arise!" our Lord shall cry:
>   "I shall arise this day
> For humble folk in servile chains
>   Who sadly waste away . . .
> I shall extol those small, dumb slaves
>   And set my Word on guard. . . ."
> Like trampled grass your thoughts will droop,
>   Your words he will discard.
> Like new-forged silver, beaten well
>   And seven times transfused

---

60. Ушкалов, "Богатство" [Ushkalov, "Wealth"], 38. In Ukrainian. See Taras Schevchenko, "A Dream (To Marko Vovchok)," translated by Mary Skrypnyk, *Shevchenko Museum*, accessed 16 September 2024, https://shevchenko.ca/taras-shevchenko/poem.cfm?poem=53.

In cauldrons on the finer's fire –
　　Such words our Lord has used!
Then let those holy words be sown
　　Throughout the entire land!
And your poor children will believe
　　The wonders of your hand [61]

For Shevchenko, the instrument of God's action is his word, which gives hope and revives "poor little children." It is the action of God through this word that is the key to the exaltation of the poor and the humiliation of the self-confident and self-reliant.

Ukrainian literary tradition retains a certain continuity with the biblical and patristic traditions. In particular, with regard to the choice of eternal riches as opposed to earthly and temporal ones and the Christological roots of the idea of voluntary poverty. At the same time, Ukrainian literature indicates that material poverty is not a good thing, it is an evil that causes suffering. Instead, it proclaims the values of freedom, prosperity, and hard work for one's own well-being and the well-being of others. The dream of well-being and prosperity is inextricably linked to the desire for freedom for oneself and for everyone else. These features are motivated by the experience of enslavement and unfair exploitation of Ukrainian peasants by their wealthy masters. This context provides a special lens through which Ukrainian writers read the biblical tradition and the experience of their people.

The Blessedness of the Poor in Spirit During the War

The experience of the Russian-Ukrainian war and its global ramifications have prompted a reevaluation of biblical texts, particularly the Beatitudes. In this section, we aim to constructively engage with the poor in spirit beatitude in light of the challenges presented by the Russian-Ukrainian conflict.

To contextualize Jesus's beatitude about the poor in spirit, it is essential to clarify what it does not imply. While material wealth is often linked to spiritual pride, there is no inherent causal relationship between the two. As previously discussed, economically capable Christians can embody spiritual humility and

---

61. Тарас Шевченко "Подражаніє 11 псалму", в *Зібрання творів*: у 6 т. Т. 2: Поезія 1847–1861 [Taras Shevchenko, "Imitating Psalm 11," in *Collection of Works*, in 6 vols. Vol. 2: Poetry 1847–1861]. (Київ, 2003), 281. For English translation see *The Poetic Works of Taras Shevchenko. The Kobzar*, translated by C. H. Andrusyshen and Watson Kirkconnel (Toronto: University of Toronto Press, 1964), 507.

possess a genuine concern for the needy. Conversely, individuals in poverty may secretly demean their benefactors or take pride in their ability to give away their possessions to others in need, only to find themselves begging. Self-aggrandizement manifests itself in various forms: material (self-interest), social (honor and recognition), and spiritual (pride). William James posits that spiritual self-aggrandizement often compensates for shortcomings in other areas of ambition.[62] In this sense, those impoverished in other domains may strive to attain spiritual wealth.

The challenge of attaining the beatitude of the poor in spirit lies in its fleeting nature; once the poor in spirit recognize their condition, they risk losing that awareness due to complacency. The beatitude of the poor in spirit stands in judgment against the rich in spirit – those who rely on their own resources to gain entry into the kingdom of God.

A rather interesting interpretation of the first beatitude is offered by Lutheran theologian Robert Smith.[63] Notably, these leaders are characterized in this Gospel as lawless and false prophets within the community rather than as external adversaries (Matt 7:15–23; 24:10–12). Smith argues that the desire for rich spiritual experiences was prevalent in both Hellenistic cults and the churches established by Paul in Corinth and Thessalonica (1 Cor 1:7; 1 Thess 5:19–22), as well as in Johannine communities (1 John 4:1) and other congregations (Rev 2:14, 20). In contrast, true followers of Jesus should be defined by their righteousness and *agape* love.

Building on this understanding of the *Sitz im Leben* of Matthew's Gospel, Smith paraphrases the first beatitude as: "Blessed are those who lack powerful charismatic gifts."[64] While this interpretation is intriguing, it appears somewhat anachronistic, as Smith introduces the hypothetical internal fragmentation of Matthew's community into Jesus's words. Even if we were to assume that Jesus foresaw potential abuses of spiritual gifts, neither he nor the other apostles opposed being filled or enriched by the Holy Spirit (Matt 10:20; cf. Luke 11:13; John 3:34; Rom 15:13, 19; 1 Cor 2:4; Eph 5:18). Therefore, the assertion that Jesus calls those who do not exhibit charismatic traits blessed is misguided. At the same time, an inflated sense of one's own spiritual authority and significance can become an obstacle, as it fosters self-reliance and diminishes awareness of one's spiritual imperfections. True charisma is a manifestation

---

62. William James, *Psychology: The Briefer Course* (New York: Collier, 1962), 123.

63. Robert H. Smith, "'Blessed Are the Poor in (Holy) Spirit'? (Matthew 5:3)," *Word & World* 18, no. 4 (1998): 389–96.

64. Smith, "'Blessed Are the Poor in (Holy) Spirit'? (Matthew 5:3)," 396.

of the Holy Spirit, and the fruits of the Spirit can only be realized through a close relationship with Jesus (John 15:4–5).

The phrase "poor in spirit" does not connote faintheartedness or timidity. Jesus cautions us not to fear "those who kill the body but cannot kill the soul; rather, fear him who is able to destroy both soul and body in hell" (Matt 10:28, 31; Luke 12:4). He underscores that genuine fear should stem not from human actions, but from God's, since he determines our eternal destiny. An awareness of one's own insignificance and vulnerability can lead to fear; however, Jesus reassures us, saying, "Do not be afraid, little flock, for your Father has been pleased to give you the kingdom" (Luke 12:32). Similarly, when a father is gripped by fear over the impending death of his daughter, the Lord encourages the synagogue leader with the words, "Don't be afraid; just believe!" (Mark 5:36).

Furthermore, spiritual poverty entails complete trust in God and an expectation that He will restore justice and divine order. This state of blessedness must therefore be accompanied by courage rather than fear and passivity. It is reasonable to assume that fear and passivity are more likely to afflict those who perceive they have something to lose – be it property, social status, or future prospects. In contrast, those who have already experienced loss of home, professional opportunities, and who lack clear prospects for the future yet rely wholly on God are truly the poor in spirit. They expect God to provide for their daily needs and see him as the guarantor of both their present and future. Thus, to be "spiritually poor" does not equate to being materially impoverished, deprived of spiritual gifts, or filled with fear.

The Beatitudes should not be viewed as moral decrees intended to secure God's approval; rather, they represent the values and principles of the kingdom of heaven. In these teachings, Jesus instructs his disciples on how to live in anticipation of the establishment of the eschatological kingdom with the coming of the king. Poverty of spirit embodies a countercultural perspective, characterized by humility rather than self-confidence, self-reliance, and ambition.[65] The poor in spirit subscribe to an unconventional view of achievement, prestige, and wealth, guided by a distinct system of values.

Those who are poor in spirit do not simply accept their spiritual state; instead, they experience a continual hunger and need for God's provision. They remain acutely aware of their intellectual insignificance, material dependence, social obscurity, and lack of influence. Importantly, this awareness is not due to any intellectual or physical shortcomings or a deficiency of entrepreneurial

---

65. Lawrence O. Richards, *The Teacher's Commentary* (Wheaton: Victor Books, 1987), 541.

talent or charisma. Rather, poverty of spirit involves a conscious acceptance of one's own spiritual inability to impress God or earn his favor. It is the recognition of personal bankruptcy that does not lead to paralysis but rather motivates individuals to seek the fulfillment of their spiritual needs in God.

As discussed in the section on the history of the interpretation of this beatitude, the poor in spirit prioritize enduring values over those prevalent in this age. In light of the message of the kingdom of God, they choose to live in such a way that their treatment of property, lives, and relationships reflects the manifestation of Christ's kingdom. According to the Lutheran theologian and martyr Dietrich Bonhoeffer (1906–1945), the poor in spirit possess no security, no property to claim as their own, nor even a piece of land to call home, nor an earthly society to which they pledge absolute allegiance. They lack the spiritual strength, experience, or knowledge that typically provide confidence or comfort. For the sake of Christ, they have relinquished everything, even their very selves.[66]

However, this loss does not result in feelings of defeat or deprivation; rather, the poor in spirit are blessed because they possess the kingdom of God. This kingdom belongs to them in the present, not merely in some uncertain future. They are blessed here and now precisely because they have chosen the kingdom, responded to its message, and reoriented their lives according to its guiding principles.

Reflecting on the outbreak of armed aggression by our eastern neighbor, I (Eduard) have grappled with feelings of inadequacy and helplessness. It has been disheartening to witness the tacit, and at times overt, support of Russian evangelicals for their government's actions. It is particularly painful that, for some, loyalty to their authorities appears to take precedence over brotherly solidarity in Christ. The religious and political leaders of the aggressor nation cloak their actions in slogans advocating for a struggle for Christian values against a perceived corrupt West. In reality, they employ methods reminiscent of the antichrist, opposing Christ through political and social ideologies, and sometimes through the outright persecution of his followers.

In recognizing our own inability to overcome these "powers and authorities" (Eph 6:12), Christians are called to focus on the biblical motif of restoring God's justice, a theme prevalent in the Old Testament prophets and echoed in the teachings of Jesus Christ and throughout the New Testament. The blessedness of the poor in spirit lies in their active pursuit of God's order. This is why Christians turn to the words of the Lord's Prayer: "Hallowed be your name,

---

66. Dietrich Bonhoeffer, *The Cost of Discipleship* (New York: Touchstone, 1995), chap. 6.

your kingdom come, your will be done, on earth as it is in heaven" (Matt 6:9–10). The Lord's Prayer serves as a manifesto of the kingdom, representing the plea and appeal of the poor in spirit to God for his protection, care, and restoration of justice.

The book of Revelation, authored by John the theologian, depicts the ultimate humiliation of the powers and authorities through the imagery of the whore of Babylon (Rev 18) and heralds the final triumph of the kingdom of God (Rev 19). The poor in spirit live in the light of this reality now, awaiting the full manifestation of God's kingdom victory in the future.

Do the values and principles of the kingdom of God change during times of war? Should the poor in spirit beatitude be supplanted by a focus on courage or strength of spirit? Can a person who is poor in spirit withstand the additional pressures of martial law without succumbing to despair?

In Ukraine, martial law appears to necessitate internal emotional endurance, fortitude, and an unbreakable will – concepts commonly emphasized by secular society and professional psychological support. However, the values of the kingdom that Jesus preached are not contingent upon the state of the nation or bound by temporal circumstances. The Beatitudes reflect the eternal nature of God, the ever-approaching reign of God, and the needs of humanity in all situations. The blessedness of the poor in spirit was countercultural during the Roman occupation, throughout the history of the Church, and remains so in the face of modern Russian armed aggression, unjust redistribution of resources worldwide, or the dominance of corrupt authorities. It is the recognition of one's spiritual insolvency and complete dependence on God that provides Jesus's followers with the spiritual resources necessary for endurance.

The source of this endurance lies not within the individual Christian but in their Lord and King. Spiritual poverty reveals to the Church that we are no better than any other sinners and do not deserve preferential treatment. It signifies that one's own strength, motivation, patience, or wisdom are insufficient to navigate the realities of instability, uncertainty, and the risks of daily life. The spiritual beggar places their hope solely in God's ability and resources to sustain their life today. They expect God to fulfill his ultimate plan and act in light of this expectation.

The war in Ukraine underscores our spiritual powerlessness in the face of evil and unchecked violence. We struggle to comprehend God's perfect purposes amidst the innocent victims of aggression and to offer reassurance to those consumed by grief and fear for their lives and the lives of their loved ones. Acknowledging one's own spiritual poverty can protect against the pitfalls often associated with self-confidence, whether in military commanders or church leaders. The kingdom of heaven is not merely a wish upon a follower of Christ who dies on the battlefield or beneath the rubble of a high-rise building destroyed by a Shahed drone but also to all those who are alive and poor in spirit.

Conclusions

The circumstances surrounding a Christian community significantly influence how it interprets biblical texts and formulates questions about them. The war of aggression initiated by Russia against the Ukrainian people has placed churches in a new interpretive context. The initial hope in international institutions, which were expected to prevent the onset of this conflict, has swiftly faded. Doubts regarding the capability of political leaders to restore a just peace are dissipating like dew under the sun. We quickly recognized that, under these conditions, we possess very limited external and internal resources to confront the horrors of war and its catastrophic consequences. The loss of economic stability, the assurance of equitable justice, and the existential threats to people's lives do not foster optimism.

So, what are we to do in such dire circumstances? The recognition of our complete dependence on God emerges as paramount. The community of believers in Jesus rejoices and remains hopeful because the kingdom of heaven is theirs. They already belong to it, and it belongs to them. They are blessed specifically because the kingdom of heaven is their inheritance. The spiritually poor must humbly continue their mission as witnesses of this kingdom, engaging in the prayerful struggle for its realization – "Thy kingdom come" (Matt 6:9) – and serving "the least of these" (Matt 25:40). The blessedness of the poor in spirit transcends personal piety and character development; it signifies the community of the kingdom, which reflects the image of its teacher and king, "meek and lowly in heart" (Matt 11:29). The poor in spirit call out to him – "Come, Lord Jesus!" (Rev 22:20).

2

"Blessed are those who mourn, for they will be comforted"

(Matthew 5:4)

Sergiy Bermas

Pain is lost in praise, the treacherous journey between pain and praise must be taken to avoid the sentimentality of both pain and praise.

Karen Dixie

The bliss of mourning
This is the lot
Not of everyone,
But only
For specially chosen
For the remnant,
When the rest are
Lost . . .
We are crying bitterly,
Because they do not stop
Hostility of strangers
And the betrayal of their own,
Morning with a summons,
Flowers at the cemetery . . .
Lost meanings
They fly with explosives . . .

When the wings are broken,
Friends are all busy
And no longer help
Tranquilizers,
Instincts affect
Psychosomatics,
Then you can simply
Sit and cry . . .
And let the tears fall,
They will sing with the downpour of God's comfort,
They will make it green
The wilderness
The withering hope of the soul.
And they will blossom
Tulips, roses, and more
As the optics of faith
Contact lenses
To see the world
Just and pure
It is only possible
Through them . . .

Oleksandr Vyalov[1]

Introduction

When I began reflecting on this chapter, I thought I understood something about lament. First, I had personally experienced the diagnosis and treatment of cancer. Second, I had shared in my people's anguish during the onset of the Russian invasion, worrying for my family, friends, and loved ones scattered across different locations and circumstances.

Today, suffering in all its forms has enveloped the nation and its people on such a scale that it is almost impossible to process rationally, morally, emotionally, or existentially. Meeting groups of refugees with disabilities and their caregivers, I witnessed suffering and struggles that began long before the war. They revealed to me the future awaiting those who, on the battlefield or in other circumstances, lost their limbs or the ability to function without the aid

---

1. Pastor of an evangelical church in Kharkiv. Used with permission.

of others or technological devices. Their battles will continue – whether in isolation or with the assistance of others.

The scale and consequences of the war will continue to echo in the laments of Ukrainian society. The tears and struggles for life await all who have lost what is most precious – their family and loved ones.

This prompts the church to reflect: Can it help such people navigate this path? Does it have the resources to address the trauma and consequences of war, particularly in the emotional and spiritual realms?

Europeans, after World War II, likely could not have imagined that the horrors of war would return to the civilized world. Yes, there were subsequent conflicts in Korea, Vietnam, numerous local wars in Africa, Yugoslavia, and the Middle East, as well as terrorist actions and counterterrorism efforts. However, the idea that a nuclear state, a participant in World War II and a permanent member of the United Nations, would invade another UN member state – a sovereign nation with recognized borders – occupying its territories, killing its citizens, engaging in terrorist actions, and committing what can be qualified as genocide against another people, seemed like the plot of apocalyptic fiction.

Yet, this is the reality faced by the Ukrainian people: missile strikes on cities and towns that not only destroy infrastructure but, most tragically, claim the lives of civilians. Horrific events like those in Bucha, which became emblematic of Ukrainian cities ravaged by barbaric violence, exposed to the world the absurdity and savagery of Russian policies toward Ukraine. The deaths of soldiers, torture in Russian captivity, the suffering of their families, grief, and post traumatic stress disorder that will linger for years – this is only a brief summary of the anguish that Ukraine endures during this aggression.

Ukrainian Christians, particularly those of the evangelical tradition, have also found themselves in a new reality. During Soviet times, the identity of evangelical believers was shaped primarily by denominational community, practice, and confession, while their national belonging was largely ignored. This led to pacifist views and a detachment from broader society. Such attitudes were influenced by the state's atheistic policies, societal ostracism, the stigma of being labelled a sect, and other pressures.

The situation changed after Ukraine gained independence. During this period, Ukrainian churches experienced freedom, expanded their congregations, and developed various ministries aimed both at the church and society. Many missionaries even served in Russia. Although societal attitudes toward evangelicals – shaped by atheistic or Orthodox worldviews – did not change significantly, generally, religious freedom facilitated the growth of churches, their openness to society, and legal relations with the state.

In the years of independence, evangelical believers and churches began to more closely identify with the Ukrainian people and their history. A new generation of Christians emerged, identifying as Ukrainians, particularly through exposure to a Ukrainian history freed from Russian imperial and Soviet mythology. This gave rise to a new generation of churches and Christians who are open to the society, history, and culture of their nation.

This identity was also forged through collective struggles for democratic values during the Maidan uprisings and later in the war since 2014. Thus, when Russia's full-scale invasion of Ukraine began, most Christians felt an assault on their very essence – as citizens of an independent country and as members of a nation. They felt not only physical danger and threats to life but also existential devastation and destruction.

Christians in Ukraine are being shaped specifically as *Ukrainian Christians*. Therefore, Russia's threats to strip us of our national identity and return us to imperial influence, branding us as an artificial nation, pose threats not only to our religious identity but also to our anthropological essence. National and religious identities are integral components of personal identity. There are no "distilled" Christians who exist apart from their civic, cultural, and ethnic identities.

Such threats have shaped a new approach and new motivations regarding war, nationhood, and the fight for freedom and independence. This has prompted a rethinking and reforming of theology, which is now laying the foundation for a new ethic, spirituality, and practice. On this journey, the Sermon on the Mount, particularly the Beatitudes, has become a central text for the Ukrainian evangelical community amid the Russian-Ukrainian war.

Part One: Biblical and Theological Analysis

"Blessed are . . . ." The Sermon on the Mount is the key text for Christian ethics, and the Beatitudes are a central part of it. Structurally, they align with the demands and promises of the kingdom of God.

The phrase "Blessed are those who mourn, for they will be comforted" may seem very simple: there are those who mourn, and they are called blessed because they will be comforted one day. But further reflection reveals something not immediately obvious – those who suffer and mourn cannot be happy, especially in their current condition. It would be more natural to say that those who mourn will be happy because they will be comforted in the future. However, according to the text, blessedness refers to their present condition, though it is connected to some future reality or event.

Thus, questions arise: How will this future event "bless" a person, making them happy? How should we understand the concept of blessedness itself?

The best attempts at reading and interpreting the Sermon on the Mount suggest recognizing its cultural location at the crossroads of the Second Temple Jewish world and the Greco-Roman tradition of virtue.[2] This understanding is based on two conceptual terms that Jonathan Pennington compares to rails: *makarios* (blessed) and *teleios* (perfect). The first concept, *makarios*, is an invitation to authentic human happiness and flourishing through Jesus. The second, *teleios*, is related to the concept of wholeness or directed devotion.[3]

Jonathan Pennington admits that translating *makarios* into English is problematic, especially when there are several variants that he believes do not match the conceptuality of the terms and lead to confusion. For example, in English translations, there are variants such as "blessed" and "happy." In his opinion, it is not appropriate to translate *makarism* with these words. To demonstrate the difference between the two, he suggests going back to the Hebrew Bible and the Septuagint (LXX).

The Bible contains a theme about human flourishing, which is depicted as the objective of God's work. This concept is represented by several ideas, one of which is shalom. Another important idea for understanding the beatitudes is *ashrê*. Of the forty-five uses of this word in the Old Testament, twenty-six appear in the Psalms and eight in Proverbs.[4] The word describes the happy state of someone who lives wisely, and in this sense it is related to shalom. Psalm 1 begins with this word and sets the tone for the frequent use of the idea of human happiness/bliss in the Psalms. In general, the wisdom literature is dominated by the idea of asherism, which refers to true happiness and prosperity in the obedience of the individual and the community to the covenant given by God. In the prophets, however, it is used only in Isaiah. Isaiah 30:18 describes the happy state of a person who waits on the Lord in the midst of suffering and trusts in him. Isaiah 32:20 describes the happy state of those who will live and prosper under the righteous rule of the king (32:1–8).[5] In general, the prophets use the term *brk* (blessed) more often.

---

2. Jonathan T. Pennington, *The Sermon on the Mount and Human Flourishing: A Theological Commentary* (Grand Rapid: Baker Academics, 2017), chap. 1, EPUB.

3. Pennington, *The Sermon on the Mount and Human Flourishing*, chap. 1, EPUB.

4. Pennington, *The Sermon on the Mount and Human Flourishing*, chap. 2, EPUB.

5. Pennington, *The Sermon on the Mount and Human Flourishing*, chap. 2, EPUB.

The Septuagint consistently translates *ašrê* as *makarios*, demonstrating an exceptional consistency in the use of terms.[6] In the New Testament, the ideas of asherism are also translated with the word *makarios*.

In the Greco-Roman environment, *makarios* was used as a synonym for the philosophical term *eudaimonia*, which means inner happiness and satisfaction, human prosperity, which semantically corresponds to the asherism of the Hebrew Bible.[7] Also in Second Temple literature, the Greek term *makarios* clearly denoted human prosperity, the fullness of earthly life.

Pennington insists on distinguishing between the terms *ašrê/makarios* and *brk/eulogetos* (blessed). The word "blessed" is usually used to translate *ascher/makarios* into English. A blessing is an action of God, a cherished promise, and it is opposed to a curse. Bliss is contrasted with sorrow. For example, in Luke 6:20–26 "blessed are you" is followed by the symmetrical "woe unto you." Therefore, Pennington tries to use transliteration rather than translation of terms more often, but sometimes suggests *flourishing* as an appropriate translation. Schematically, this can be depicted as follows:[8]

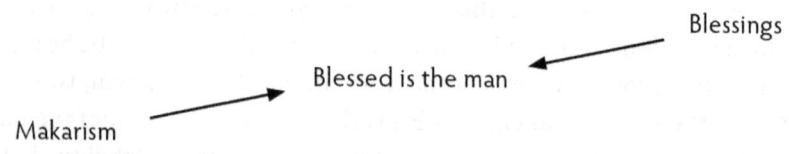

Blessings (and curses), according to Pennington, is divine, effective language. Makarisms (and woe) is human, descriptive language, so we should not confuse the genre of makarism with the genre of vow or blessing.[9]

This "division of powers" of terms reveals the difficulties that arise when translating and choosing certain meanings in a modern language, including Ukrainian. Pennington found a way out by translating the idea of asherism/macarism as flourishing. But in Ukrainian, flourishing/prosperity has mostly economic connotations, which will make it difficult to understand the Beatitudes. Such subtleties have merit but we need a wider range of perceptions of the concept of asherism/macarism.

---

6. Pennington, *The Sermon on the Mount and Human Flourishing*, chap. 2, EPUB.
7. Pennington, *The Sermon on the Mount and Human Flourishing*, chap. 2, EPUB.
8. Pennington, *The Sermon on the Mount and Human Flourishing*, chap. 2, EPUB.
9. Pennington, *The Sermon on the Mount and Human Flourishing*, chap. 2, EPUB.

To summarize the significance of Pennington's concept of macarism, let us present a second rail of understanding: *teleios* (perfect). He points out that, unlike the terms *ašrê/makarios*, between which there was a surprising consistency in the Septuagint, *teleios* does not have a single referent. This word is used to translate a variety of terms.[10] Pennington repeatedly emphasizes that the Hebrew Bible constantly repeats the theme of salvation as human flourishing. It does this in several ways, along with such significant concepts as *ashrê* (happiness), *tamim* (wholeness), and *shalom* (peace, prosperity).[11]

The term shalom is used frequently and on various occasions, consistently focusing on the concept of wholeness with implications of well-being. The greeting shalom signifies a wish for prosperity and a state free of conflict. A person can be considered thriving when all aspects of life are functioning in harmony and completeness. However, shalom is often translated as "peace" (both in English and Ukrainian), which may provide a narrower interpretation. Typically, "peace" implies the absence of conflict and war, which remains relevant for people globally. According to Nicholas Wolterstorff, the Bible presents a clear vision of what God desires for creation – a vision of human flourishing and destiny, beyond just individual bodyless contemplation of God.[12]

Along with the term shalom the Bible contains another term, *tamim*, which is understood as "completeness" and "wholeness." It conveys, depending on the context, the concepts of completeness, faultlessness, justice, honesty, perfection, and peacefulness. The main idea associated with each of them is authenticity and reliability. Especially important is the connection between wholeness and holiness. Therefore, the Old Testament, using different words and their connections, agrees with the idea of *teleios* as the wholeness, completeness, and perfection of a person in the sense of devotion to God with all one's heart.

Plato, Aristotle, and Philo each saw *teleios* as a blissful goal and a state of bliss, human happiness. For Aristotle, by the way, *teleios* is when the goal (*telos*) for which something exists is achieved.[13]

Pennington's overview of the terms *makarismos* and *teleios* revealed that the Beatitudes encompass meanings linked to other concepts, forming a notion of bliss that, first, is difficult to express with any single, narrowly technical term. The meaning of *asherism/macarism* is so rich and profound that the precision

---

10. Pennington, *The Sermon on the Mount and Human Flourishing*, chap. 3, EPUB.
11. Pennington, *The Sermon on the Mount and Human Flourishing*, chap. 3, EPUB.
12. Pennington, *The Sermon on the Mount and Human Flourishing*, chap. 3, EPUB.
13. Pennington, *The Sermon on the Mount and Human Flourishing*, chap. 3, EPUB.

of one term may limit the range of its interpretations. Second, in this context, there is a need for a more general term that is accessible to a broader audience.

We find the connection of makarism with "perfection" in James, who, also in the tradition of the wisdom of asherism/makarism, calls for patience in trials, because it has a perfect (*teleion*) effect and leads to perfection (*teleioi*), which corresponds to the idea of integrity as the goal of Christian life (James 1:2–3). He speaks of the perfection of Abraham's faith, the perfect gifts of the Father, the perfect Law – all of which are united by the concept of *teleioi*. Paul, in his letter to the Colossians, defines his mission and pastoral task as follows: "To make every person perfect (*teleios*) in Jesus Christ" (Col 1:28, author's translation). In Paul's writings, there is often a connection between goal and wholeness/perfection, expressed through words related to *teleios* (for example, Phil 3:12–15). There are many examples of *teleios* in the New Testament, and it is an important theme for Christian life and pastoral ministry.

James uses makarisms three times (1:12, 25; 5:11). In 1:12, the blessed person is the one who has overcome temptation and trials and will receive the crown of life. The blessed person should be filled with bliss, prosperity, fullness, shalom, and all that fills the gift of eternal life. James goes on to call blessed the person who freely fulfills and lives the perfect (*teleios*) Law (1:25). If in 1:12 bliss is associated with a future gift, then a person already experiences the bliss of a holistic and harmonious life in which internal intentions and values coincide with external actions that the person freely performs. All the terms and concepts in Pennington's research refer to this state.

In order to understand the concept of asherism/macarism, I propose to apply the idea of good or goodness. That is, "it is good for the one . . .". This is a simple and understandable idea that aligns with the deepest desire and yearning of every person. The idea of good runs through all philosophical and religious traditions. An illustration of this understanding is the statement of the apostle Paul: "We know that all things work together for good to those that love God" (Rom 8:28 NKJV). A person whose life is filled with goodness – goodness from God – is blessed.

Since the themes of blessedness, happiness, and good in Christian life are important because they reflect the meta-theme of God's action and purpose for creation, research on both biblical, historical, and practical nature is urgently needed for Ukrainian theological thought and pastoral theology.[14] It is crucial to overcome the distortion of the idea of *asherism/makarism* in

---

14. Useful examples include Ellen Charry, *God and the Art of Happiness* (Grand Rapids: Eerdmans, 2010); John Michael Rziha, *The Christian Moral Life: Directions for the Journey to*

some speculations, manipulations, and sometimes even frauds from the so-called "prosperity theology," as well as in some exaggerated forms of piety that reject happiness as something secular and hedonistic. John Rzhia asserts that humans were created to participate in God's happiness, and that happiness is connected to actions for which we were created, through which we experience the meaning and joy of life.[15] Often, popular evangelical preaching rhetoric has included slogans such as "God created us not for happiness, but for holiness." Pennington's previous conclusions counter this claim.

"*. . . Those who mourn.*" The idea of happiness and flourishing, to which God desires to lead all creation, is shattered by the reality of human everyday life. Suffering and evil in the world is too broad a topic to even begin addressing here. It is as deep as it is banal due to its obviousness, especially in the times we are currently experiencing. We see the consequences of evil in those who mourn. The main question researchers on the Sermon on the Mount have raised is: who mourns and why?

The list of the eight Beatitudes does not seem like a selection of unrelated propositions but rather a cluster of cumulative revelations of the conflict between the kingdom of heaven and the earthly realm. In this conflict, the disciples will live at the intersection of worlds, the struggle between Spirit and flesh (Gal 5:16–21). After the Beatitude for the poor in spirit, those who mourn appear. Mourning as a continuation of spiritual poverty leads to a thirst for justice, peace, meekness, and is the result of persecution by this world, which pushes the faithful to the margins of life. The list of Beatitudes concludes with a sort of summary – the ninth Beatitude – rejoicing when the disciples undergo persecution for their faith and loyalty to Jesus (cf. Jas 1:2–4; 5:11).

Mourning in Matthew begins at the outset of Jesus's story and ends with his cry on the cross. Matthew cites the text of the prophet Jeremiah 31:15 about the cruel killing of infants. The phrase "Rachel weeping for her children and refusing to be comforted, because they are no more" dramatizes the intensity of her mourning, emphasizing that she will not accept comfort. The grief is so immense that comfort is impossible, although from Jeremiah's perspective on the future, mourning will cease when Israel returns from exile.[16] In the

---

Happiness (Notre Dame: University of Notre Dame Press, 2017); Miroslav Volf, *For the Life of the World: Theology that Makes a Difference* (Grand Rapids: Brazos, 2019).

15. Rziha, *The Christian Moral Life*, 40.

16. David L. Turner, *Matthew*, Baker Exegetical Commentary on the New Testament (Grand Rapids: Baker Academics, 2008), 95.

Bethlehem story, hope must be realized through Jesus the Messiah.[17] However, the final cessation of mourning is seen at the end of the story (Rev 21:4), when God will wipe away every tear. Until that moment, as Paul writes, all creation groans as in pain (Rom 8:22).

The mention of Rachel's weeping takes on a paradigmatic function of both the figure and the state of weeping. Elizabeth Eklund aptly notes that Rachel's weeping still echoes when we hear the beatitude of those who mourn.[18] Billman and Migliore make several important points about Rachel's lament:

> It is Rachel's refusal to be consoled that grabs our attention. She does not remain silent while facing the loss of her children. She weeps and laments, and her weeping is bitter. She resists the comfort extended to her because she refuses to be reconciled to the injustice and violence of her world.[19]

Rachel's weeping and her bold refusal to be comforted reveal two aspects of her suffering. First, she weeps for herself and grieves over her loss. Second, she is angry at the senseless murder of her children. But the text also includes the promise of God, who hears her cry and responds with a promise: there is hope that the children will return to their country; justice and peace will reign on the earth (Jer 31:16).[20]

Rachel's figure in Matthew retrospectively points to the earlier biblical tradition of weeping, which has been lost in contemporary churches. They try to build, at least Sunday services, in the style of "everything will be fine." The singing, testimonies, sermons are all aimed at overcoming problems and achieving a state of "okay" as understood by certain communities. Even under the pressure of problems or, worse, suffering caused by catastrophes or war, churches sing songs that do not correspond to the current state. Federico Villanueva gives the example of a pastors' meeting where they were asked not to speak about problems because it was not seen as a blessing – this is a time for joyful witnessing.[21] Only stories with a "Christian happy ending" are invited to the

---

17. Turner, *Matthew*, 95.
18. Eklund, *The Beatitudes through the Ages*, chap. 4, EPUB.
19. Kathleen D. Billman, Daniel D. Migliore, *Rachel's Cry of Lament and Rebirth of Hope* (Cleveland: United Church Press, 1999), 2.
20. Billman and Migliore, *Rachel's Cry of Lament and Rebirth of Hope*, 2.
21. Federico G. Villanueva, *It's OK to Be Not OK: Preaching the Lament Psalms* (Carlisle: Langham Preaching Resources, 2017), also G. Geoffrey Harper, *Finding Lost Words. Foreword* (Eugene: Wipf & Stock, 2017), 2, Kindle.

stage because the world needs positivity.²² And if a problematic or tragic story occurs, it is given the status of a prayer request, focused only on its positive resolution. Understandably, this is natural because, as we mentioned earlier, people long for happiness, which aligns with the purpose of creation. But life is filled with suffering, which does not fit into the script or plot of such joyful Sunday services. The issue is not only with Sunday services, but with the fact that they reflect the goal of Christian life that the believers of this community strive for. And when suffering or war appears on the horizon, it shatters the Christians' imagination of a proper life. This state is characteristic of a church that has lived in a peaceful and successful period of history.

Now the whole of Ukraine is a Rachel, continuously crying and not wanting to be comforted. Weeping not only becomes a condition of the church, but calls for weeping as a tradition and practice of prayer for help and comfort should be heeded. But is there a place for crying in the church?²³ It would seem that the church is a community of compassion. Sadly, in reality as one Christian woman who lost a loved one in the war noted, "the church is mostly a place of active speaking, not listening." The situation of pain is common to Christians in different countries. Eliana Ah-Rum-Koo connects the theology of Jeremiah's Lamentations to the Korean tradition of lamentation and notes that preachers are tempted to circumvent the reality of suffering by proclaiming hope too quickly or by misinterpreting the gap between the reality of suffering and the world promised by God. He (Але це жінка) calls for the involvement of weeping in the sermon, which can be one way to help overcome suffering. Weeping is mainly related to the human condition itself, rather than to finding out the cause of suffering, and is opposed to the attempt to quickly escape from pain.²⁴

Weeping as a stage of life and a state of the soul is described by other images and ideas. For instance, Old Testament scholar Walter Brueggemann describes the human condition in the book of Psalms through the scheme of "orientation – disorientation – reorientation."²⁵ The first phase of life marks a state where people experience prosperity and happiness. Life is understandable to them; the principles of covenantal relationships are clear, they understand God, and they enjoy his generosity and care. If we take Psalm 23 as a model,

---

22. Scott Harrower and Sean M. McDonough, eds. *A Time for Sorrow: Recovering the Practice of Lament in the Life of the Church* (Peabody: Hendrickson, 2019), Introduction, EPUB.

23. Harrower and McDonough, *A Time for Sorrow*, Introduction, EPUB.

24. Eliana Ah-Rum Ku, *Lament-Driven Preaching. Proclaiming Hope and Suffering* (Eugene: Pickwick, 2014), Introduction, EPUB.

25. Walter Brueggemann, *The Message of The Psalms: A Theological Commentary* (Minneapolis: Augsburg, 1984), 19.

this is the part of life where the Lord is the good shepherd who meets the person's needs for blessings and safety. But later, everything radically changes (Psalm 73). The person suffers hardship, difficulties, and losses (Job), or the person loses the meaning of life (Ecclesiastes). This condition is reminiscent of another part of Psalm 23, where darkness is mentioned: there is no clear path, no understanding of what is happening, and no sense of God's presence. All prior understanding of the world and God is shattered. Yet, in this darkness, the person finds new paths, new experiences, and a deeper knowledge of God. This is vividly depicted in the final part of Psalm 23: the person once again enjoys God's gifts, but now with enriched experience, deeper faith, and renewed devotion.

This scheme is not linear, and the cycle can repeat itself. Exploring the narrative movement in the book of Psalms, Federico Villanueva discovered that it is not only the shift from weeping to praise, but also the reverse – praise can change into weeping.[26] Bruce Demarest, in his book *Seasons of the Soul*, considers Brueggemann's scheme useful for practical theology.[27] He applies it in several chapters dedicated to describing the state of disorientation. In Chapter 4, he refers to another traditional classification of this state – the "dark night of the soul" by John of the Cross.

The development of this scheme and practical advice can also be seen in the book by Bill and Kristi Gaultiere, *The Journey of the Soul*, which describes seven stages of Christian life, forming the acronym CHRIST corresponding to each stage.[28] In the middle between CHR and IST is the stage W – the wall of weeping, which marks the transition from "spirituality before the wall" to "spirituality after the wall." This is a period in life that Brueggemann identifies with disorientation.

Who is mourning and why? Beatitudes scholars have wondered who exactly has this "blessed" mourning. Rebecca Ecklund provides an overview of the history of the interpretation of the beatitude of mourning, in which one can see a certain departure from the biblical tradition of weeping in the

---

26. Federico G. Villanueva, *The "Uncertainty of Hearing": A Study of the Sudden Change of Mood in the Psalms of Lament* (Leiden: Brill, 2008).

27. Bruce Demarest, *Seasons of the Soul: Stages of Spiritual Development* (Downers Grove: InterVarsity Press, 2009).

28. Bill and Kristi Gaultiere, *Journey of the Soul: A Practical Guide to Emotional and Spiritual Growth* (Grand Rapids: Revell, 2021). Respectively: C is for Confidence in Christ; H is for Help in Discipleship; R is for Responsibilities in Ministry; then the Transition: Through The Wall; next is I for Inner Journey; then S for Spirit-led Ministry; and, finally, T for Transforming Union.

Old and New Testaments. The church fathers believed that the beatitude of weeping implied a weeping of repentance, a weeping over one's sins. Jerome, referring to the principle of the Stoics, who considered death to be natural, the fear of which must be overcome, wrote that the lament of Matthew 5:5 is not intended for "those who died according to the general law of nature." Augustine also wrote that sadness over the "loss of dear ones" is an emotion that will be rejected when people turn to God and learn to love what is eternal. In his Confessions, Augustine describes hesitating whether he should cry over the death of his own mother.[29] Unlike these thinkers, Tertullian, one of the fathers who most resisted the merger of Christian thought with secular (Greco-Roman) philosophy, did not interpret beatitude as repentance of one's sins. This tendency may also have been influenced by the fact that in Israel there was a decline in lamentation as a prayer and an increase in penitential prayer after the exile and a rethinking of the experience of captivity in Second Temple Judaism.[30]

However, as Turner notes, it is impossible to separate sorrow on the account of one's sin from weeping due to one's suffering. Those who mourn for sin turn away from it, while those who turn away from sin encounter suffering at the hands of sinners. In any case, those who mourn now will find comfort in the future through the anointed servant in Isaiah 61.[31]

During the Reformation, Luther and Calvin rejected the notion that mourning pertains solely to sin, noting that mourning is a natural state of human existence, arising from the trials of life.[32] Perhaps the rejection of monastic life with its focus on penance for sins prompted Luther to dismiss such views and practices. He believed that people see the world as it is in its sinfulness, and this causes them sorrow. For Luther, it was appropriate, even pleasing to God, to mourn the death of a good friend. He also urged Christians to mourn with faith and hope, cautioning that their sorrow should not be excessive. However, as Migliore counters, mourning shallowly is to mourn inadequately and distortedly.[33]

In contrast to the narrow views of penitential mourning, Eklund reflects on whether the post-Reformation tradition became too broad, making mourning and weeping "everything that breaks the heart" (Dallas Willard). In such

---

29. Also in Billman and Migliore, *Rachel's Cry of Lament and Rebirth of Hope*, 47–48.
30. Eklund, *The Beatitudes through the Ages*, chap. 4, EPUB.
31. Turner, *Matthew*, 151.
32. Turner, *Matthew*, 151.
33. Billman and Migliore, *Rachel's Cry of Lament and Rebirth of Hope*, 55.

a case, mourning becomes too vague to be meaningful. However, Scripture promises comfort specifically to those with broken hearts: "The LORD is near to the brokenhearted" (Ps 34:18). Eklund notes, in particular, that modern interpretations continue the general tone of mourning and weeping found in previous traditions, asserting that the righteous mourn because, prior to the eschatological reversal, one cannot be satisfied with the status quo.[34]

The Bible pays a great deal of attention to mourning, sorrow, and suffering. Beginning with the narrative of Israel's exodus from Egypt, wisdom literature (Job), the prophets (Jeremiah's Lamentations, Habakkuk), and the book of Psalms, of which approximately forty percent are psalms of lament,[35] it reveals the full range of human emotions that were poured out in prayer before God. Reducing mourning to repentance or reducing it to a limited list of "pious lamentations" in history and the modern church does not coincide with the biblical tradition. Daniel Migliore makes the following points about the biblical tradition of weeping in the Old and New Testaments:[36]

The Biblical Old Testament Tradition	The New Testament Trajectory of Weeping
1. The prayer of lamentation is a bold and disturbing form of prayer.	1. Prayers, including the Lord's Prayer, are full of passion and a sense of urgency.
2. The biblical prayers of lamentation have a specific life context.	2. New Testament prayers also have their own specific life context.
3. Many of the psalms of lamentation implicitly or explicitly reject the idea that all suffering is caused by sin.	3. In the New Testament, prayer includes, but is not limited to, asking for forgiveness of sins.
4. Prayers of lamentation often contain expressions of intense anger and calls for revenge against enemies.	4. Although the call for vengeance against enemies is much less frequent in the prayers of the New Testament than in the Old, its presence reminds us of the seriousness of evil and the reality of divine judgment.
5. The tradition of biblical lament contrasts trust and doubt, lament and praise, sometimes in extreme tension.	5. As seen in the prayer of Jesus in Gethsemane and the prayer of the apostle Paul for the removal of his "thorn in the flesh," prayer can involve deep struggle.

---

34. Eklund, *The Beatitudes through the Ages*, chap. 4, EPUB.
35. Harrower and McDonough, eds., *A Time for Sorrow*, chap. 1, EPUB.
36. Billman and Migliore, *Rachel's Cry of Lament and Rebirth of Hope*, 27–40.

The Biblical Old Testament Tradition	The New Testament Trajectory of Weeping
6. The prayer of lamentation sometimes contains an element of protest, when the one praying enters into an intense, even angry dispute with God.	6. While the prayer of lamentation and protest is evident in relatively few of the Gospel accounts, some passages that are mostly overlooked contain its spirit.
7. The prayer of lamentation implies the realization of God's freedom and hiddenness.	7. The acceptance of the prayer of lamentation in Christianity is finally confirmed by the cry of Jesus on the cross.
8. In the same biblical tradition that contains prayers of lamentation, there is evidence that God also mourns and grieves with the people of Israel over their sin and suffering.	8. Because the New Testament community sees Jesus in the most intimate relationship with God, Jesus's weeping becomes the basis for the Christian claim that God weeps too.
9. In the prayer of lamentation, Israel recalls hope.	9. In the New Testament prayer, memory and hope are closely linked.

Thus, the biblical overview points to the importance of recognizing mourning and grieving as a major theological, pastoral and practical issue. Against the background of humanity's achievements in the technological and humanitarian spheres, evil has not diminished its power so sadness, suffering, and mourning accompany the world and the people of God. How to reduce suffering, how to help those who grieve, what resources does the church have?

One of the actions of the church is to give voice to those who mourn in prayer, preaching, and pastoral care, especially in the context of national tragedy. The biblical tradition of lamentation, especially the Israelite tradition, is closely linked to national and corporate tragedy.[37]

In the context of a national tragedy shared by the Ukrainian church community, it is crucial to strengthen its resources, which are drawn from the biblical narrative as the metanarrative of its faith, meanings, values, and virtues.

---

37. There are many studies on the tradition of biblical lamentation and its implementation in local cultures. For the Korean experience see Eliana Ah-Rum Ku, *Lament-Driven Preaching*; for Latvian see Ruth Sonia Ziedonis, *Healing and Wholeness Through Sharing One's Latvian Grief Story* (Riga: University of Latvia, 1997); for African see Emmanuel Katongole, *Born from Lament. The Theology and Politics of Hope in Africa* (Grand Rapids: Eerdmans, 2017); and for the Filipino context see Villanueva, *It's OK to Be Not OK*.

During this time, many people are experiencing both personal and corporate mourning. What can the church offer in these times?

At the onset of the war, the intense, focused activity into which most believers immersed themselves fostered a sense of solidarity, care, and empathy. It transformed fear and feelings of helplessness into responsibility and optimism. However, over time, fatigue, discouraging news from the front lines, bombings of cities, social media reports of the deaths of soldiers and civilians, and personal losses increasingly weighed on the hearts of believers. Even when they were called to sing "victory" songs on Sundays, questions still arose in prayer or reflection as they grappled with the realities of the day. Preachers also strive to encourage their congregations. Yet, the songs and sermons of peacetime do not always bring comfort to those who mourn with the cry of Ukraine's Rachel.

Part Two: Practical Advice for Pastoral Theology

"For They will be Comforted." Humans seek comfort, meaning, and love as inherent aspirations of human existence.[38] Comfort is an eschatological hope and event, tied to the full coming of the kingdom of God, which we are called to desire above all else in this life (Matt 6:10, 33).[39] Yet, future comfort often seems too distant, and amidst intense suffering and mourning. It can provoke dissatisfaction and the thought: "Yes, this is doctrinally correct, but right now, I am in unbearable pain."

Shallow eschatological faith, or comforters who hastily apply "eschatological therapy," can lead to rejection. As one Christian soldier, a father of two and a mission worker who has preached extensively about eternal life in Christ, candidly admitted, he is "not particularly drawn to heaven." The reality of dying – even as a Christian – and "going to the Father in heaven" does not comfort him because he does not know what awaits him there, while life with his family, wife, and children is tangible and familiar. Similarly, a Christian woman who devoted much of her time and energy to ministry during the war lost her fiancé on the front lines. She said, "I don't want to be with him in heaven; I want him to be with me here on earth." These examples do not

---

38. Ilit Feber and Paula Schwebel, *Lament in Jewish Thought: Philosophical, Theological, and Literary Perspectives* (Berlin: Walter de Gruyter, 2014), 11.

39. Understanding the concept and theology of the kingdom of God is important for interpreting the Sermon on the Mount. For a brief overview of the topic, see J. B. Green, "Kingdom of God/Heaven," in *Dictionary of Jesus and Gospel* (Downers Grove: IVP Academic, 2013). R. T. France. "The Church and Kingdom of God. Some Hermeneutical Issues," in *Biblical Interpretation and the Church: Text and Context*, ed. D. A. Carson (Exeter: Paternoster, 1984).

indicate a loss of faith but rather an honest expression of feelings and thoughts. They raise a critical question: Can the church listen to such stories without judgment and give them a voice within the community?

The primary question for both the mourners and those offering comfort remains: When do the mourners receive their consolation? Is it only in the future? Helen Cherry states: "The gap between eschatological happiness and temporal happiness needs to be addressed because people experience hardship and grief that sets them off balance, and they wonder whether they can ever be happy again in this life, or whether life amounts to nothing more than a vale of tears simply to be slogged through somehow in hopes of a heavenly reward."[40]

Rebecca Eklund answers: "Both in this life and in the next. The consolation received in this life, for both ancient and modern interpreters, is but a foretaste of the heavenly consolation to come."[41]

But how does consolation come? The way to it consists of the action of God and the actions of the church and man.

God's Action and Help. How does God act during our suffering and mourning, especially in times of war? This question carries both theological and practical significance.

During this war, many believers rely more heavily on Old Testament texts than on New Testament ones. Observing social media reveals how Christians use certain passages and reflections to explain events, determine actions, and anchor their hopes. It appears that many approach God as if Christians and the church possess the covenantal promises given to Israel, along with their associated blessings and curses. Some extreme groups, often holding questionable views, have even suggested that Ukraine suffers divine punishment for permitting events such as LGBTQ+ pride parades. Another recurring theme is the expectation that God will inevitably punish Ukraine's enemies for violating its borders.

The application of Scripture during wartime is a complex issue, and much of it suggests that Christian expectations of God remain within the framework of Brueggemann's orientation phase: the belief that God will inevitably restore order and justice. However, as in the case of Job, the reality often seems far more complex and slow to resolve. As a result, both the church and individual believers may begin to feel disoriented, leading to questions about how God acts, how He can be influenced, and what to hope for.

---

40. Charry, *God and the Art of Happiness*, ix.
41. Eklund, *The Beatitudes through the Ages*, chap. 4, EPUB.

In their desire for a swift resolution, some Christians may turn to prayer with increased fervor, believing that God will respond if they act correctly or petition strongly enough. However, this mindset often resembles denial of the reality and complexity of the situation. The next step in this journey is the acceptance and acknowledgment of disorientation. Believers come to realize that the situation may not be quickly resolved, that God does not conform to human desires, and that his ways are often beyond comprehension.

In such moments, prayer itself may feel pointless. Yet, this reflects the raw reality of disorientation – a state poignantly captured in Nicholas Wolterstorff's *Lament for a Son*, where he processes the death of his son during a shared mountain climb. Wolterstorff's reflections embody the experience of grappling with profound disorientation:

> Faith endures; but my address to God is uncomfortably, perplexingly altered. It's off-target, qualified. I want to ask for Eric back. But I can't. So I aim around the Bull's-eye. I want to ask that God protect the members of my family. But I asked that for Eric. . . . I must explore the Lament as a mode of my address to God?[42]

Church Action. I am writing these thoughts during a time of war, as suffering and mourning continue unabated for the Ukrainian people. Most likely, it will only be after the war, when the long-awaited peace arrives, that a fuller awareness of the scale of losses – and the pain associated with them – will emerge. This will lead to a deeper understanding of the pathways and therapeutic methods needed to address grief and all forms of trauma. For now, aid is being provided to those affected, but unfortunately, the war persists. As a result, the pain not only remains but multiplies and intensifies. Christians, too, are seeking psychological help during this time. The church is also striving to offer spiritual support to people.

Both biblical and church history is deeply marked by suffering and mourning. It offers comfort by drawing on God's revelation and the faithfuls' experiences, helping individuals endure difficult periods of life while cultivating spiritual virtues. Mourning is an integral part of biblical history. It encompasses individual and communal laments as essential components of one's relationship with God. This is a biblical means for individuals and groups who experience profound pain or sorrow to turn toward God – even when God may seem to be the source of their suffering. In essence, lament is a "canonical" provision

---

42. Billman and Migliore, *Rachel's Cry of Lament and Rebirth of Hope*, 104.

from God, enabling us to sustain and deepen our relationship with him when our experiences fail to align with our faith.[43]

A Prayer of Lamentation. The first and most important question we should ask about prayer, especially petitionary prayer: Is there a point to it? God is unchanging and omniscient, so he does not need information about our condition.[44] Drawing on Aquinas, Simon Oliver and Judith Wolf argue that prayer is, among other things, an attempt to interpret and order our lives by asking or pleading with God for what is appropriate to achieve our ultimate goal of desiring God and all that God desires.[45] In other words, prayer is both *an eschatological* and *hermeneutical* practice. It is eschatological because whether it is a petition, a lament, a confession, or a praise, it seeks first of all to recognize our ultimate goal and the means to achieve it when we open ourselves to God.[46] And it is hermeneutical because it is a context for interpreting our needs and desires in relation to the divine will.[47] These characteristics point to the importance of the narrative context of prayer.[48] The Sermon on the Mount provides us with such a context. It calls us to pray (Matt 6:10) and seek (Matt 6:33) the kingdom of God (in the tension between "already" and "not yet"), to interpret and implement its commandments and virtues (Matt 7:24–27).

In other words, prayer is a task of reading the signs of our lives, even the signs of history, in relation to our final end. An important aspect of such a task is to make ourselves present to God in all our "incompleteness and uncertainty – to practice what Chrétien calls 'anthropophany'" (insofar as prayer expresses our deepest desires, laments, and praise, it stretches toward God as our final end and expresses, however fleetingly, eschatological hope).[49]

Kathleen Billman and Daniel Migliore, in their book *Rachel's Lament*, remind us that prayer has many voices and many seasons – joyful and lamenting prayers, summer and winter. The summer and winter voices of prayer cannot be separated without harming the life of faith; together they remind us that the danger of praise without weeping is triumphalism, and the danger of

---

43. June F. Dickie, "The Importance of Lament in Pastoral Ministry: Biblical Basis and some Applications," *Verbum et Ecclesia* 40 (1) (2019), 1. https://dx.doi.org/10.4102/ve.v40i1.2002.

44. Simon Oliver and Judith Wolfe, "A Narrative and Apocalyptic Philosophy of Prayer: Being towards God," in *Biblical Narratives and Human Flourishing?* Eleonore Stump and Judith Wolfe, eds. (London and New York: Routledge, 2024), 165.

45. Oliver and Wolfe, "A Narrative and Apocalyptic Philosophy of Prayer," 166.

46. Oliver and Wolfe, "A Narrative and Apocalyptic Philosophy of Prayer," 166.

47. Oliver and Wolfe, "A Narrative and Apocalyptic Philosophy of Prayer," 166.

48. Oliver and Wolfe, "A Narrative and Apocalyptic Philosophy of Prayer," 166.

49. Oliver and Wolfe, "A Narrative and Apocalyptic Philosophy of Prayer," 166.

weeping without praise is hopelessness.[50] The Winter Prayer is associated with the lament of Rachel, who refuses to be comforted because of her inconsolable grief. The authors argue that adding the prayer of lamentation to all aspects of Christian life and ministry (along with our prayers of praise, thanksgiving, intercession, and confession) can help sustain a life of faith in the "winter times."[51] They observe, "Rachel's cry needs to be reclaimed in Christian prayer, the liturgy of the church, and pastoral ministry."[52]

Weep with Those who Weep. Paul calls the church to "weep with those who weep" (Rom 12:15). Some churches avoid weeping in worship and prayer, fearing a "complaint culture" that could undermine the popularity of a culture of joy and praise where praise is good, and weeping is not. As this logic goes, weeping as a manifestation of suffering should not be public, because we should always give thanks, and suffering should be silent and patient, without complaining.[53] Some in the church try to avoid suffering at all costs, so avoiding such mourners is part of the behavior or strategy of avoiding suffering and loss. This can lead to "toxic shame" when a populist and false belief is formed (like Job's friends) that good things happen to good people and bad things happen to bad people.[54] As a result, mourners may ask God why this happened to them, what is their fault? The culture of complaints can form a distorted culture of victimization, in which everyone demands a special victim status for themselves and avoids responsibility. However, a proper understanding of the prayer of lamentation does not undermine, but strengthens, a person's sense of responsibility and supports a sense of solidarity in the community and society.[55] The ability to express one's pain provides people with a tool to deal with uncertainty and fear, and when it is shared, it provides an antidote to the extremes of modern individualism. This is important because silencing, minimizing, and ignoring the suffering of people in the church community gradually leads to a toxic indifference of the church to the wider society.[56]

June Dickie indicates that although lament has been neglected in practice, research interest in this area has seen a resurgence in recent years. Additionally, the study of trauma as it relates to biblical studies has also contributed.

---

50. Billman and Migliore, *Rachel's Cry of Lament and Rebirth of Hope*, 5.
51. Billman and Migliore, *Rachel's Cry of Lament and Rebirth of Hope*, 104–105.
52. Billman and Migliore, *Rachel's Cry of Lament and Rebirth of Hope*, 4.
53. Dickie, *The Importance of Lament in Pastoral Ministry*, 2.
54. Nathaniel A. Carlson, "Lament: The Biblical Language of Trauma," in *Cultural Encounters* 11, no. 1 (2015): 50–68. doi:10.11630/1550-4891.11.01.50.
55. Billman and Migliore, *Rachel's Cry of Lament and Rebirth of Hope*, 16.
56. Dickie, "The Importance of Lament in Pastoral Ministry," 2.

Furthermore, advances in cognitive psychology and neurotherapy intersect with biblical studies, indicating that the act of lament can facilitate social, spiritual, and even physical healing.[57]

Of course, war breaks down misguided attitudes and the tendency to ignore suffering. However, within the church, a taboo on lament remains – especially collective and public lament – because the church itself lacks the language of mourning. The church often seeks positive answers, believing that its mission in the "Good News" lies in offering encouragement and providing answers to all questions. Yet lament raises many inconvenient and difficult questions. Meanwhile, Rachel – that is, the nation of Ukraine – continues to weep ever more profoundly.

Understanding and Accepting a Person and Society in a State of Mourning. In suffering and pain, we regress to a childlike state.[58] We cling to "childish" convictions, believing that the more we trust or remain faithful, the less we will suffer. This reflects a faith tied to a state of orientation. Suffering isolates individuals, leaving them alone in both personal and societal spaces. Pain renders people voiceless because it destroys meaning, shatters the familiar world, and leaves them without words to describe their feelings.[59]

Psalms of lament are marked by the physical state and reactions of the sufferer, while psalms of imprecation are characterized by verbal expressions. In September 2024, a group of Ukrainian soldiers returned from Russian captivity after spending nearly two years imprisoned. Among them was a twenty-two-year-old man who had lost his ability to speak. According to his mother, when he finally spoke, his first question was, "How can people harbor so much evil?" – referring to his torturers. This tragic example illustrates how evil can literally destroy a person's capacity for speech.

On the one hand, internal pain robs individuals of their voice; on the other, the church often fails to provide space for expressing pain because it does not adequately recognize lament and lacks a language for it. This regression, isolation, and voicelessness not only demand the church's attention but also provide her with a unique opportunity.

First, the church, by sharing in the lament of individuals and society – particularly during times of war – manifests care for their condition. By honoring personal lament, the church ensures that no one is left alone: "Carry each other's burdens, and in this way, you will fulfill the law of Christ" (Gal

---

57. Dickie, "The Importance of Lament in Pastoral Ministry," 2.
58. David F. Ford, *The Shape of Living* (London: HarperCollins, 1997), 143.
59. Billman and Migliore, *Rachel's Cry of Lament and Rebirth of Hope*, 105.

6:2). Isolation pushes those who mourn to the margins of life. In such a state, individuals face profound needs due to the loss of loved ones, productivity, or social engagement. The presence of a community is essential to prevent people from remaining in isolation. By staying close to those who grieve, the church cultivates the virtue and practice of love and care, breaking down barriers of alienation and overcoming the marginalization of those who suffer.

Second, the church cultivates the virtues of solidarity and compassion, especially when lament is provoked by injustice or pervasive threats, as during war. In such times, the church, which itself endures suffering, does not separate itself from the collective hardship and tragedy. It not only comforts the victim but also prophetically denounces injustice and evil. However, this is not enough – the church must also work to address the root causes of injustice.

Following the Beatitudes in the Sermon on the Mount comes the call to be "salt" and "light" (Matt 5:13) – metaphors of influence and ubiquitousness, of kenotic immersion and moral guidance in society. During war, when suffering overwhelms the community, faith is not only tested but can also be lost – not just in the religious sense, but in the very belief that goodness and justice still exist in the world. The church, as the herald of good news, reveals an alternative story – the gospel of the kingdom of God (Mark 1:14–15) – through both word and action.

Matthew 25 provides a list of actions that will ultimately be deemed the most important: feeding the hungry, giving drink to the thirsty, welcoming strangers, clothing the naked, visiting prisoners, and caring for the sick.[60] This passage is an invitation to the Ukrainian church (and others) to orient itself around these deeds, both in public and private life, "playing its role in the ongoing drama of compassion"[61] amid the devastation of war.

The continuation and embodiment of this "alternative story" (Matt 25) include the church's presence and support during memorial services for fallen soldiers and civilian victims of bombings. In these acts, the church manifests its calling as a witness to God's justice and mercy, providing hope and light in the darkest of times.

Liturgy and Weeping. The liturgy of the church can become a subversive practice that draws attention to the human condition and society. Communion, in the words of Johann Baptist Metz, is the center of "dangerous memory." He explains, "Every time we remember the passion and death of Jesus, especially in the context of partaking of the bread and wine in the Eucharistic meal, we

---

60. Ford, *The Shape of Living*, 144.
61. Ford, *The Shape of Living*, 144.

encounter the power of God's renewing promise and grace. For the memory of his passion, while singular and irreplaceable, also exposes and brings to judgment the countless instances of injustice and brutality in human history. 'The cross of Christ' . . . reveals the suffering of all God's preferred ones – the forgotten, the oppressed, and the marginalized of all history."[62]

The cross symbolizes not only a "yes" to solidarity, but also a resounding "no" to suffering and its perpetrators.[63] From this perspective, communion highlights that the Savior's suffering also represents solidarity with those who endure specific manifestations of evil. Ukrainian Christians, particularly Evangelicals, are concerned about the support from some Russian churches and their leaders for actions against Ukraine. They are also troubled by perceived indifference to suffering and ignoring its causes by Christians both in Russia and abroad. It is understandable that individuals in Russia may find it difficult to openly oppose the war and instead pray for peace due to the current government. However, there are immigrant Christians in the West who maintain a non-political stance and do not express solidarity or protest.

Preaching and Mourning. In times of personal or collective suffering – of which war is the epitome – it often feels as though God is silent or hidden. Preachers strive to fill this "silence of God" with their sermons. But does this approach work? Paradoxical as it may sound, there is something to be heard in God's silence. Preachers frequently address the problem of suffering either from a human perspective or through an eschatological lens.[64] However, simplified and hurried eschatological consolation can diminish both the value of eschatology itself – the gift of eternal life – and, conversely, the significance of this earthly life, along with its suffering and pain.

Preachers often gravitate toward familiar topics, rarely venturing into the Psalms of lament or other Scripture passages centered on lamentation. Historically, lament was an integral part of ancient liturgies. "Where is this in our churches?" Allen Verhey asks.[65] As previously noted, in the state of lament, believers can lose their words, overwhelmed by disorientation, unsure of what to say – or even whether certain things should be said, especially within the church context.[66]

---

62. Billman and Migliore, *Rachel's Cry of Lament and Rebirth of Hope*, 118.
63. Billman and Migliore, *Rachel's Cry of Lament and Rebirth of Hope*, 119.
64. Ku, *Lament-Diven Preaching*, chap. 4, EPUB.
65. Allen Verhey, *Reading the Bible in the Strange World of Medicine* (Grand Rapids: Eerdmans, 2003), 124.
66. Verhey, *Reading the Bible in the Strange World of Medicine*, 124.

Thus, the preacher's mission is to teach the biblical language of lament, mourning, protest, and even questioning God, all rooted in Scripture. The preacher must reveal the God who laments and leads his people and creation through lament toward ultimate redemption. They must also articulate that the power of evil – the focal point of eschatological wrath[67] – still exerts a strong influence over creation (cf. Rom 8:18–27), which groans for its Savior. As theologians remind us, "Nothing is excluded from the fated suffering, and no period of time has been free of lament and pain."[68]

A sermon on lament is less a solitary address and more a communal act of listening and reflecting on the story of God's response to human lament. It is crucial to illuminate the dual dimensions of lament – human and divine – by drawing more heavily on the candid and probing narratives of Scripture rather than on dogmatic defenses of axioms like God's immutability, impassibility, invulnerability, or self-sufficiency.

The sermon calls worshipers to prayer and adoration of the God who, in the garden of Gethsemane, confessed, "My soul is overwhelmed with sorrow to the point of death" (Matt 26:38). Before that moment, he wept at Lazarus's tomb (John 11:35). In both cases, though he knew resurrection would follow death, the moments between these events – chronologically brief yet existentially weighty – were filled with lament. In those moments, he became for us and with us "a man of sorrows, acquainted with grief" (Isa 53:3).

"We do not honor God by attributing to him what Alfred North Whitehead termed 'metaphysical compliments,'" write Billman and Migliore.[69] The God of biblical testimony is far from being an impassive metaphysical absolute, unaffected by creation. Instead, he is "responsive" to prayer. Passionate prayers of lament and protest assume that God is touchable, that he is moved by the cries and questions of the sufferers.[70] Revealing in the sermon the God who weeps invites believers into more honest and open prayer – prayers of lament that confront the pressures of evil while yearning for the Savior himself, rather than for the preacher's theodicy.[71]

Pastoral Care and Practical Ministry and Mourning. Billman and Migliore emphasize three key convictions that encourage the use of prayers

---

67. Fleming Rutledge, *The Crucifixion: Understanding the Death of Jesus Christ* (Grand Rapids: Eerdmans, 2015), 377, 382.
68. Ku, *Lament-Driven Preaching*, chap. 4, EPUB.
69. Billman and Migliore, *Rachel's Cry of Lament and Rebirth of Hope*, 113.
70. Billman and Migliore, *Rachel's Cry of Lament and Rebirth of Hope*, 113.
71. More about mourning in preaching see in Eliana Ah-Rum Ku, *Lament-Driven Preaching*, chap. 4.

of lament in pastoral care. First, voicing one's experience of suffering is vital for healing and hope. It is an act of faith – entrusting God with the honest transformation of our experiences. Second, a sense of structure or flexibility within that structure is also crucial for those who suffer. Third, lament requires community, as hope is rooted in the experience of relationships.[72]

According to Billman and Migliore, pastoral theology concludes that the prayer of lament:[73]

- offers a language of pain;
- confirms the value of an embodied life;
- gives permission to grieve and protest;
- prepares the way for a new understanding of God;
- strengthens the understanding of a person as a responsible agent;
- cleanses from anger and desire for revenge;
- gives solidarity with all those who suffer;
- revitalizes praise and hope.

In practical terms, the ministry of prayer of lamentation is embodied in:

- worship practice;
- practice of pastoral care;
- the practice of rehabilitation and reconciliation;
- practice of communal theological reflection;
- holistic prayer and holistic Christian service.

June F. Dickie explains how mourning helps in pastoral ministry. First, it provides those who suffer an opportunity to share their story. A victim finds assurance that they are heard and no longer alone. Second, the practice of lament renders today's Christian witness authentic. Let us consider her question in the Ukrainian context: How can we sing, "The Lord is my Shepherd; I shall not want. He makes me lie down in green pastures; He leads me beside still waters" (Ps 23:1–2), when the victims of bombings lie buried beneath the rubble? How can we refrain from lamenting when we hear of children dying, being maimed, or left orphaned? If we aspire to be a community of care, Dickie asserts, we must *listen*, offering our presence to those who suffer.[74]

Third, lament enables us to confront reality honestly, correcting misconceptions about the Christian life. It teaches that challenges in a believer's jour-

---

72. Billman and Migliore, *Rachel's Cry of Lament and Rebirth of Hope*, 101.
73. Billman and Migliore, *Rachel's Cry of Lament and Rebirth of Hope*, chap. 5.
74. Dickie, "The Importance of Lament in Pastoral Ministry," 3.

ney are not signs of failure but rather normal and expected.[75] Dickie points to Scripture and the early church, which incorporated numerous hymns of lament, providing a language capable of addressing suffering. Through this ancient vocabulary of lament, we gain a means to name the unnamed, address God, and identify situations that are unbearable: "We need to retrieve the language of lament if we hope to find the language of hope."[76]

Fourth, lament challenges faulty perceptions of God that rely on convenient theology and ignore pain.[77] For Dickey, the practice of lament counters shallow, one-dimensional understandings of God's character. Instead, "expressed and processed pain" lays the foundation for a renewed relationship with God – one that is more mature and capable of enduring life's difficulties.

June Dickey goes on to cite interesting findings from neuropsychology about the physiological benefits of crying.[78] She researched and suggested the following practices:

- Careful reading of "crying texts" in a support group.
- Using the psalms of lament to create your own prayerful lamentations in a group setting, where participants considered the following questions:
    1. Is there anything that upsets me that I would like to complain to God about (a problem with others, God, or myself)?
    2. What would I like to ask God to do in my situation?
    3. Do I feel a need for justice? Do I need to ask God to "deal" with the person who has caused me pain?
    4. What do I know about God or what have I received from God in the past that gives me hope now?
- Using the Psalms of lament to compose laments for community worship.[79]

Theological and Spiritual Virtues and Mourning. The basis and deepening of human existence are found in three virtues that, in Christian tradition, are defined as theological virtues – faith, hope, and love. In the tradition of the

---

75. Dickie, "The Importance of Lament in Pastoral Ministry," 3.

76. J. Cilliers, "Breaking the Syndrome of Silence: Finding Speech for Preaching in a Context of HIV and AIDS," in *Scriptura* 96 (2007): 391–406. https://doi.org/10.7833/96-0-1164.

77. Dickie, "The Importance of Lament in Pastoral Ministry," 3. The author recalls Jürgen Moltmann's assertion that the true God is recognized not through his power and glory in the world but through his helplessness and death on the cross of Jesus.

78. Dickie, "The Importance of Lament in Pastoral Ministry," 3–4.

79. Dickie, "The Importance of Lament in Pastoral Ministry," 4–6.

church, these virtues were distinguished from the cardinal virtues (courage, justice, prudence, and temperance). An analysis of the New Testament lexicon reveals that, at least in the writings of Paul, these virtues frequently appear as markers of Christian life. Faith, hope, and love often appear together as a triad in Paul's letters. It is tempting to contrast these virtues with vices as dichotomies – faith/doubt, hope/despair, love/hatred. However, when we consider virtues and vices, it is useful to recall Aristotle, who presented virtue not as a dichotomy but as a continuum, with virtue occupying a space of moderation between extremes.[80]

These virtues reflect not only the spiritual-ethical expression of a Christian's life but also its existential foundation. Faith, hope, and love are not just external manifestations, but deep-rooted principles of life; they are inner structures of the human spirit and soul. For example, in 1 Thessalonians 1:3, Paul greets the believers with a triadic list – the work of faith, labor of love, and patience of hope. The work, labor, and patience represent the visible (essential) aspect of life – they can be seen, as Paul noticed in the Thessalonians. However, faith, love, and hope themselves are grounded in the acceptance of God and living in him (1 Thess 1:6–10) as a deep internal conviction and existential foundation. They are the pillars of the spiritual nature of humanity. Here, faith is not merely a matter of acknowledgment but a profound trust in God, which is the basis for hope (Heb 11:1 – faith is the confidence in what we hope, see also Heb 10:38), and hope does not disappoint because it is rooted in God's love for us (Rom 5:3). Love, or rather perfect love, as John writes (1 John 4:18), drives out fear, which brings suffering. These virtues are not just important; they are the guarantee of a blessed life. They are interconnected and function as one mechanism that leads a person toward blessedness and perfection (Jas 1:4; 2:22).

By accepting the continuity of spiritual virtues – at least faith, rather than simply opposing them to their corresponding vices – we can understand the dynamics of faith in a state of lament. Faith does not disappear; rather, it undergoes a transformation, as indicated in Breuggemann's schema of orientation, disorientation, and reorientation. At different stages of life, the believer will live and respond differently. Therefore, in a state of lament, the Christian's faith undergoes changes, transformation, and growth, but this is not a linear or ascending process. On the contrary, the journey may be cyclical, regressive,

---

80. Troy DuJardin, M. David Eckel, eds., *Faith, Hope, and Love. Theological Virtue and Their Opposites*, Boston Studies in Philosophy, Religion and Public Life, 10 (Cham: Springer, 2023), 1–2.

or even appear to be the loss of faith altogether. In such a state, the person raises difficult but sincere questions about God – questions such as: Where is he? Why does he not respond? Why did he allow this? Why did this happen in the first place? Who is to blame? And, of course, when faith wavers, there is a corresponding oscillation in hope and love. In this state, believers may face misunderstanding from the community and leaders, as it may seem as though they are doubting God, losing faith in him, or that their perception of God is distorted. Many books have been written on the subject of faith and doubt.[81] Doubt is the shadow of faith, and the loss of faith is not an uncommon phenomenon, especially in an era of widespread criticism of religion, and particularly during difficult times. After the death of his wife, C. S. Lewis wrote: "But go to him when your need is desperate, when all other help is vain, and what do you find? A door slammed in your face, and a sound of bolting and double bolting on the inside. After that, silence. You may as well turn away. . . . The real danger is of coming to believe such dreadful things about him. The conclusion I dread is not 'So there's no God after all,' but 'So this is what God's really like.'"[82]

The issue is not merely losing faith and saying, "God does not exist," but rather coming to the conclusion that God is not good, merciful, or loving. Not many believers can express such thoughts, especially within the church. Returning to Brueggemann's schema, we recall that a person in a state of lament is in total disorientation when the familiar world is being destroyed, and for some, it already has been. Thus, it is important for the church to understand and accept the state of a person and society in such a time and to offer comfort, drawing on the resource it possesses – the wisdom of God in his Word, the history of the church, and the wisdom of the saints who have been able "to grasp . . . and know this love of Christ that surpasses knowledge" (Eph 3:18–19). This wisdom has helped navigate the horrific traumatic experiences and circumstances faced by churches and the people of Ukraine. Biblical practices of lament, as seen throughout history and in the studies referenced, have become one of the useful means of overcoming trauma and pain, as well as growing in faith, hope, and love.

Concerning Individual Mourning. It is challenging to offer advice and support to someone in this regard, and even harder to go through it alone. No matter how tangible our need for help may be, we must understand that those

---

81. Of note are the works by Philip Yancey, *Where is God when It Hurts?* and *Disappointment with God* or Ruth Tucker, *Walking Away from Faith*.

82. C. S. Lewis, *A Grief Observed* (New York: HarperCollins, 1996), 5–7.

who try to comfort us are limited by their own experiences and abilities, even if they have the appropriate expertise or simply a sincere desire to help and a good heart. Unfortunately, we endure suffering personally. During my "winter period of the soul," unlike Job's surroundings, I had family, friends, and church community by my side who sincerely sympathized and helped as best as they could. But the feeling that you are almost on the other side of the river of life, which separates you from your loved ones, filled my heart with cold loneliness. Job's story is a good biblical example of this feeling (fortunately, we are mostly surrounded by more sincere and kind people than Job was).[83] It is profoundly biblical, strange as it may sound. Job invited God to meet. The idea is that, as the tradition of lament demands, God speaks. Yes, this book is for reading and reflection. But when we suggest turning to the book of Job, we must understand that the main thing is the encounter with God. This encounter is not literary, not just in reading the text, as if God is only a literary character. The God of the Bible, if he is as described, does not dwell in "man-made texts." We need a personal encounter. It can be different; we can describe it differently, and it doesn't matter that this leads to subjectivism.

Another example is the text of James. James writes that when people face trials, they should understand that it is a testing of faith (Jas 1:2–3). It is difficult, but it is something that must be personally endured (therefore, he goes on to talk about patience and perfection 1:3-4). In the moment of uncertainty, when I was waiting for my diagnosis, I heard the words: The diagnosis is not a verdict, but a testing of faith. The words were valuable because the one who said them relied on their own experience. It didn't bring joy, but it made me think that I am a person of faith, and everything in my life happens as with a person of faith. This is not what I wanted, but it is what tests me, my faith. James further writes: "If any of you lacks wisdom," meaning that this is indeed the case, "let him ask of God" (Jas 1:6). This is where all exegetical analyses and hermeneutical practices end – only prayer and the gift of understanding, wisdom. Admitting one's own helplessness before God is a stage of testing and acquiring faith.

In writing the First Letter to the Thessalonians, Paul draws attention to their grief for the deceased (1 Thess 4:13) and desires to comfort them so that they "do not grieve like others who have no hope." He does not say, "Do not grieve," because grief is and will still be present. But the apostle distinguishes grief without hope and grief with hope. To the Philippians, Paul wrote from

---

83. To reflect on Job's experience, I recommend the book by Bill and Will Kynes, *Wrestling with Job: Defiant Faith in the Face of Suffering* (Downers Grove: InterVarsity Press 2022).

prison, anticipating death. He wanted Christ to be exalted in his body, "whether by life or by death" (Phil 1:20), explaining: "For to me, to live is Christ and to die is gain" (1:21). When I asked God to help me, to teach me, to prepare me "to die rightly with Christ," a thought came to me later: Before thinking about how to die with Christ, we need to think about how to live with him. This is the sequence in Paul: "For to me, to live is Christ," and then, and only then, will death become gain. For Paul's life can be described in his words: "It is no longer I who live, but Christ lives in me; and the life which I now live in the flesh, I live by faith in the Son of God, who loved me and gave himself for me" (Gal 2:20).

Therefore, faith, hope, and love are not lost but are tested and tempered in these troubled times; they become the pillars of our soul and life through which we lean on God and in which we grow, awaiting the final promise – the comfort of the coming kingdom of God.

3

"Blessed are the meek, for they will inherit the earth"

(Matthew 5:5)

Stanislav Stepanchenko

They say it's easy to give up land,
where you haven't buried anyone yet,
but when that happens and the land accepts your people,
you seem to grow into it.
We are all tied to this land forever.
it has taken in too many of us.

Marichka Paplauskaite, "Reporters"

Introduction

Documentary photographer Serhiy Polezhaka has been capturing images of the Russo-Ukrainian war since 2014, yet he remains amazed by how tenaciously Ukrainians hold onto their frontline vegetable gardens, flowerbeds, and orchards. The people he encounters along the line of fire water roses amidst the ruins of their homes and clear mines from fields in their villages by hand, enabling them to pasture their livestock. They continue these actions without waiting for a ceasefire – under shelling, in occupation, and in villages wiped off the map.[1]

---

1. Сергій Полежака, Дар'я Безрученко, "Наївні сади", *Reporters*, доступ 1 грудня 2024 року [Serhiy Polezhaka, Darya Bezruchenko, "Naïve Gardens," *Reporters*, accessed 1 December 2024], https://theukrainians.org/naivni-sady/.

For Ukrainians, land has always held significant value, something nearly sacred. At the same time, generations of Ukrainians have continually fought over this very land. Collectivization, the Holodomor, deportations, and wars – all centered around Ukrainian soil – form part of our history and collective memory.

"Now that Ukrainians own this land, cultivating it for sustenance and investing their time and resources, they exhibit stubbornness," reflects Serhiy Polezhaka. "I witnessed this stubbornness in a village near Kyiv, where a woman carefully tended vibrant flowerbeds amidst the burned remains of what had once been her home. On the other side of the house lay a plowed field, evidently waiting to be sown."[2]

It appears as though the land to which Ukrainians cling is akin to the land mentioned in the Sermon on the Mount – the land we inherited, lost, and now struggle not to lose again. In this context, what does the first part of the beatitude – "blessed are the meek" – mean for us? What does meekness entail in the third year of a full-scale war?

Perhaps it means being friendly and companionable in relationships, even with enemies? Such an interpretation is grounded in the general usage of the word "meekness" throughout other New Testament texts. Or does it mean demonstrating meekness as a spiritual virtue? Then meekness becomes closer to humility before God's will and his plan. Such meekness manifests itself in trust. Alternatively, should these two approaches be combined – expressing meekness both as a virtue in interactions with people and as an attitude toward God that involves accepting everything he provides?

Should we perhaps interpret the third beatitude strictly through the prism of Matthew's Gospel? In this case, followers of Jesus ought to cultivate meekness in the sense demonstrated by Christ himself. Or, drawing upon Old Testament texts, should meekness be understood as the social condition of a person? Then "blessed are the meek" refers to those who are oppressed and unable to defend their rights. They would prefer to change their situation but lack the means to do so independently. Their only recourse is humble reliance on God who, ultimately, will establish justice. Thus, the meek will inherit their land – either during their lifetime or after death.

In this chapter, we aim to delve deeper into the third beatitude of the Sermon on the Mount. First, we will overview key variations in interpretative approaches. Next, using biblical research tools, we will examine the text itself

---

2. Полежака, Безрученко, "Наївні сади" [Polezhaka, Bezruchenko, "Naïve Gardens"].

to discern the author's intent. Finally, we want to explore whether it is possible to contextually interpret this beatitude through Ukrainian eyes.

Living amid war while upholding the beatitudes creates tension. It is one thing to read the Sermon on the Mount and another to live it out. However, we hope this tension will not distort our reading of the biblical text but instead provide a fresh perspective, allowing us to see the Sermon on the Mount through the eyes of the meek.

A Survey of Interpretations

There are a variety of significantly different interpretations of the Sermon on the Mount in general and of the Beatitudes in particular.[3] Approaches differ strikingly, ranging from one-dimensional and superficial understandings to claims that the Sermon on the Mount simultaneously proposes numerous ideas, rendering it incorrect to reduce it to a single overarching goal or singular conclusion.[4] Below, we will examine key approaches to understanding the third beatitude.

In the Gospel of Matthew, those aspiring to fulfill Christ's new law should dedicate themselves to the ideal of meekness, kindness, and gentleness. Meekness is not simply a passive state or weakness, but rather an active posture based not on anger, cruelty, or hostility, but solely on goodness.[5]

Dale Allison interprets the phrase "inherit the earth" as "to possess the kingdom of heaven," because "humanity's ideal future was frequently imagined as the possession of the land of Israel or even the entire earth."[6] Perhaps there is an allusion here to Genesis 1:26–28, where God gives Adam and Eve dominion over the whole earth. Accordingly, the third beatitude promises the restoration of the entire earth – that is, returning to the original state of Adam and Eve's dominion over the land. Jesus promises that "the future will reverse the present. If now the powerful rule the world, in the future the meek will have charge."[7]

In composing his Gospel, Matthew attempts to present Jesus as a new Moses. On multiple occasions, the stories of Jesus and Moses resonate with each other here. Looking closely at the third Beatitude through this lens, it

---

3. Warren S. Kissinger, *The Sermon on the Mount: A History of Interpretation and Bibliography* (Metuchen: Scarecrow Press, 1975).

4. Dale C. Allison, Jr., *The Sermon on the Mount: Inspiring the Moral Imagination* (New York: Crossroad, 1999), 7.

5. Allison, *The Sermon on the Mount: Inspiring the Moral Imagination*, 47–48.

6. Allison, *The Sermon on the Mount: Inspiring the Moral Imagination*, 47.

7. Allison, *The Sermon on the Mount: Inspiring the Moral Imagination*, 47.

is difficult not to notice certain parallels between Moses, meekness, and the promise of inheriting the land. About Moses it is written: "Now Moses was very meek, more than all people who were on the face of the earth" (Num 12:3). Likewise, Moses promised the inheritance of a new land to the Israelites. Yet Moses himself never entered or inherited this land. One can hardly disagree with Allison's conclusion that the third beatitude promises something Moses himself never received. According to this interpretation, the followers of Jesus are more blessed than the great Moses: if in the past the meekest man did not enter the land, in the future "the meek will inherit the earth."[8] Craig Blomberg expresses a similar thought, stating that the text of the third beatitude echoes not only Psalm 37:11 but also Isaiah 61:1–7 as it appears in the Septuagint. While in Isaiah, pious Israelites inherit the land, here the reference is to Christ's followers, who inherit the entire world.[9]

Ulrich Luz, the renowned scholar of Matthew's Gospel, refrains from offering a defined interpretation regarding the word "meek." In his view, it is complicated by extraordinary semantic openness. Luz is not persuaded by the interpretation common in early church tradition, where "meek" is primarily set against "angry." He attempts to establish Matthew's own usage, which, according to Luz, is influenced more significantly by Judeo-Greek usage, since the third beatitude is a quotation from Psalm 37:11 in the Septuagint. The Greek and its Hebrew equivalents of "meekness" were typically understood as ethical attitudes, which has informed the modern interpretation of the word "meekness."[10] Clarifying its specific meaning, Luz proposes: "A look at Jewish parenesis shows that the nuances of humility and kindness can hardly be separated from each other. Thus, πραΰτης is humility which is demonstrated in kindness."[11]

According to Craig Keener, the Beatitudes in Matthew's Gospel were initially perceived by the earliest listeners as direct promises of the coming kingdom of God which would be inaugurated at the end of time. The Beatitudes not only outlined certain moral ideals or life values but primarily served as prophetic statements concerning the ultimate establishment of God's order, transcending merely earthly existence.[12]

---

8. Allison, *The Sermon on the Mount: Inspiring the Moral Imagination*, 48.

9. G. K. Beale and D. A. Carson, eds., *Commentary on the New Testament Use of the Old Testament* (Grand Rapids: Baker Academic; Apollos, 2007), 77.

10. Ulrich Luz, *Matthew: A Continental Commentary* (Minneapolis: Fortress, 1992), 236.

11. Luz, *Matthew: A Continental Commentary*, 236.

12. Craig S. Keener, *A Commentary on the Gospel of Matthew* (Grand Rapids: Eerdmans, 1999), 373–74.

Citing Psalm 37:9, 11, Keener suggests that the author wished to emphasize that not those who strive to establish the kingdom by political or military means, but those who humbly rely upon God, will "inherit the earth." There is a possibility that the Hebrew word for "land" in this Psalm is used more narrowly, referring to "tribal inheritance" (Ps 25:13). However, in Jesus's time, Jews, relying upon numerous Old Testament texts promising victory and dominance for God's people, nurtured hopes that ultimately God's people would rule over the entire earth.[13] Such expectations were shaped within the context of eschatological hopes for the restoration of justice and the re-establishment of God's order, when the promised dominion would become a reality for the entire world. Thus, the concept of "inheriting the earth" was part of the theological worldview of Jews awaiting the time when the Lord would fulfill his promises and God's people would reign in a new, restored world. By quoting this Psalm, Jesus emphasizes that only those who trust in God and live according to his righteousness will receive the promised inheritance that will extend over the entire earth in the ultimate establishment of God's kingdom.

Donald Hagner offers a somewhat different emphasis in his commentary. He agrees with most scholars of Matthew's Gospel that Jesus quotes the Septuagint's version of Psalm 37:11: οἱ δὲ πραεῖς κληρονομήσουσιν τὴν γῆν. According to Hagner, the term πραεῖς corresponds to the Hebrew עֲנָוִים (ʿănāwîm), also appearing in Isaiah 61:1, where it is translated as πτωχοί ("poor"). This indicates a semantic connection between the third and first beatitudes. In both cases, it is not merely about people characterized by humility, meekness, or lack of self-assertion but rather about those "who are humble in the sense of being oppressed (hence, 'have been humbled'), bent over by the injustice of the ungodly, but who are soon to realize their reward. Those in such a condition have no recourse but to depend upon God."[14]

Here, Hagner places a different emphasis: Meekness is not primarily a character trait that followers of Christ must demonstrate, nor a manifestation of Matthew's new righteousness. It also is neither friendliness, as Luz suggests, nor simple humility, as Keener proposes. Instead, Hagner argues for a forced meekness – a degree of helplessness in the face of circumstances leaving no other choice but reliance on God. Humiliation and oppression by unjust people

---

13. Craig S. Keener, *The IVP Bible Background Commentary: New Testament*, 2nd ed. (Downers Grove: InterVarsity Press, 2014), 108.

14. Donald A. Hagner, *Matthew 1–13*, Word Biblical Commentary (Waco: Word, 1993), 476.

drive individuals toward this meekness, as victims are incapable of resisting their enemies through their own power.

Donald Turner explains his perspective on the third beatitude as follows: "God's inaugurated reign will eventually result in humble disciples, not arrogant tyrants, inheriting the earth."[15] Turner concurs with Hagner's idea that Matthew speaks not abstractly but specifically about those humiliated and oppressed by injustice. This context aligns closely with Psalm 37:9, 11, echoed in the beatitude. Turner, however, places a slightly different emphasis than Hagner. He believes true meekness (πραΰς) is humility expressed through reliance on God, renouncing any independent efforts to escape oppression or fulfill desires. As an illustration, he cites Christ, who perfectly embodied this humble meekness. According to Turner, it is precisely such individuals who will inherit the earth.[16] R. T. France expresses a similar viewpoint.[17]

David Garland, referencing several Old Testament texts, argues that the "meek" are the powerless.[18] Besides the well-known passages from Psalm 37 and Isaiah 61, he points to Isaiah 11:4; 29:19; and 57:15. For instance: "Once more the humble will rejoice in the Lord; the needy will rejoice in the Holy One of Israel. The ruthless will vanish, the mockers will disappear, and all who have an eye for evil will be cut down" (Isa 29:19). The context here indicates that Israel is oppressed by enemies, humble or meek, yet now they will be liberated because "the ruthless," "the mockers," and those "who have an eye for evil" will be destroyed. In other words, Israel's condition of poverty and meekness will be transformed into victorious status because Yahweh himself intervenes against their oppressors. Here, meekness or humility is not an active state or moral virtue but rather a condition of oppression, resulting from injustice and violence by those who hold greater power. Meekness here is not submission to God but subjugation by an enemy through force. The meek are blessed because they are more inclined to accept God's authority, whereas current earthly rulers are not interested in God's kingdom, as it inevitably promises to remove worldly rulers from their thrones.[19]

Garland rightly suggests that for Matthew, "the earth acquires a spiritual significance, signifying God's new world. The earth comes not through violent

---

15. Turner, *Matthew*, 151.
16. Turner, *Matthew*, 151.
17. R. T. France, *Matthew: An Introduction and Commentary* (Downers Grove: InterVarsity Press, 2015), 168.
18. David E. Garland, *Reading Matthew: A Literary and Theological Commentary* (Macon: Smyth & Helwys, 1993), 56.
19. Garland, *Reading Matthew*, 57.

conquest but as an inheritance, a gift from God."[20] Yet Garland's interpretation may overlook the perspective of the meek themselves, who, under pressing circumstances, are forced into this status. Does Matthew have only eschatological and spiritual realities in mind? Or does the third beatitude encompass a realization of inheriting the promise of land here and now, within the lifetime of the meek – in other words, reclaiming their status as free individuals, no longer burdened by oppression and forced humility? Does this beatitude exclude reclaiming the land by one's own means when possible, or does Matthew indeed consider meekness a permanent trait and status of the oppressed, without the possibility of change through their own efforts?

Another view on the third beatitude involves comparing "meekness" directly with descriptions of Jesus himself in Matthew's Gospel, where he is called meek. Accordingly, the beatitude is read through texts such as Matthew 11:29 and 21:5. Wilkins asserts that meekness in the third beatitude does not signify weakness, as Jesus describes himself in these terms: "Take my yoke upon you, and learn from me, for I am gentle and lowly in heart, and you will find rest for your souls" (Matt 11:29).[21]

Likewise, the promise of inheriting the earth is viewed as an allusion to Christ's earthly reign.[22] The second half of the beatitude is thus understood through texts related to Christ, such as Matthew 25:35.

D. A. Carson considers the interpretation of "meek" as lack of pretentiousness but generally emphasizes meekness and the self-control it implies. He rejects interpretations linking the third beatitude directly with nonviolence and compliance with the law as methodologically unpersuasive. Carson uniquely references another group of New Testament texts, including 1 Peter 3:4, 14–15, and James 3:13. From this perspective meekness is viewed as a character trait one can either develop or neglect. This trait should be demonstrated toward other people, not toward God. Such individuals will inherit the earth – entry into the new heaven and new earth, or, in other words, realization of the messianic kingdom.[23]

Thus, we can identify four approaches to interpreting the third beatitude:

---

20. Garland, *Reading Matthew*, 57.

21. Michael J. Wilkins, "Matthew," in *Zondervan Illustrated Bible Backgrounds Commentary: New Testament* (Grand Rapids: Zondervan, 2011), 1:132.

22. Wilkins, "Matthew," 1:132.

23. D. A. Carson, "Matthew," in *The Expositor's Bible Commentary: Matthew–Mark (Revised Edition)*, edited by Tremper Longman III and David E. Garland (Grand Rapids: Zondervan, 2010), 299.

1. The word "meek" is understood as an instruction. A follower of Christ must demonstrate meekness in relationships with others. Consequently, the second part of the beatitude is perceived as the result of fulfilling this instruction. Inheriting the earth is seen as a reward for meekness.

2. The second approach suggests that "meekness" should be directed toward God. Here, meekness is also regarded as a character trait, a spiritual virtue. The key difference is that the word "meekness" acquires another semantic nuance – "humility." Individuals must exhibit humility toward God's will and his plans. Such a person, fully trusting in God, will inherit the earth. It is important to note that some authors combine these first two approaches. Meekness as a virtue should actively be expressed toward people and passively toward God, accepting everything he provides.

3. The third approach significantly differs from the first two. Meekness here refers to a person's social status. It describes people who are oppressed by society and lack the means or resources to defend their rights. Though they desire to change their situation, they are unable to do so independently. Thus, their only recourse is to humbly rely on God, who will ultimately establish justice. Consequently, the meek will inherit their land either in this life or thereafter.

4. The final approach suggests viewing the third beatitude exclusively through texts in Matthew that reference Jesus's own meekness. Followers of Jesus should cultivate the same meekness demonstrated by Christ himself.

Having outlined these primary interpretive approaches to the third beatitude, let us now examine the text itself more closely within its immediate literary context.

Literary Analysis

In this section, we will provide several hermeneutical keys to help frame our interpretation of the third beatitude, specifically highlighting features of the literary form of the Beatitudes, structural context, and word analysis.

Genre issues. Is it possible to identify the literary characteristics of the "Beatitudes" genre and interpret them through this lens, particularly the third beatitude: "Blessed are the meek, for they will inherit the earth"? Indeed, when interpreting the Beatitudes collectively and their individual statements and words specifically, it is essential to bear in mind that they represent a unique literary form. It is known that beatitudes were a widespread literary form in both the ancient Near East and the Mediterranean region to the west.[24] Beatitudes constitute a recognizable Old Testament formula.[25]

Though there is some debate about specific features of the beatitude genre, Eduard Lipinski suggests that understanding the original meaning and significance of this genre in the Bible necessitates primarily consulting texts in the Psalms.[26] Most beatitudes in the Old Testament occur within the Psalms (twenty-six of the forty-five total occurrences).[27] Yet, analysis of these texts reveals that while contained within the Psalms, they often exhibit characteristics of wisdom literature. Certain Psalms, such as Psalm 1, fully embody the form known as "wisdom psalms."

Why are wisdom literature forms, particularly wisdom psalms, similar to the form of beatitudes? Matthew Goff convincingly argues that the foundation for this similarity lies in the fact that biblical beatitudes align broadly with the tradition of wisdom literature. Both wisdom literature and beatitudes share an eudaimonistic character, which considers happiness or blessedness as the ultimate goal of human life. According to Goff, these literary forms aim to cultivate intellectual skills and moral conduct, ultimately leading to a fulfilled, happy, blessed life. Both genres serve a pedagogical function, motivating others to emulate the blessed.[28]

This is the first significant conclusion that should guide the interpretation of biblical beatitudes, regardless of the perspective chosen concerning the genre's *Sitz im Leben*, whether wisdom literature or liturgical temple function.

New Testament beatitudes are strongly influenced by the Old Testament. According to Lipinski, in the Judeo-Christian context, this genre evolved and somewhat transformed. As previously mentioned, the form of beatitudes was widely popular within Jewish literature, and it is unsurprising that by New Testament times, this literary form had developed a broad spectrum of variations.

One notable variation includes apocalyptic beatitudes. Lipinski associates apocalyptic makarism with the final judgment, where the faithfulness of those

---

24. Julius Steinberg, "Macarism," *Encyclopedia of the Bible and Its Reception Online*, edited by Brennan Breed, et al. (Berlin: Walter de Gruyter, 2011), 3:674.
25. Keener, *The IVP Bible Background Commentary*, 39.
26. E. Lipiński, "Macarismes et psaumes de congratulation," *Revue Biblique* (1968): 330.
27. For instance, Pss 1; 2; 32; 33; 34; 41; 45; 49, and others.
28. Steinberg, "Macarism," in *Encyclopedia of the Bible and Its Reception*, 3:674–75.

who endure trials is rewarded. Clear examples are found in Jewish literature of the Second Temple period.[29] Luz believes that eschatological beatitudes emerge alongside apocalyptic literature, as the relationship between action and fate became impossible without involving the eschaton.[30]

The central idea of eschatological beatitudes is that those who remain righteous, walk the path of righteousness, and fulfill covenant conditions will receive their reward despite current realities and oppression. However, there is a significant nuance – previously, observing the law guaranteed a good, blessed, and peaceful life here and now, the condition remains the same, but its fulfillment shifts to an eschatological dimension.

This is the second crucial conclusion regarding interpreting beatitudes as explicitly eschatological. According to Lipinski, many New Testament period *makarisms* continue this tradition of eschatological beatitudes.[31] Matthew's beatitudes, including the third one, acquire a paradoxical nature. Unlike Old Testament beatitudes aimed at pedagogical instruction, those now considered blessed are individuals perceived by the world as unhappy and oppressed. These individuals will rejoice at history's culmination, as God's kingdom in the new world will have different values.[32] Their oppression will end and God will establish justice, punishing the wicked and rewarding the good.

One apparent structural pattern in Matthew's text is its division into five major blocks of teaching alternating with narrative sections, framed by an introduction and conclusion.

The Sermon on the Mount, the first teaching block, is preceded by texts outlining the start of Jesus's ministry. Initially, he calls disciples, then begins preaching and performing miracles. Christ's central message was the nearness of God's kingdom. After proclaiming this message, the Sermon on the Mount follows. This kingdom is not merely a destination in the afterlife but relates broadly to God's presence, particularly here and now. At the end of history, God will destroy all forces of evil, exalting the oppressed and humbling those in positions of power.

Given this understanding of God's kingdom, how should we interpret the subsequent beatitudes? Jesus proclaims the arrival of the kingdom, invites participation, and then lists the beatitudes. Do these beatitudes specify conditions listeners must fulfill to become kingdom members? Is Jesus explicitly

---

29. E.g., Enoch 81:4.
30. Luz, *Matthew: A Continental Commentary*, 185.
31. Lipiński, "Macarismes et psaumes de congratulation," 366.
32. Там само.

instructing people to become meek in order to inherit the earth? Bart Ehrman suggests understanding the Beatitudes as assurances for those currently humbled, oppressed, weak, and suffering, promising that when the kingdom of heaven arrives, they will receive their reward. Thus, the Beatitudes primarily describe future hope and justice for the downtrodden rather than imposing rigid entry conditions.[33]

The subsequent narrative block in Matthew (8:1–9:34), immediately following the Sermon on the Mount (5:1–7:20), recounts Jesus's miracles. What Jesus preached, notably in the Beatitudes, begins to be realized, at least in part, as we are presented with manifestations of God's future kingdom. Jesus heals a leper, a centurion's servant, Peter's mother-in-law, calms a storm, heals two demon-possessed men and a paralytic, raises a synagogue leader's daughter, heals a woman with bleeding, restores sight to two blind men, and heals a mute demon-possessed man.

All these narratives of Christ's miraculous interventions in people's lives demonstrate what the kingdom of God brings. Indeed, those mentioned in the Beatitudes already experience the kingdom of God's actions partially in the present. Thus, perhaps the Beatitudes are not conditions for entering this new kingdom but rather descriptions of what the kingdom can provide.

Therefore, as outlined above, the Beatitudes are best understood as eschatological beatitudes, meaning complete liberation and reward will be received in the eschatological future. Yet, within Matthew's structure, the kingdom proclaimed by Jesus already provides answers to the oppressed and downtrodden who encounter him.

Having outlined interpretative contours of the third beatitude, we will examine what "meek" means in the Bible, who these people are, and what "inheriting the earth" signifies.

The concept of inheritance is complex in both the Old and New Testaments. Several key points relevant to our study should be highlighted. In the third beatitude, the verb κληρονομέω, meaning "to inherit," is used. In the Old Testament, inheriting land has a dual meaning. Silva's analysis concludes that when the Old Testament speaks of Israelites inheriting the land, it primarily refers to the idea of "possession." Why? Because the land belongs to Yahweh, and the Jews consider it their inheritance from him.[34] But what does it mean

---

33. Bart D. Ehrman, *The New Testament: A Historical Introduction to the Early Christian Writings*, 2nd ed. (New York: Oxford University Press, 2000), 93.

34. Moisés Silva, ed., *New International Dictionary of New Testament Theology and Exegesis* (Grand Rapids: Zondervan, 2014), 2:693.

that the land belongs to Yahweh and the Jews are heirs? Does it automatically transfer to the control of God's people? No. It becomes their inheritance only after Joshua distributes the land among the tribes by lot. This represents the second stage and meaning of inheritance.

Thus, the word carries a sense of promise: God promised the land to Abraham. This aspect of inheritance is crucial – it was promised by Yahweh. However, it must still be allocated by Joshua, that is, the Jews must enter into the inheritance, literally inhabiting it. This is the second nuance. Between these two stages lies a critical condition – between the promise and entering the inheritance is a challenging period of conquest. The Hebrews had to literally conquer the land. Certainly, Yahweh supports his people and fights for them, but their participation is decisive.

Another critical aspect is that after conquest and receiving the land by lot, the land does not become Israel's eternal and absolute possession. Because the land still belongs to Yahweh, he sets the conditions for living in it. Remaining in the inheritance depends on Israel's efforts.

Looking at the New Testament dimension of inheriting the land, we see eschatological and soteriological elements.[35] The idea of possessing the land transitions from a literal to a theological meaning. Christ fulfills all promises God gave Abraham, as described by Matthew and other New Testament authors. However, this does not imply the land literally loses all meaning. Yes, in Christ, God has globally achieved his purposes, and the future of those accepting the new kingdom of God and its authority is decided – it will be realized at history's end when God ultimately establishes justice and peace. When Jesus says the meek shall inherit the earth, does he mean only the eschatological dimension? It is likely, but why specifically the meek? Does this promise exclude the desire to possess and live on one's own land literally? Let us examine the complex meaning of the word "meek," which should clarify the concept of inheritance.

The adjective πραΰς (meek) appears 17 times in the Septuagint, translating two related Hebrew words: עָנָו and עָנִי. According to Moisés Silva, although these words can have varied meanings, their semantic distinction is sometimes neutralized, giving both words the sense of "humble," or "submissive."[36] In Hebrew, these words have nuances, including "humble or submissive" in the context of low social status or oppression. They also denote character traits, demonstrating humility or submission.

---

35. *New International Dictionary of New Testament Theology and Exegesis*, 2:693.
36. *New International Dictionary of New Testament Theology and Exegesis*, 4:124.

Importantly, in the Septuagint, these Hebrew concepts are also translated by other Greek synonyms for πραΰς, such as πτωχός and ταπεινός, indicating poverty and low social status, sometimes resulting from oppression by unjust people.

The noun πραΰτης appears fewer than 10 times, and the verb πραΰνω only twice.

Let's explore contexts where "meek" appears in the Old Testament: "He leads the humble (πραεῖς) in justice, and he teaches the humble (πραεῖς) his way" (Ps 25:9). David begins this Psalm by declaring his hope solely in God: "I trust in you; do not let me be put to shame, nor let my enemies triumph over me" (v. 2). The reason for this prayer is a request for help against enemies: "do not let me be put to shame" and "nor let my enemies triumph over me" as well as "but shame will come on those who are treacherous without cause" (v. 3). David then confesses his sins openly before God, convinced that God will regard him and his humility: "Good and upright is the Lord; therefore he instructs sinners in his ways" (v. 8). Interestingly, David acknowledges himself as a sinner, which is a key to God's mercy. The following verse reinforces this idea: "He guides the humble in what is right and teaches them his way" (v. 9). Thus, πραεῖς here means acknowledging one's guilt before God and humility before him, but this humility aims to attract God's attention, prompting him to deliver David from his enemies.

Many scholars believe that Psalm 37, in particular verse 11, influenced the content of the third beatitude. In fact, the beatitude reproduces almost verbatim the first half of verse 11 in the Septuagint:

οἱ δὲ πραεῖς κληρονομήσουσιν γῆν καὶ κατατρυφήσουσιν ἐπὶ πλήθει εἰρήνης (BGT).

μακάριοι οἱ πραεῖς, ὅτι αὐτοὶ κληρονομήσουσιν τὴν γῆν (NA28).

וַעֲנָוִים יִירְשׁוּ־אָרֶץ וְהִתְעַנְּגוּ עַל־רֹב שָׁלוֹם: (Ps 37:11 WTT).

Similar to other Psalms discussed above, we observe the recurring theme of contrast between the weak and the powerful. The author exhorts readers to remain faithful to God, even when the wicked appear to prosper: "Do not fret because of him who prospers in his way, because of the man who carries out wicked schemes." There is also a clear motif of the oppression of the poor and needy by the wicked: "The wicked draw the sword and bend the bow to bring down the poor and needy, to slay those whose ways are upright" (v. 14). The context makes it evident that this is a socio-economic setting of domination by the strong over the weak. The psalm encourages the meek to wait on

God and to ignore the seeming successes of the wicked: "Better the little that the righteous have than the wealth of many wicked" (v. 16). The text contains strong themes of waiting, endurance, and loyalty to Yahweh. The author reassures: "A little while, and the wicked will be no more; though you look for them, they will not be found" (v. 10). In other words, the time of oppression, poverty, and the arrogant rule of the wicked over the righteous will not last forever, for "the meek will inherit the land and enjoy peace and prosperity" (v. 11). This verse reads as a promise, and although its fulfillment is claimed to be near, the current circumstances remain unchanged. Therefore, the meek (πραεῖς), the poor, and the needy must continue to demonstrate faithfulness to Yahweh, though the reward is deferred.

Another compelling example is found in Psalm 76, where the psalmist describes God's majesty and power. There is a contrast between God's strength and human strength: "The valiant lie plundered, they sleep their last sleep; not one of the warriors can lift his hands. At your rebuke, God of Jacob, both horse and chariot lie still" (vv. 5–6). Those who were once strong, brave, and triumphant are now powerless, for God will judge them. The reason God reveals his might through judgment is to save the meek (πραεῖς) of the earth. The meek are contrasted with the mighty. God intervenes on their behalf and delivers them: "He breaks the spirit of rulers; he is feared by the kings of the earth" (v. 12). The meek here are those who suffer under kings and rulers. The word designates a social condition – oppression and weakness in the face of the powerful.

From these uses of "meek" in the Old Testament,[37] we can draw several conclusions. In the Psalms, David describes himself as meek, humble, and submissive. However, this meekness consistently appears in the context of conflict with enemies. In times of distress, when his enemies were stronger and he had no way out, David cried out to God for help. Other texts in the Old Testament show that David was not naturally meek – his military campaigns were often brutal and highly successful. But in situations where he lacked the resources or opportunity to win, he demonstrated meekness (πραΰς). This meekness reflects both his circumstances in the conflict and, as a result, his submission to God.

Other texts describe people who occupy a particular socio-economic status, one defined by the dominance of the wealthy and the wicked. Despite

---

37. A complete list of passages where the adjective πραεῖς is used: Num 12:3; Job 24:4; Job 36:15; Pss 25:9; 34:3; 37:11; 76:10; 147:6; 149:4; Sirach 10:14; Isa 26:6; Dan 4:19; Joel 3:11; Zeph 3:12; Zech 9:9; 2 Mac 15:12.

the oppression that offered no resolution for the poor, they were called to trust that God would rescue them.

Moisés Silva clarifies the socio-cultural context of these meek (πραεῖς) individuals: "In Israel the poor consisted of those who had no landed property. They were wrongfully restricted, disinherited, and deprived; hence they were often the victims of unscrupulous exploitation. Yahweh, however, is the God of the defenseless and oppressed (Ps 25:9; 34:2; 149:4), and he will finally reverse all that is not now in their favor."[38]

Silva rightly notes that in the Old Testament texts examined above and others using the word πραεῖς, one can observe "a semantic shift from 'those who are materially poor' to 'those who humbly seek help from Yahweh alone.'"[39]

It is important to highlight that the word πραεῖς appears in contexts that convey a sense of hopelessness and oppression. Although these texts may not state this directly, it is clear that the meek (πραεῖς) do not choose these circumstances and cannot change them by their own power. The context is one of domination – the strong over the weak, the rich over the poor. If the weak and poor had the resources to change their situation, they would do so, whether referring to David's desperate circumstances or the socio-economic oppression of the impoverished by the wealthy. If they had the ability to escape the status of "meek," they would do it. Thus, their only remaining hope is that God will one day intervene and change the situation.

In the New Testament, the adjective "meek" appears only four times, and the noun "meekness" eleven times. Jesus describes himself as meek and humble: "For I am meek and lowly in heart" (Matt 11:29). These two terms are used synonymously here. The context in which Matthew places this statement is within the narrative block (Matt 11:1–12:50) that follows Jesus's second discourse on mission (Matt 9:35–10:42). Interestingly, after Jesus's invitation – "Come to me, all who labor and are heavy laden, and I will give you rest. Take my yoke upon you, and learn from me, for I am meek and lowly in heart, and you will find rest for your souls. For my yoke is easy, and my burden is light" (Matt 11: 28–30) – come narratives of conflict with the Pharisees regarding Sabbath interpretation. Matthew seeks to show his audience the difference between the letter and the spirit of the Law. The mercy and goodness Jesus shows to his

---

38. *New International Dictionary of New Testament Theology and Exegesis*, 4:125.
39. *New International Dictionary of New Testament Theology and Exegesis*, 4:125.

hungry disciples and the man with the withered hand demonstrate the spirit of the Law, and that the disciples have taken on the yoke of Jesus's law.[40]

This helps us understand Jesus's invitation: "Come to me, all who labor and are heavy laden, and I will give you rest." The yoke Jesus offers is not the yoke of the Law's letter, which was burdensome for ordinary people. In Judaism, the image of the yoke symbolized submission and obedience. Jews claimed to bear the yoke of the Law in obedience to it. Jesus, however, speaks of his yoke, which brings true rest. This likely echoes Jeremiah 6:16, where God promises to restrain his wrath if Israel returns to him and stops following the words of religious leaders.[41] Thus, the meekness and humility of Jesus primarily reflect his attitude toward the true spirit of the Law, which he exemplifies in the following Sabbath narratives. True rest is found only in fulfilling the spirit of the Law.

Another noteworthy text Matthew uses concerns Jesus's request for a donkey to ride into Jerusalem. This important image reads: "This took place to fulfill what was spoken through the prophet: 'Say to Daughter Zion, "See, your king comes to you, gentle and riding on a donkey, and on a colt, the foal of a donkey."'" (Matt 21:4–5). This is a quotation from Zechariah 9:9. Moisés Silva suggests that the image of Christ on an animal associated with lower social classes points to the fact that this messianic king's path is directed toward the poor and oppressed. Moreover, the mission of this king is peaceful, unlike a king who comes riding a war horse.[42]

The noun "meekness" ($\pi\rho\alpha\ddot{\upsilon}\tau\eta\varsigma$) appears mostly in Pauline texts – eight times in Paul, and also in James 1:21; 3:13; and 1 Peter 3:16. The word "meekness" is listed among virtues, as an expression of Christian love (Gal 5:23) and true wisdom (Jas 3:13). It is also used as counsel for how Christians and non-Christians should coexist (Titus 3:2). A specific group of texts uses the noun in reference to how to treat Christians who have sinned or erred (1 Cor 4:21; Gal 6:1; 2 Tim 2:25). Meekness as a character trait must also be demonstrated in contexts of hostility and persecution (1 Pet 3:16).[43]

As Silva rightly notes, when the New Testament calls for meekness ($\pi\rho\alpha\ddot{\upsilon}\tau\eta\varsigma$), it does not refer to a disposition produced solely by human effort. Meekness is a fruit of the Spirit; it is not a virtue in the ordinary sense but a

---

40. John Nolland, *The Gospel of Matthew: A Commentary on the Greek Text* (Grand Rapids: Eerdmans, 2005), 1162.
41. Keener, *The IVP Bible Background Commentary*, 58.
42. *New International Dictionary of New Testament Theology and Exegesis*, 4:126.
43. *New International Dictionary of New Testament Theology and Exegesis*, 4:126.

potential that can grow and be realized only in relationship with Christ and conformity to his image.[44]

Thus, the meek are the oppressed segments of society, whose suffering may come through economic hardship or military persecution. This condition is not their choice. It is a condition of helplessness, similar to the situations David and the Israelites experienced during foreign oppression. Were the meek to have the power or means to change their circumstances and throw off their subjugation, they would. But the situation is so dire that they lack the resources to do so. Their only hope is salvation from God. One day, God will intervene and change everything. Here the eschatological dimension of the Beatitudes emerges. The situation is so crushing and hopeless that hope must be transferred to the future, when God will establish justice.

Accordingly, inheriting the earth can have two meanings. In the New Testament context, after Christ, inheritance in any sense is transferred to the coming age of God's reign. But in the Old Testament context, inheriting the land does not necessarily shift to the future age if there is a present opportunity to reclaim one's land. Inheriting the land never implied passively receiving it as a gift. It had to be fought for, settled, and defended. The meek are blessed because the kingdom of God – under God's rule – offers them a way out of their distress. Meekness is not the condition for inheriting the land; it is the condition to which God's authority responds with a gift.

Ultimately, the key to understanding the third beatitude is best sought in a space where the voices of the meek can be heard. What follows is an attempt to listen to their voice.

Contextual Reading

An exegetical reading of the third beatitude amid war presents a challenge. We propose looking at the story of a Ukrainian human rights defender, soldier, and former prisoner of war as a living illustration of how the third beatitude is embodied today during the Russian-Ukrainian war.

Maksym Butkevych, a Ukrainian journalist and human rights advocate, volunteered at a military enlistment office on 24 February 2022, despite his pacifist convictions. Within days, he became an active-duty officer, and soon after, a platoon commander. In June 2022, Maksym was captured by Russian forces. A fabricated trial sentenced him to thirteen years in prison. On 18 Octo-

---

44. *New International Dictionary of New Testament Theology and Exegesis*, 4:126.

ber 2024, after nearly two and a half years in captivity, Maksym Butkevych was exchanged along with ninety-four other prisoners of war. He returned home.

Inheriting the earth may seem like a passive expectation, but if the land and all it represents are truly valuable, it implies a readiness to defend and protect it.

"Sometimes love is expressed by picking up a rifle,"[45] Maksym Butkevych says. For him – a pacifist and human rights defender, yet also an officer and soldier – there was no internal conflict in taking up a weapon designed to take life in order to protect it. The meekness of which Jesus speaks is not expressed merely in kindness toward others but in steadfastness and faithfulness to God amid severe trials.

Old Testament texts shed light on the meaning of meekness in the third beatitude of the Sermon on the Mount. Meekness is a social condition, and the "blessed are the meek" refers to people who are oppressed and unable to defend their rights.

"The sense of freedom I have now is so tangible, you can almost touch it," Maksym Butkevych said after his release. "It's the most basic form of freedom – freedom of choice: what to drink, what to eat, whether to go right or left, to speak or remain silent, to make plans for the day or for life, to respond to someone or say nothing at all. In captivity, none of these questions exist. You drink what you're given – if anything. You eat what you're given – if anything. You go where you're told. If they say stand, you stand. Lie down, you lie down. Push-ups – you do them. Squats – you do them. Crawl – then crawl. Head down, hands up, punch to the liver – you feel it all, and you have no choice."[46]

The beatitude points toward the age to come, but its foretaste can sometimes be experienced here on earth.

A few days after his release, Maksym Butkevych recorded a video address to Ukrainians and the international community, expressing gratitude to all who waited and supported him. In that same video, he reflected on freedom: "To be free is happiness; it is the most natural state of a person – the very essence of being human. Therefore, the attempt to enslave others, to turn them into property, objects for manipulation, is a disgrace and a crime of catastrophic proportions. If I may add one more thing to my gratitude, it is a heartfelt plea: Please do not forget the enslaved and the oppressed, those in danger, whose dignity is constantly under assault. Let us do all we can to bring about their

---

45. "Надія – це те, на чому ми тримаємось", *HB* ["Hope is What is Holding Us," *NV*], accessed 5 December 2024, https://nv.ua/ukr/opinion/maksim-butkevich-rozpoviv-shcho-vidchuvaye-pislya-polonu-maybutnye-ukrajinciv-50469398.html.

46. "Надія – це те, на чому ми тримаємось", *HB* ["Hope is What is Holding Us"].

release. Because as long as one person remains a captive, none of us is truly free."⁴⁷

In the language of the Beatitudes, Maksym Butkevych's experience and words might be rendered: "Blessed are the meek, for they shall inherit the earth. And blessed are those who do not forget the meek."

For Ukrainians, land is profoundly sacred. Perhaps no one captured this more fully than one of the world's greatest filmmakers, Oleksandr Dovzhenko, in his 1930 film *Earth*. The director reveals "a powerful connection to the land, which becomes a symbol of both the nurturing mother and of spirituality – encompassing the people's history and culture – and even linked to eternity, for it preserves the memory of the people."⁴⁸ And this is the very value that others have tried – and continue to try – to strip away from us. The Holodomor, deportations, wars . . . all these painful historical events have revolved around the land.

In May 2024, the literary reportage magazine *Reporters* released an issue devoted to the land. It featured stories of daredevils harvesting crops under fire, a woman growing buckwheat in demined fields while waiting for her husband to return from the front, and the journey of Ukrainian grain – from a farmer near the Russian border in Chernihiv to bakeries in Italy and Lebanon.

One of the pieces, "About Love for the Work You Do and the Land You Fight for," was written by Ukrainian soldier Bohdan Tyshchenko.⁴⁹ His first-person account could also serve as an illustration of the third beatitude, as it is deeply about both meekness and inherited land worth protecting.

Amid war, horror, and death, bunkers, and conversations with fellow soldiers, Bohdan confesses that he loves what he does because he sees purpose in it. He cannot imagine leaving it all behind. He longs to return to his loved ones, yet understands: "The front must be here, as far from home as possible. So that there can be a home. And dreams. And a chance for those dreams to come true."

---

47. "Надія – це те, на чому ми тримаємось", *НВ* ["Hope is What is Holding Us"].

48. Марія Фока, "Сугестія підтекстових смислів у кіноповісті 'Земля' та в однойменному фільмі Олександра Довженка", *Вісник ЛНАМ. Серія: Культурологія*. Вип. 29. (2016) [Maria Foka, "Suggestion of Senses behind the Text in the Cinematic Novel 'The Earth' and Oleksander Dovzhenko's Film of the Same Title," *Herald of LNAM. Series: Cultural Studies*, Issue 29]: 101.

49. Богдан Тищеко, "Щоб був дім. І були ми", *Reporters, доступ 1 грудня 2024 року* [Bogdan Tyschenko, "For House to Exist. And for Us to Exist"] https://theukrainians.org/shchob-buv-dim-i-buly-my/.

Near a temporary military shelter, Bohdan once noticed an abandoned flowerbed. The earth around it had been ravaged by an explosion. It seemed to cry out for life to return. So he spent his free time restoring the neglected patch of ground: he tilled the soil, cleared away shards of glass, and bought flower seedlings from elderly women at a local market. Locals and fellow soldiers looked on with kind-hearted curiosity. Only one man, another soldier, questioned him with disdain: "What's the point? No one's going to thank you."

"Can't you just do something for its own sake? For yourself, for those around you? Just to make it beautiful? It's our land," Bohdan replied.

A few months later, the flowers bloomed. Bohdan sat in his vehicle near the flowerbed he had restored and watched passersby. A seven-year-old girl noticed the flowers, ran to them, touched and smelled them, and smiled. She asked her mother to take her picture with the flowers.

"I was still sitting in the car, watching white, pink, and violet flowers growing against the backdrop of a wall scarred by shrapnel. I saw someone's wife taking a photo of her smiling little daughter. I sat there, smiling too – and crying a little."

Blessed are the meek, for they shall inherit the earth.

4

"Blessed are those who hunger and thirst for righteousness, for they will be filled"

(Matthew 5:6)

Ivan Rusyn

Introduction

> Blessed are those who act justly,
> who always do what is right. (Ps 106:3)

Certain texts within the Bible evoke an ironic smile from me, and the collection of beatitudes in the Gospel of Matthew seems a focal point for such passages. Few texts are at once so familiar and yet so perplexing. The Beatitudes resonate with a deceptive simplicity, particularly when considered from a place of abundance, joy, and security. However, in the context of a full-scale war, amidst the devastation of places like Bucha or Mariupol, these same pronouncements give rise to questions, even bewilderment. What do they truly signify? How are they to be lived out in the quotidian? Amidst ruins and uncertainty, they appear detached from reality. Has the world ever witnessed the impoverished in spirit inheriting anything? Can happiness truly coexist with tears? Has anyone observed the meek defending the earth? The ironic smile, in truth, is a clumsy attempt to conceal perplexity, sorrow, and even lamentation, much like Sarah's initial reaction to the promise of a son. In this chapter, we shall explore one of the paradoxical beatitudes: "Blessed are those who hunger and thirst for righteousness, for they shall be satisfied" (Matt 5:6).

Everything is New: Teacher, Covenant, Torah, Community

The opening words of the fifth chapter, which introduce the Sermon on the Mount, signal that what is about to be spoken is of profound significance. Jesus, surveying the crowd, ascends a mountain. In Matthew's Gospel, mountains are the setting for many pivotal events: temptation (Matt 4:8), the Sermon on the Mount (Matt 5:1), prayer (Matt 14:23), healings (Matt 15:29), the transfiguration (Matt 17), teaching (Matt 24:3), a special time of prayer before the passion (Matt 26:30), the crucifixion, and the Great Commission (Matt 28:16–20). Matthew further emphasizes the gravity of the moment by noting that when Jesus sat down, his disciples gathered around him. This posture echoes that of the rabbis, who would read texts while standing in the synagogues but teach while seated (Luke 4:16, 20).[1] The phrase "he opened his mouth and taught them, saying" underscores the solemnity of the occasion and its biblical character. It is a Semitic idiom denoting an important and public discourse.[2]

This scene and the subsequent narrative evoke Old Testament associations. The reason is that the mountain played a significant role in the Old Testament, symbolizing the special presence of God and the proclamation of his teachings. Several details in the preceding chapters hinted at this, and now it becomes evident. Matthew draws parallels and contrasts between Moses and Jesus, the Torah and the gospel, the people of Israel and the church. Let us outline the most significant ones.

The gospel text can be divided into five parts. The newborn Moses's life was threatened by Pharaoh, Jesus's life was threatened by Herod. Both Pharaoh and Herod murdered newborns. Moses and Jesus both found refuge in Egypt. Both fasted in the wilderness for forty days before proclaiming teachings from a mountain. Moses led the people through the sea, Jesus walked on water. After encountering God, Moses's face shone, Jesus's clothing became as white as light. On the Mount of Transfiguration, Moses and Elijah – embodying the Law and the Prophets – conversed with God. Perhaps it was there that the prophecy of a new prophet, whom God would raise up for Israel, was fulfilled (Deut 18:15, 18). The final episode of Moses's life occurs on a mountain, from which he

---

1. C. S. Keener, *The Gospel of Matthew: A Socio-Rhetorical Commentary* (Grand Rapids: Eerdmans, 2009), 164.

2. Hagner, *Matthew 1–13*, 86.

views the promised land. His community would continue the journey without him. His burial place remains unknown. The final episode of Jesus's earthly life also takes place on a mountain. He reveals to his disciples the vast scope of their mission, giving them a special commission. We know the location of Jesus's tomb, but it is empty. Unlike Moses, he is present through the Spirit within the church. Matthew shows not only similarities but also, in a certain contrast, the superiority of Jesus. Jesus is not merely a new or second Moses. He is greater than the temple and the Sabbath (Matt 12:6, 8), Jonah and Solomon (Matt 12:42–42). He is a unique figure; the Christ, the Son of the Living God (Matt 16:16). Reading Matthew's Gospel against the backdrop of the Pentateuch, we see a familiar divine pattern, yet we also discover something radically new: in Emmanuel, God has come to dwell with us personally.

Moses proclaimed the Law during a period of profound change in the life of the people. Through God's intervention, they had emerged from Egypt and stood before an unknown future. God established a covenant with them and gave them the Law, which shaped their identity in religious, legal, cultural, and economic spheres. Israel's righteousness, defined by God's righteousness, set them apart from other nations. Israel's history and uniqueness had a missionary dimension: They were a window into God's purposes for all nations. The Old Testament prophets reminded Israel of their righteousness, particularly focusing on issues of social justice (Isa 58:6–7).

Community formation was also part of God's mission in the New Testament. Jesus embodies a new exodus, proclaims a new Torah, and establishes a new covenant.[3] Matthew particularly emphasizes the formation of the church, a matter of great importance to him. He is the only evangelist to use the word "ekklesia" (16:18; 18:17). The evangelist underscores that the church's origin, essence, and mission are grounded in the Lord's will: Even "the gates of hell shall not prevail against it" (16:18). Matthew wrote his gospel not to provide information about events but to shape and instruct the community through the content of those events.[4] He was motivated by pastoral and missionary concern for the church, which was facing political and religious persecution.[5] They were a minority among their Jewish brethren as disciples of Christ and, as Jews, among Christians, the majority of whom were Gentiles. Moreover,

---

3. Christopher J. Mertens, *The Beatitudes: A Pathway to Theosis* (Oosterhout: Orthodox Logos, 2020).

4. W. Carter, *Matthew and the Margins* (London: Bloomsbury Academic, 2005), 8.

5. Robert H. Gundry, *Matthew: A Commentary on His Handbook for a Mixed Church Under Persecution* (Grand Rapids: Eerdmans, 1994), 8–10.

there was the break with Judaism, which had already occurred or was nearing completion.[6] All of this exacerbated the church's identity crisis, which threatened its existence and mission.

Matthew organizes his gospel as a constitutional document. Against the backdrop of the Old Testament, Jesus emerges as the new teacher, proclaiming the Law of the kingdom of heaven for the new covenant community. Matthew does not sever ties with the old; rather, he roots the new in the old. He rewrites history in a new way in the first chapter because he understands that history and memory shape and preserve identity.[7] This history reveals not only where everything begins but also where it is headed – to Jesus. It opens up perspectives for the future and defines the church's role within it. The gospel's hearers understand that they are the community of the kingdom of heaven amidst an earthly kingdom, a minority with a great mission for the whole world. This essence and purpose imply an identity built on the values of the kingdom, or, in the language of the gospel, a new righteousness.

New Righteousness: The Incarnation of Righteousness as a Sign of the Kingdom Community

The primary instrument through which the gospel shapes the community's ethos is the Sermon on the Mount.[8] The sermon commences with an unexpected manifesto – a sequential proclamation of beatitudes. It appears suddenly and unexpectedly.[9] Through their unique style and radical content, the beatitudes "cut" into the listener's consciousness. Their purpose is to ensure easy memorization and maximum impact on the hearer.[10] With this manifesto of kingdom values, Jesus causes an earthquake in the listeners' minds, prompting a fundamental reevaluation of everything in light of the gospel. The beatitudes serve as markers of the kingdom community's identity. One of them reads: "Blessed are those who hunger and thirst for righteousness, for they will be filled."

---

6. J. A. Overman, *Matthew's Gospel and Formative Judaism: The Social World of the Matthean Community* (Minneapolis: Fortress, 1990), 72.

7. Dale C. Allison, Jr., *The New Moses: A Matthean Typology* (Eugene: Wipf & Stock, 2013), 277.

8. Rudolf Schnackenburg, *The Gospel of Matthew* (Grand Rapids: Eerdmans, 2002), 10.

9. M. Green, *The Message of Matthew: The Kingdom of Heaven* (Downers Grove: InterVarsity Press, 2000), 89.

10. France, *The Gospel of Matthew*, 159.

The adjective "blessed" translates from the Greek *makarios*, which signifies fortunate, happy, blessed, or blissful.[11] Perhaps, McKnight exaggerates by asserting that "the entire passage stands and from this one word the whole list hangs."[12] Nevertheless, the meaning of this word is crucial for understanding the passage.

In Greek literature, *makarios* described the life of the gods, free from suffering and death.[13] Later, this word depicted those fortunate individuals who enjoyed prosperity.[14] A genre of macarisms even developed – stylized formulas of blessedness that celebrated fortune and congratulated the fortunate.[15] The cause of blessedness could be honor, wisdom, a wife, or children. However, *makarios* was most often associated with the wealthy, whose abundance allowed them to be unconcerned with the troubles of the poor.[16] Participants in religious rites were also called blessed, as it was believed they drew a person closer to the divine.[17] This word also appears in epitaphs, indicating a belief in the possibility of blessedness after death.[18]

Makarios is the New Testament equivalent of the Hebrew *ashrê*, which signifies happiness, satisfaction, blessing, and blessedness.[19] The Old Testament contains over forty makarisms, primarily in the Psalms and Wisdom Books.[20] Unlike Hellenistic literature, Old Testament makarisms are applied exclusively to humans.[21] God is not called blessed, as he is the sole source of

---

11. J. P. Louw and E. A. Nida, *Greek-English Lexicon of the New Testament: Based on Semantic Domains* (New York: United Bible Societies, 1996), 301.

12. Scot McKnight, *Sermon on the Mount* (Grand Rapids: Zondervan, 2013), 32.

13. F. Hauck and G. Bertram, "Μακάριος, Μακαρίζω, Μακαρισμός," in *Theological Dictionary of the New Testament*, ed. G. Kittel, G. Bromiley, and G. Friedrich (Grand Rapids: Eerdmans, 1964), 4:362.

14. H. Cremer, *Biblico-Theological Lexicon of New Testament Greek* (Edinburgh: T&T Clark, 1895), 776.

15. Hauck and Bertram, "Μακάριος," in *Theological Dictionary of the New Testament*, 4:363.

16. M. Vincent, *Word Studies in the New Testament* (New York: Charles Scribner's Son, 1887), 33.

17. Hauck and Bertram, "Μακάριος," in *Theological Dictionary of the New Testament*, 4:363.

18. G. Kittel, G. Friedrich, and G. W. Bromiley, *Theological Dictionary of the New Testament: Abridged in One Volume* (Grand Rapids: Eerdmans, 1985), 548.

19. U. Becker, "Μακάριος," in *The New International Dictionary of New Testament Theology*, ed. C. Brown (Grand Rapids: Zondervan, 1986), 1:215.

20. R. Guelich, "The Matthean Beatitudes: 'Entrance-Requirements' or Eschatological Blessings?," *Journal of Biblical Literature* 95, no. 3 (1976): 64.

21. Hauck and Bertram, "Μακάριος," in *Theological Dictionary of the New Testament*, 4:363.

blessedness.[22] Similar to Hellenistic texts, the cause of blessedness can be honor, wisdom, children, and so on (Ps 127:5; Prov 3:13). However, makarisms are most often used to describe a relationship with God – blessed is the one whose sins are forgiven (Ps 32:1–2), who belongs to God (Ps 33:12; 65:4; 84:4; 89:15; 144:15), hopes in him (Ps 34:8; 40:4; 84:12; 146:5; Prov 2:12; Isa 30:18), keeps his commandments (Pss 1:1; 112:1; 119:1, 2), and who learns from the Lord even in suffering (Job 5:17; Ps 94:12). Blessed as well is the one who cares for the poor (Ps 41:1; Prov 14:21), upholds justice, and always acts righteously (Ps 106:3; Prov 20:7; Isa 56:2). Thus, there is a clear contrast with the extra-biblical use of blessedness, as in the Old Testament, it is directly related to a relationship with God and does not always correspond to common external criteria of happiness. Old Testament beatitudes also have an eschatological nuance.

In the New Testament, the word *makarios* is used fifty times, most often in the gospels of Luke and Matthew, as well as in Revelation. Although its meaning often resonates with the Old Testament, it acquires new shades in the New Testament. Here, *makarios* conveys the fullness of spiritual joy and happiness from participating in salvation and belonging to God's kingdom. In the Old Testament, blessedness is primarily understood as practical wisdom, while in the New Testament, it is more of an eschatological proclamation. In 1 Timothy 1:11 and 6:15, God is called blessed, likely due to polemics with the imperial cult. Sometimes *makários* is used in a general sense. For example, the apostle Paul calls himself blessed because he can defend himself before Agrippa (Acts 26:2).

In general, Matthew uses "blessed" in a general biblical sense. However, there are several peculiarities. Firstly, we know of no other instance where as many as nine makarisms are collected. Secondly, some of Matthew's beatitudes appear contradictory. For example, in extra-biblical literature, beatitudes are conventional. The causal nature of beatitudes is also evident in other Bible texts. The exclamation is quite understandable: "Where there is no revelation, people cast off restraint, but blessed is the one who heeds wisdom's instruction" (Prov 29:18). But in Matthew, it is the opposite: the beatitudes are not conventional.[23] Jesus calls blessed those whose blessedness is not at all obvious, honors those whom the world would mock as failures. Jesus turns everything upside down, proclaiming the unhappy as happy. If the beatitudes are taken seriously, one must be prepared to reevaluate values. For example, wealth better

---

22. C. Spicq and J. Ernest, *Theological Lexicon of the New Testament* (Peabody: Hendrickson Publishers, 1994), 2:434.

23. France, *The Gospel of Matthew*, 160.

suits blessedness, but Jesus proclaims the poor as blessed. In popular culture, joy is a sign of happiness, but the Lord proclaims those who weep as blessed. In a culture of success and external image, a pure heart is not respected and adds no advantage. Therefore, one wants to confidently answer "no!" to almost all the beatitudes.

But there is one factor that permeates the content of the gospel, forever changing the perception of reality – the kingdom of God. Having ascended the mountain and viewed everything from the perspective of the kingdom of heaven, we discover the horizon of a new reality, in which everything is not just the opposite, but everything is truly real. John, Jesus, and the disciples unanimously preach: "Repent, for the kingdom of heaven is at hand." To repent is to return to the appropriate position, to an observation deck that allows one to see everything from the necessary angle. Thus, the beatitudes appear true, though this does not make them easier. Indeed, the beatitudes are "sacred paradoxes."[24]

Their opposite can highlight aspects of "blessedness." Boring argues that the antonym of "blessed" is not unhappy but cursed.[25] In the parable of the kingdom of God, the cursed are those whom God does not favor and who cannot enter the kingdom (Matt 5:44; 25:41). Another option is the word "woe," which Jesus proclaims eight times to the Pharisees. Beatitudes and curses form an important contrast in Matthew. Interestingly, the words "blessed" and "woe" are used thirteen times in Matthew.

Blessedness is more than a subjective feeling; it is an objective reality, though invisible from the perspective of the earthly kingdom. It belongs to the present and future and signifies a special favor from God.[26] To be blessed is deep, comprehensive happiness and blessing from participating in salvation and anticipating God's kingdom.

Jesus proclaims the hungry and thirsty for righteousness as blessed. This beatitude is also found in the Gospel of Luke. However, it is somewhat shorter and seems to have different accents: "Blessed are you who hunger now, for you will be satisfied" (Luke 6:21). Matthew strengthens the emphasis on need by adding the word "thirsty" and defines righteousness as the object. "Hungry and thirsty" is a well known biblical image (Ps 107:5–9; Isa 49:10; 55:1–2; 65:13). In pairs, these words reinforce each other, sharpening the emphasis on need.[27]

---

24. Hauck and Bertram, "Μακάριος," in *Theological Dictionary of the New Testament*, 4:368.
25. M. Eugene Boring, "The Gospel of Matthew," in *New Interpreter's Bible*, ed. Leander E. Keck, vol. 8 (Nashville: Abingdon, 1994), 177.
26. Turner, *Matthew*, 146.
27. Nolland, *The Gospel of Matthew*, 202.

In a region where food and water were often scarce, these metaphors had a powerful impact.[28] The Greek *peináō* and *dipsáō*, along with their Hebrew equivalents, have literal and metaphorical meanings. Primarily, they speak of literal hunger and thirst, resulting from a prolonged lack of food, or a state of exhaustion during a long journey. As metaphors, they can speak of deprivation or the lack of something necessary.[29] For example, the oppressed are sometimes called hungry or thirsty (Ps 107:36; Isa 41:16). And in Matthew 25:31–46, Jesus speaks of himself as a sick prisoner, deprived of food and water. Also, in a symbolic sense, "hungry and thirsty" can express the idea of a passionate desire for something. Often in Scripture, the object of hunger and thirst is God (Ps 41:3; 42:2; 62:2).

Righteousness is a key theme in Matthew, although he uses the word only seven times – five times in the Sermon on the Mount and twice in the Beatitudes.[30] Righteousness is the main and most complex word of the fourth beatitude. The problem is that the noun *dikaiosynē* has a broad spectrum of semantic and theological nuances. There is ongoing debate about the meaning of "righteousness" in Matthew among scholars. Currently, there are four main options, and the rest are variations of these: (1) righteousness is a gift from God; (2) righteousness is justification by God; (3) righteousness is the state and action of a person, manifested in the conscientious observance of God's commandments;[31] and (4) righteousness is both a gift from God and a requirement from humanity.[32] Proponents of various interpretations will find confirmation of their views in the gospel of Matthew, as righteousness is a multifaceted concept. Rejecting other options in favor of one is not advisable. It is more appropriate to consider the key aspects of righteousness that the evangelist seeks to convey, combining them with additional aspects present in the text. When discussing righteousness in Matthew, it is important to refrain from reading the texts in light of the apostle Paul. To assert that righteousness

---

28. W. Bauder, "πεινάω," in *New International Dictionary of New Testament Theology*, ed. C. Brown (Grand Rapids: Zondervan, 1986), 2:264.

29. Kittel, Friedrich, and Bromiley, *Theological Dictionary of the New Testament*, 820, 177.

30. Grant R. Osborne, *Matthew*, Zondervan Exegetical Commentary on the New Testament (Grand Rapids: Zondervan, 2010), 168.

31. W. D. Davies and D. C. Allison, Jr., *Matthew 1–7*, International Critical Commentary (London: T&T Clark, 2004), 453.

32. R. Guelich, *The Sermon on the Mount: A Foundation for Understanding* (Dallas: Word Books, 1982), 84–85.

in Matthew is primarily justification by God would be incorrect.[33] An analysis of the Gospel of Matthew leads to the conclusion that the key meaning of righteousness in Matthew 5:6 is righteousness as a gift, commandment, and promise. Let us focus on righteousness as a commandment.

The Greek *dikaiosynē* is equivalent to Hebrew words derived from the root *sdq*, in particular *sedeq* and *sedaqa*, which convey a whole constellation of meanings, though righteousness and justice are dominant.[34] First of all, righteousness characterizes the nature and actions of God regarding creation and humanity. God's righteousness is manifested in holiness and justice. In the Old Testament, righteousness is directly related to the covenant. Righteousness also describes the state and actions of a person. Human righteousness is manifested in faithfulness in covenantal relationships with God and in the observance of the Torah's decrees.[35] Righteousness is a relational concept, encompassing the relationship between God and humanity, as well as between people.

In Matthew, there is an obvious emphasis on ethics, and the Sermon on the Mount has an ethical sharpness.[36] He uses righteousness in an anthropological and moral sense. In Matthew 3:15, Jesus states that it is fitting for him "to fulfill all righteousness," and in Matthew 6:33, he calls on listeners to seek first the kingdom of heaven and its righteousness. In Matthew 21:32, John's ministry is defined as "the way of righteousness," and in Matthew 28:16–20, Jesus calls on the disciples to teach all nations to observe what he has commanded. Clearly, righteousness is the fulfillment of commandments, the essence of which Jesus now reveals.[37] The words of Christ to his disciples are telling: "For I tell you, unless your righteousness exceeds that of the scribes and Pharisees, you will never enter the kingdom of heaven" (Matt 5:20 ESV). The problem of the scribes and Pharisees was not the absence of God's gift, but rather insufficient righteousness, which manifested itself in certain actions or inaction. Their actions were inconsistent with the Law and especially with the righteousness of the New Covenant.

The communication device by which Jesus conveys the essence of the new righteousness in contrast to the righteousness of the Law deserves special attention: "You have heard that it said," "but I say to you." These statements

---

33. B. Przybylski, *Righteousness in Matthew and His World of Thought* (Cambridge: Cambridge University Press, 2004), 105–106.

34. J. V. Brown, "Justice, Righteousness," in *Dictionary of Jesus and the Gospels*, ed. J. B. Green, P. J. K. Brown, and N. Perrin (Grand Rapids: InterVarsity Press, 2013), 463.

35. Luz, *Matthew 1–7*, 196.

36. Luz, *Matthew 1–7*, 169.

37. France, *The Gospel of Matthew*, 167.

are antitheses. However, one must be cautious with this formulation, as it can create a false impression of the Law's nullification. Jesus came not to abolish but to fulfill the Law (Matt 5:17–19). The contrast between the old and new righteousness shows the continuity between the new and the old. Jesus not only reveals the true meaning of the law but goes beyond its boundaries.[38] The six contrasts demonstrate that the new righteousness presupposes something deeper and greater. The righteousness of the kingdom is not only a righteous act but also a righteous word and, most importantly, a righteous motive. In other words, the new righteousness is primarily about who a person is, not just what they do.[39]

The six contrasts culminate in the most challenging – non-resistance to evil and love for enemies. In the context of Matthew's Gospel, enemies are those who persecute the Christian community, including religious and political forces. Jesus radicalizes the Law and reveals a new level of righteousness. This is a super-righteousness, manifested in the integrity and unity of intention and action, thought and word, inner and outer. Such righteousness is rooted in a person's worldview and identity. Jesus concludes his teaching on contrasts with words that demonstrate the meaning of righteousness: "Be perfect, therefore, as your heavenly Father is perfect" (Matt 5:48).

Righteousness has synonyms in Matthew. Primarily, it is the phrase "God's will."[40] To be righteous is to do God's will. The embodiment of God's will is a precise marker of belonging to his community. Those who do so are Jesus's true "brother, sister, and mother" (Matt 12:46–50). They will enter the Kingdom, not those who cry "Lord, Lord" (Matt 7:21). The new righteousness is manifested not in religious rhetoric but in concrete fruits (Matt 7:15–20).

The second synonym for righteousness is the word "disciple." Matthew does not use the word "righteous" in relation to disciples. The scribes and Pharisees can be righteous to a greater or lesser degree. The righteous are those who keep the Law, but the followers of Jesus's law are called disciples.[41] As Barth observed, true righteousness is accomplished only in the context of discipleship.[42] To be a disciple means to embody the righteousness of God's kingdom. The beatitudes have an implicit imperative, so they are a call to acts

---

38. E. P. Sanders, *Jesus and Judaism* (London: SCM Press, 1985), 261.
39. M. Dibelius, *The Sermon on the Mount* (New York: C. Scribner's Sons, 1973), 137.
40. Przybylski, *Righteousness in Matthew and His World of Thought*, 115.
41. Przybylski, *Righteousness in Matthew and His World of Thought*, 111.
42. Przybylski, *Righteousness in Matthew and His World of Thought*, 112.

of righteousness.[43] By using the article before the word "righteousness," Matthew indicates that it refers to all righteousness.[44]

Righteousness can be mistakenly perceived as exclusively personal spirituality, manifested or even limited to the performance of rituals. However, Jesus revolutionizes the understanding of righteousness by linking it to mercy. Interestingly, Jesus calls those righteous who, in the parable, cared for him in prison, sickness, hunger, and thirst (Matt 25:37, 46). At the coming of the kingdom, caring for others will be decisive. In opposition to the righteous stand not the unrighteous, but the evil (Matt 13:49). Joseph is also called righteous (Matt 1:19). His righteousness prompted him to choose a norm of the Law that would preserve not only Mary's honor but also, likely, her life. His actions demonstrated faithfulness to the commandment and mercy towards a person. Interestingly, people who saved Jews during the Holocaust are called righteous among the nations. Righteousness in Matthew gives life to another.

The reason for the harsh criticism of the Pharisees was their narrowing of righteousness to religious rituals and their indifference to the needs of vulnerable people. The Pharisees meticulously calculated the tithe but neglected the most important – justice, mercy and faithfulness (Matt 23:23). They devised ways to evade the duty to care for parents, which is the fifth commandment, through the promise of a temple offering (Matt 15:5–6).[45] They saw God in the commandment, so they observed the Sabbath, but they could not recognize him in the suffering neighbor, so they were indignant at the healing on the Sabbath (Matt 12:9–15). This manifested "small" righteousness, which not only did not promote helping the vulnerable but, on the contrary, oppressed them. Jesus showed that according to the Pharisees' righteousness, cattle had greater value than a destitute person. He reminded them that true righteousness promotes good, not limits it (Matt 12:12). In fact, God desires mercy, not sacrifice (Matt 12:7).

It is worth noting that the beatitudes on righteousness and mercy go hand in hand.[46] Righteousness seems to lead to mercy, and mercy stands on righteousness. The spirit of the Law and the prophets is to do to others what we expect from them (Matt 7:12). The entire Law is contained in two commandments: love God and love your neighbor as yourself (Matt 22:37–38).

---

43. Boring, *The Gospel of Matthew*, 178.
44. G. Strecker, *The Sermon on the Mount: An Exegetical Commentary* (Nashville: Abingdon, 1988), 37.
45. Osborne, *Matthew*, 586.
46. Eklund, *The Beatitudes through the Ages*, chap. 6, Apple Books.

In English, as in many other languages (including Ukrainian), there is a difference between the words "righteousness" and "justice." However, the Greek *dikaiosynē*, like the Hebrew *sedeq* and *sedaqa*, considers righteousness and justice so interconnected that it is sometimes difficult to understand which one is meant.[47] In light of that it is appropriate to ask whether Matthew 5:6 has personal righteousness or social justice in mind? Hagner believes that Matthew 5:6 refers specifically to justice.[48] He points out that the first beatitudes speak of those who suffer social injustice and that Matthew uses the word "righteousness" unsystematically. Therefore, "the hungry and thirsty" are those who are deprived of justice and suffer oppression.[49] They long to see God's righteousness, which will be manifested in the triumph of justice.[50] It is known that the first readers of the Gospel were in unfavorable conditions, which likely led to little faith (Matt 6:30; 8:26; 14:31; 16:8; 28:17).[51] However, to assert that Matthew 5:6 refers only to social justice is incorrect.[52] But it is equally wrong to insist that in Matthew 5:6, *dikaiosynē* means only personal righteousness.

I believe that it is not necessary to choose between righteousness and justice. The point is that it is impossible to separate righteousness from justice.[53] In the Old Testament, which is the semantic matrix for Matthew, *sedaqa* contains the meaning not only of personal righteousness but also of truth, equity and justice.[54] Often *sedaqa* is used with *mišpāṭ*, which also means justice. Biblical righteousness is a holistic and multifaceted concept that encompasses righteousness, truth, equity and justice. The source of this righteousness is God himself. Righteousness and justice are the foundation of his throne (Ps 89:14). Jesus links righteousness to the kingdom of heaven and calls on listeners to seek above all the kingdom and its righteousness (Matt 6:33). The kingdom is one of the central and formative themes of the Gospel. It is mentioned ninety-six times in thirty-one verses. The kingdom frames the Sermon on the Mount and Jesus's ministry with miracles (Matt 4:23; 9:35). In Matthew, the gospel is at

---

47. G. P. Anderson, "Righteousness," in *Lexham Theological Wordbook*, ed. D. Mangum (Bellingham: Lexham Press, 2014).

48. Hagner, *Matthew 1–13*, 93.

49. A. Wierzbicka, *What Did Jesus Mean?: Explaining the Sermon on the Mount and the Parables in Simple and Universal Human Concepts* (Oxford: Oxford University Press, 2001), 35.

50. Powell, "Matthew's Beatitudes," 469.

51. Gundry, *Matthew*, 6.

52. Allison, *The Sermon on the Mount*, 50.

53. Betz, *The Sermon on the Mount*, 129.

54. John Goldingay, *An Introduction to the Old Testament: Exploring Text, Approaches & Issues* (Downers Grove: InterVarsity Press, 2015), 232.

the service of the kingdom. Except for one instance, he always speaks of "the gospel of the kingdom." No other evangelist uses this phrase. The kingdom is mentioned in the first and eighth beatitudes, framing all the beatitudes. It is worth noting that the future tense is used in all the beatitudes, but the present tense is used where the kingdom is mentioned. The kingdom is already present.

In the Gospel, the kingdom of heaven does not mean space but God's reign.[55] The kingdom is the comprehensive and dynamic dominion of God, which extends to everything and everyone. It speaks not only of a new era and new values, it also speaks of comprehensiveness and integrity. The kingdom goes together with righteousness, and for Matthew, this is fundamental. Where Luke says, "Seek his kingdom" (Luke 12:31), Matthew says, "Seek first his kingdom and his righteousness" (Matt 6:33). Although the fullness of the kingdom belongs to the future, it is present now in Jesus and the ministry of the disciples. The disciples pray that the kingdom may come and that his will may be done on earth as it is in heaven (Matt 6:10). The kingdom is made present to a certain extent when the disciples continue Jesus's mission in word and deed. Where God's kingdom is present, his justice is present. Beatitudes have spiritual and political, moral and social dimensions.[56]

Those who desire righteousness seek God's justice, which is a sign of his kingdom. To seek righteousness means to embody it in personal and social life, to be concerned with personal spirituality, the needs of the environment, and issues of social justice. Any limitation of the embodiment of righteousness is a limitation of God's reign. The new righteousness not only motivates mercy towards the destitute but also acts of justice that eliminate the cause of destitution. The new righteousness has not only a moral and social dimension but also a public and even political one.[57] True righteousness is manifested in justice, and justice is impossible without personal righteousness. Stott calls such righteousness "social righteousness."[58]

Beatitudes make the church a visible community of the kingdom of heaven amidst the earthly kingdom. Textually, the Beatitudes lead to the missionary proclamation of the essence and purpose of the church in the world. Jesus proclaims: you are the salt of the earth, you are the light of the world (Matt 5:13–16). With the Beatitudes as markers of identity, the church becomes a

---

55. T. Ålöw, *The Meaning and Uses of βασιλεία in the Gospel of Matthew: Semantic Monosemy and Pragmatic Modulation* (Leiden: Brill, 2024), 1.

56. Eklund, *The Beatitudes through the Ages*, chap. 2, Apple Books.

57. Gundry, *Matthew*, 170.

58. Stott, *Christian Counter-Culture*, 45.

missionary community. With the metaphors of salt and light, Jesus says that the purpose of the church is not escapism but prophetic interaction with the world. In such an environment, the hearers of the gospel hear a call not to conformism, which will make life easier, but Jesus's call to public otherness.

Public mission, which includes promoting justice, will certainly cause persecution. Thus, the fourth beatitude gives a promise, and the eighth warns that the church will be persecuted for righteousness. It is strikingly noticeable how much attention is paid to oppression in the beatitudes. The blessed will be persecuted for righteousness, which has a socioeconomic dimension, and for the name of Jesus Christ, which has a dimension of political loyalty.[59] The righteousness of the kingdom is a challenge to any economic system that stands on injustice. The gospel of the kingdom is a challenge to any political system that affirms itself by the propaganda of lies and idolatry. The gospel and the righteousness of the kingdom are a judgment on the "righteousness" of the world and its structures of totality. Jesus's teaching was a theological challenge to imperial propaganda and a social challenge to the empire.[60] Public and new righteousness will allow the church not only to survive in the world but also to revive it. Such righteousness is visible but not for show. Thus, Matthew is more focused on forming the church and its mission than on transforming the world. But through mission, the church can transform the world.[61]

Bernardino of Siena believed that righteousness has three components: to God – through reverence, love, and fear; to oneself – through purity of heart, restraint of tongue, and discipline of body; to one's neighbor – through obedience, harmony, and benevolence.[62] In light of the fourth beatitude, it is necessary to add: to society – through the promotion of justice, freedom, and well-being.

The beatitudes contain an implicit imperative. To be hungry and thirsty for righteousness means not passive expectation, but the active embodiment of righteousness here and now. The most accurate proof that a person truly cannot live without the justice of the kingdom is the promotion of justice today.

There is another facet of righteousness, indicated by the first and last word of the beatitudes. Righteousness is not only a duty but a gift and a promise. Righteousness in the fourth beatitude seems to be embraced by grace. On one hand, there is the proclamation of blessedness, and on the other, the proclama-

---

59. Osborne, *Matthew*, 167.
60. W. Carter, *Matthew and Empire* (Harrisburg: Bloomsbury Academic, 2001), 170.
61. Luz, *Matthew 1–7*, 389.
62. Boxall, *Matthew Through the Centuries*, 116.

tion of an eschatological gift. The beatitude begins with grace and ends with a promise. Similarly, in the Old Testament, grace preceded the commandments. God first liberated the people and only then gave the Law.[63] In the New Testament, Jesus proclaims the listeners blessed and then delivers the teaching about the new righteousness.[64] The promise of satisfying hunger indicates that the fullness of righteousness can be received as an eschatological gift. Yes, Matthew does not say directly that righteousness is a gift, but he notes that salvation is a gift from God (Matt 1:21).[65] Here, he almost sounds in unison with Paul, without using the word "righteousness."[66] Thus, righteousness in Matthew is a gift, a commandment, and a promise. Matthew uses the Beatitudes not as wisdom teachings, but as eschatological proclamations.[67] In light of this, the Beatitudes are better called "promises" rather than "commandments" of blessedness (as they are typically referred to in Ukrainian). The emphasis on morality is present in Matthew, but his ethics are not moralizing.[68] Yes, righteousness is important for entering the kingdom of God, but to call it a criterion would be an exaggeration. It is better to say that those who have received the gift of salvation and enter the kingdom are righteous. Without considering the gift, the beatitudes turn into legalism and impossible conditions for entering the kingdom. Du Toit calls the Beatitudes "soft imperatives," which are more encouraging than prescriptive.[69]

In an attempt to outline at least the contours of the complex and multifaceted concept of righteousness in Matthew, we can say that it is a gift and a duty, an act of God and man, a sort of synergy between God's grace and human free will.[70] The Beatitudes stand at the head of the Sermon on the Mount just as the Ten Commandments precede the Law of Moses.[71] They do contain an indirect imperative, but to equate them only with commandments means to

---

63. Davies and Allison, *Matthew 1–7*, 427.

64. L. Morris, *The Gospel According to Matthew*, Pillar New Testament Commentary (Grand Rapids: Eerdmans, 1992), 95.

65. Przybylski, *Righteousness in Matthew and His World of Thought*, 106–107.

66. Przybylski, *Righteousness in Matthew and His World of Thought*, 107.

67. Davies and Allison, *Matthew 1–7*, 440.

68. E. Brunner, *The Word and the World* (New York: SCM Press, 1931), 172.

69. Andrie B. du Toit, "Revisiting the Sermon on the Mount: Some Major Issues," *Neotestamentica* 50, no. 3 (2016): 82.

70. Mertens, *The Beatitudes*, chap. 6.

71. L. Farley, *The Gospel of Matthew: Torah for the Church* (Chesterton: Ancient Faith, 2009), 64.

diminish their depth. They speak the language of grace, but to ignore the call to virtuous living they attest to is to miss their true meaning.[72]

Those who seek the new righteousness above all will be satisfied. Matthew uses the strong word *chortazomai*, which means "to be well fed," as we say, "to the brim."[73] This word probably reminded the listeners of God's provision of manna and water in the desert on the way from Egypt. It is used three more times in Matthew. Once, the disciples confusedly state that they have no idea where to get bread for the multitude (Matt 15:33). Jesus twice miraculously fed the people so that they "ate their fill" and there was still some left over (Matt 14:20; 15:37). Although the fourth beatitude does not say directly that God will satisfy those hungry for righteousness, the context clearly indicates this.[74] The word "will be satisfied" is used in the passive voice, also referred to as "divine passive" in scholarly vernacular, noting that the hungry will be fed not by their own efforts, but by God's action.[75] In fact, it is not hunger that makes a person blessed, but God's action.

The meaning of being satisfied with righteousness depends on how the reader understands the phrase "hunger and thirst for righteousness." If this need is interpreted as a desire for one's own and God's righteousness, then this hunger is satisfied by an encounter with God. If hunger and thirst for righteousness are understood as a lack of justice and oppression, then in the eschatological time, God will vindicate his disciples by establishing justice. The fullness of God's justice will be revealed in God's kingdom.

The full satisfaction of the hunger for righteousness will occur in the future. The Sermon on the Mount, on the one hand, reminds listeners of Mount Sinai, where God gave the Law, and on the other hand, Mount Zion, the place of God's future triumph. God had long promised to gather the nations on Mount Zion for a great feast, where the messianic banquet, hinted at in the Beatitudes and the feeding of the people, would take place (Isa 25:6–9). This event will be the Lord's historical response to the prayers of the saints for the coming of the kingdom and the fulfillment of God's will on earth.

At the same time, it is important to emphasize that eschatology in Matthew is not limited to the future. In Jesus, the kingdom of God is already present. In his teaching, miracles, and shared meals, the kingdom manifests as a present reality. Matthew structured the Gospel to show Jesus as the model and content

---

72. Allison, *The Sermon on the Mount*, 29.
73. France, *The Gospel of Matthew*, 168.
74. Davies and Allison, *Matthew 1–7*, 423.
75. Osborne, *Matthew*, 168.

of the mission of his disciples. After the ministry in words and deeds, Jesus instructs the disciples to continue his mission – to preach and act according to his example (Matt 10). Seeking righteousness and completing the ministry according to Christ's example, the disciples not only proclaim the kingdom but also, to some extent, carry it within themselves.

Bruner rightly warns about the importance of balance between the present and future dimensions of the Beatitudes. If the community does not pay due attention to the eschatological dimension, then the Beatitudes become too individual and thus insufficiently universal. In other words, the second part of the beatitude is as important as the first. Without it, the Beatitudes risk turning into insipid commandments that can lead to self-righteousness or disappointment. Ignoring the eschatology and the "divine passive" in the beatitude excludes "the question of God" in history.[76] This can lead to activism and positivism, a false understanding that the kingdom can be built by humans. It is worth remembering that God builds the kingdom.

On the other hand, when the community loses its understanding of the essence of the "already and not yet" aspect of biblical eschatology it ceases to testify to the values of the kingdom and embody them in life. Then the world ceases to be a place for the realization of righteousness and becomes a waiting room. Then the church isolates itself from the world, losing the opportunity to fulfill its calling. A disciple of Christ in this case becomes an *expectator spiritalis* – a "spiritual waiter."

The metaphor of hunger and thirst emphasizes the constant need for righteousness and that it is a daily active search, not passive expectation.[77] Just as the daily search for food is an instinct for a person, so is the search for righteousness an instinct for a disciple of Christ. Righteousness is not just a burning desire but a vital necessity. A person cannot live without it, just as they cannot live without food and water. In other words, blessed are those who seek righteousness first and foremost. It is important to note that it is not about the righteous, but about those who seek righteousness. This does not mean that righteousness is unimportant, but it means that righteousness is never enough. A person cannot achieve its fullness, and therefore it is an immunity from self-righteousness, which Jesus constantly contrasts in the gospel.

Through the Sermon on the Mount and the Beatitudes, Matthew lays the foundation for the identity of the church. Identity is the basic values and beliefs that define a person's existence and actions. When the markers of the kingdom

---

76. Bruner, *Matthew: A Commentary, Vol. 1: The Christbook, Matthew 1–12*, 172.
77. Davies and Allison, *Matthew 1–7*, 451.

become markers of identity, the community embodies these values with joy and without coercion, acting according to them always: both when no one sees it and even against the majority. Identity allows the values of the kingdom to be realized even in times of oppression and vulnerability. The church lives by these values not because it is obliged, but because it is its essence, and it does not want and cannot be otherwise. Identity plays a crucial role in the life of the community, especially in times of crisis. It allows it not only to survive but also to fulfill its mission. It inspires the church to remain a community of the kingdom of heaven amidst the earthly kingdom, of righteousness among unrighteousness, a voice of truth in the cacophony of lies. Loss of understanding of identity and belonging threatens to transform the church into something else and fall under anyone's influence. Identity is not about opportunism or activism. The church is and acts according to its inner nature. Identity allows doing the right things the right way and at the right time.

The Beatitudes are important because they combine realism and optimism. They soberly recognize that life can include weeping and suffering, but at the same time, they open up a perspective of hope and prophetic vision. The Beatitudes offer not only a new view of the present but also radically change the perception of the future.[78] Moreover, they make the church a pre-experience of the future.

Reception of the Text in History

The Sermon on the Mount gained significant importance from the very beginning of church history. It is mentioned in pastoral instructions and polemical works starting from the Didache and the works of Justin Martyr. However, the first systematic interpretations specifically of the Sermon on the Mount belong to Gregory of Nyssa and Aurelius Augustine. The teachings of the church fathers have two common features – symbolic and ethical interpretations of the Beatitudes. The Beatitudes were perceived as a holistic and logically interconnected list, intended to lead a person gradually to higher levels of perfection, heaven, and union with God. They illustrated this purpose of the Beatitudes

---

78. Carter, *Matthew and Empire*, 33.

with various metaphors, such as the "golden chain,"[79] "ladder,"[80] "steps"[81] or "boundary posts,"[82] "levels and maxims."[83] The fathers perceived the Beatitudes as virtues and ethical maxims. In them, they saw the characteristics of Christ, which his followers should acquire.[84] The Beatitudes are ideals that a person achieves by doing God's will in their own life. This is especially evident in the fourth beatitude.

For Gregory of Nyssa, righteousness was a central concept that defines the ideal of Christian life. The pursuit of righteousness is manifested in the desire to achieve salvation and fulfill God's will.[85] Explaining the fourth beatitude, the bishop uses illustrations from the field of medicine and even dietetics. Natural appetite is suppressed by false satiety when the stomach is filled with unhealthy things. With the help of medicine, a person can restore their appetite and eat with pleasure. Not all food is beneficial. It is the same with spiritual food. The pursuit of glory and wealth poisons, while the pursuit of righteousness satisfies and strengthens a person. The problem also lies in the fact that a person is tempted to satisfy needs in an unnatural way. The devil tempted Jesus to satisfy his hunger by turning stones into bread.[86] If stones were nutritious for humans, God would have created the world differently – the bishop asserts. A person must distinguish what is beneficial and what is harmful and also satisfy hunger in God's appointed way. The true bread for the soul is doing God's will, so being hungry for righteousness means striving for salvation and doing God's will. Gregory notes that righteousness is an inclusive term that encompasses other virtues. A virtue that is separate from others cannot be perfect. The path to *theosis*, the restoration of God's image, and union with

---

79. John Chrysostom, *Homilies on the Gospel of St. Matthew* (NPNF 10:96), 96.

80. Gregory of Nyssa, *The Lord's Prayer: The Beatitudes* (Westminster: Newman Press, 1954), 96–97, 117.

81. Saint Ambrose, *Commentary of Saint Ambrose on the Gospel according to Luke* (Dublin: Elo Press, 2001), 133, 38.

82. М. Горяча, "Блаженства як основа духовного росту християнина: духовна екзегеза Мт. 5:3–8 у гоміліях Псевдо-Макарія", *Наукові записки УКУ: Богослов'я* 2 (2015) [M. Horyacha, "Beatitudes as the Foundation of Spiritual Growth of a Christian: A Spiritual Exegesis of Matthew 5:3–8 in the Homilies of Pseudo-Macarius," *Scientific Proceedings of UCU: Theology* 2]: 150.

83. Augustine of Hippo, *Commentary on the Lord's Sermon on the Mount with Seventeen Related Sermons*, vol. 11, The Fathers of the Church (Washington, DC: Catholic University of America Press, 2010), 213.

84. A. B. Lawrence, *Comparative Characterization in the Sermon on the Mount: Characterization of the Ideal Disciple* (Eugene: Wipf & Stock, 2017).

85. Gregory of Nyssa, *The Lord's Prayer: The Beatitudes*, 124.

86. Gregory of Nyssa, *The Lord's Prayer: The Beatitudes*, 121.

God involves the embodiment of all virtues.[87] Commenting on the essence of righteousness, Gregory concludes that righteousness in Matthew 5:6 is God himself, accordingly, seeking righteousness means seeking God. Such hunger and thirst will be satisfied in fullness. The fourth beatitude for the bishop is both a task and a reward.[88]

Augustine tended towards allegorical interpretation, symbolism of numbers, and ethical interpretation of the Beatitudes. According to him, the Sermon on the Mount is "the highest morality and the perfect standard of Christian life." Augustine called those who hunger for righteousness "lovers of true and unwavering good."[89] The righteousness that Jesus teaches is rooted in the righteousness of the Old Testament but surpasses it. For example, if the righteousness of the Law forbids murder, then the new righteousness forbids being angry with one's neighbor in the heart without cause. Doing God's will is the bread that feeds, and Christ himself gives the living water. In this way, one's hunger and thirst for righteousness will be satisfied. Augustine preached that the Beatitudes are Christian maxims and levels of spiritual growth. He associated each beatitude with a gift of the Holy Spirit (according to Isaiah 11:2 in the Latin translation): wisdom, understanding, counsel, strength, knowledge, piety, and fear of God and the Lord's Prayer.[90] Augustine correlated the fourth beatitude with the strength of spirit and the request for daily bread in prayer.[91]

Ambrose believed that righteousness is the essence of all virtues.[92] John Chrysostom argued that Matthew 5:6 is not about general righteousness, but about that which opposes greed.[93] He favors a literal interpretation of the text, which ensures the understanding of the Beatitudes as commandments that must be embodied in life. This interpretation also determines the understanding of the reward. It will be real, not just mystical and eschatological.[94]

Jerome drew attention to the insufficiency of merely desiring righteousness if there is no hunger for it. Righteousness is never enough, so the search

---

87. Rebekah A. Eklund, "Blessed Are the Image-Bearers: Gregory of Nyssa and the Beatitudes," *Anglican Theological Review* 99, no. 4 (2017): 735; Mertens, *The Beatitudes*, Chapter 6.

88. Gregory of Nyssa, *The Lord's Prayer: The Beatitudes*, 128–29.

89. Augustine of Hippo, *Commentary on the Lord's Sermon on the Mount with Seventeen Related Sermons*, 11, 19, 23.

90. Augustine, *Commentary on the Lord's Sermon on the Mount with Seventeen Related Sermons*, 11, 213.

91. Betz, *The Sermon on the Mount*, 46.

92. Saint Ambrose, *Commentary of Saint Ambrose on the Gospel according to Luke*, 138.

93. John Chrysostom, *Homilies on the Gospel of St. Matthew*, 94.

94. Mertens, *The Beatitudes*, Chapter 6.

for righteousness must be constant.⁹⁵ Hilary of Poitiers also interpreted the Beatitudes in an ethical way and noted that the full satisfaction of the hunger for righteousness will take place in heaven.⁹⁶

Commenting on Matthew 5:6, the church fathers speak of personal righteousness and say almost nothing about social justice or the embodiment of righteousness in public life. However, Gregory of Nyssa used illustrations from public life, defining righteousness as justice in the equal distribution of resources and a fair court decision.⁹⁷ Clement of Alexandria noted that the embodiment of righteousness and persecution go hand in hand. Jesus proclaims blessed those who seek righteousness and those who are persecuted for it. Clement encourages listeners with the words: "Let us remember that any trial is a good opportunity to stand as a witness." He also notes that the pursuit of righteousness is the pursuit of truth.⁹⁸

Although the interpretation of the church fathers is dominated by the understanding of righteousness as a requirement to do God's will, Tertullian and Augustine mention God's grace. Tertullian calls the Beatitudes and the Sermon on the Mount the official proclamation of Christ. He notes the fact that Jesus begins his teaching with the Beatitudes speaks volumes about God.⁹⁹

In the Middle Ages, Thomas Aquinas also interpreted the Beatitudes ethically, perceiving them as perfect virtues.¹⁰⁰ Aquinas speaks of the possibility of different understandings of righteousness. Righteousness can be general (*iustitia generalis*), which like an umbrella covers all virtues and corresponds to the fulfillment of the Law, or particular (*iustitia particularis*), which is one of the cardinal virtues and is manifested in equality and the distribution of what is due to everyone.¹⁰¹ He notes that general righteousness is genuine only if it is voluntary. Forced righteousness or righteousness without joy is not what Jesus speaks of. Also, general righteousness is perfect and imperfect. A person cannot achieve perfect righteousness by their own efforts. However, Jesus calls

---

95. St. Jerome, *Commentary on Matthew* (Washington, DC: Catholic University of America Press, 2008), 76.

96. Hilary of Poitiers, *Commentary on Matthew*, The Fathers of the Church, vol. 125 (Washington, DC: Catholic University of America Press, 2012), 61.

97. Gregory of Nyssa, *The Lord's Prayer: The Beatitudes*, 119.

98. Clement of Alexandria, *Writings of Clement of Alexandria*, vol. 1 (*ANCL* 4:158).

99. Q. S. F. Tertullianus, *The Five Books of Quintus Sept. Flor. Tertullianus Against Marcion*, ed. P. Holmes (Edinburgh: T&T Clark, 1868), 224.

100. St. Thomas Aquinas, *Summa Theologica*, vol. 9 (London: Oates & Washbourne, n.d.), 240.

101. Thomas Aquinas, *Commentary on the Gospel of St. Matthew* (Camillus: Dolorosa Press, 2012), 150.

his disciples to be lovers of righteousness.[102] In other words, achieving the fullness of righteousness is beyond human power, but striving for righteousness is their responsibility. If we are talking about particular righteousness, then Jesus illustrates its essence against the backdrop of the behavior of greedy people. Just as a greedy person cannot say "enough," so righteousness will never be enough in this life. The theologian notes that the fullness of blessedness belongs to the future, but given the presence of the kingdom, a certain experience of blessedness is real now. Since doing God's will is the true bread, the pursuit of righteousness can be partially satisfied in this life.[103]

It is worth paying attention to Rupert of Deutz's (1075–1129) understanding of the fourth beatitude. He interpreted the hunger for righteousness as the lack of justice experienced by the Old Testament prophets.[104]

The Reformation opened a new page in the understanding of the Beatitudes.[105] For Martin Luther, the question of righteousness was central. He emphasized the connection between inner and outer righteousness, as well as between God's righteousness and human righteousness. Luther called inner righteousness "righteousness before God" (*coram Deo*) and outer righteousness "righteousness before neighbor" (*coram hominibus*).[106] Luther believed that it is about outer righteousness – righteousness in relation to neighbors – that Jesus speaks of in the fourth beatitude. He argued that a person who "persistently and diligently seeks to promote the common good, the proper behavior of everyone, and supports this in word and deed, advice and action" is truly blessed.[107] Luther emphasized that such righteousness requires "great seriousness, ardent readiness, and unceasing diligence" from a person. After all, in a world wounded by sin, sincere deeds often encounter ingratitude and even persecution.[108] Because of this, many people become disillusioned and choose seclusion, going into the desert or monasticism, believing that the world cannot be changed. Luther called such self-removal feigned holiness and indifference – the opposite of what Jesus calls for. Luther insisted that Christ's disciples are called not to hide in a corner, but to embody righteous-

---

102. Thomas Aquinas, *Commentary on the Gospel of St. Matthew*, 151.
103. Thomas Aquinas, *Summa Theologica*, vol. 9.
104. Eklund, *The Beatitudes through the Ages*, chap. 6, Apple Books.
105. Betz, *The Sermon on the Mount*, 14.
106. Eklund, *The Beatitudes through the Ages*, chap. 6, Apple Books.
107. Martin Luther, *Commentary on the Sermon on the Mount* (Philadelphia: Lutheran Publication Society, 1892), chap. 1, Apple Books.
108. Luther, *Commentary on the Sermon on the Mount*, chap. 1, Apple Books.

ness "with all sincerity, firmness, and strength" through care for their neighbor. "If a person cannot make the whole world righteous, let them do what they can," he concluded. Righteousness, according to Luther, should manifest itself both in church ministry and in professional activity. It should be embodied in the life of an evangelist, as well as a "righteous ruler," because every person through their work can be an instrument of God's will.[109]

John Calvin considered the fourth beatitude in the context of the persecution of the church. He saw a connection between the first beatitude, "Blessed are the poor in spirit," and the fourth, "Blessed are those who hunger and thirst for righteousness." According to Calvin, to be hungry for righteousness means to be in a state of lack of the most necessary things for life. This desire is not about excesses or luxuries, but about receiving only what is just and proper. In this blessedness, Jesus gives his disciples hope: One day he will satisfy their righteous aspirations. The Scripture reminds us that he feeds the hungry (Luke 1:53).[110]

For Erasmus, the Sermon on the Mount is a compendium of Christ's teachings. The paradoxical statements and metaphors inherent in the Sermon on the Mount are rather rhetorical devices that encourage reflection rather than set unattainable requirements. The Beatitudes should be viewed not as a list of strict laws to be literally fulfilled, but as examples and moral guidelines that contribute to the education of an ethical lifestyle of a Christian and can be used in different conditions.[111]

Over the past hundred years, the Beatitudes and the Sermon on the Mount have been popularized even outside of Christianity. It is important to pay attention to the development of an understanding of righteousness as holistic, which necessarily involves social justice. This shift in the understanding of righteousness has inspired many initiatives for social transformation and broadening the understanding of the essence of the church's mission. One striking example is liberation theology.

The Beatitudes played a significant role in the views of Gustavo Gutierrez, a leading popularizer of liberation theology that emerged in Latin America.[112] The political and social reading of the Bible that liberation theologians

---

109. Luther, *Commentary on the Sermon on the Mount*, chap. 1, Apple Books.

110. Jean Calvin, *Commentary on a Harmony of the Evangelists Matthew, Mark, and Luke*, 2 vols., vol. 1 (Bellingham: Logos Bible Software, 2010), 263.

111. Betz, *The Sermon on the Mount*, 47.

112. J. B. Nickoloff, ed., *Gustavo Gutiérrez: Essential Writings* (Minneapolis: Fortress Press, 1996), 162.

used revealed that the Beatitudes speak not only of spiritual but also of social poverty.[113] Gutierrez concluded that socio-economic poverty is central to the Scriptures, and the poor have an advantage in God's story.[114] The Gospel must address both spiritual and physical hunger. Freedom, dignity, and justice are integral parts of the biblical concept of salvation, as it embraces the whole person. Any form of poverty, inequality, and exploitation is a sin against man as the image of God and therefore is a "radical rejection of the will of God."[115] Gutierrez emphasized that the liberation offered by Jesus is universal and holistic, and that it "attacks the foundations of injustice and exploitation."[116]

Liberation theology grounds this vision in the concept of the kingdom of God, the example of the exodus from Egypt, the ministry of Jesus Christ, the holistic nature of the gospel, and God's commitment to the marginalized. These factors broaden the understanding of righteousness. Righteousness is a gift and a requirement, and it is holistic, consisting of personal spirituality and social justice. Liberation theology especially emphasizes the importance of human rights, particularly of the disadvantaged or, in other words, social justice. Sobrino noted that it is impossible to belong to God and his kingdom without the embodiment of love and justice. Justice is a form of love in a particular time. Fidelity to the gospel is impossible without raising questions about social injustice. Thus, the fourth beatitude is a call to decisive action in the realization of social justice, which begins with solidarity with the oppressed and is a movement that must overcome any form of deprivation.[117] This movement can only be effective if it is organized and counteracts systemic and institutional evil. If sin has distorted the social institutions that produce injustice, they must be renewed. Personal holiness necessarily manifests itself in social holiness, which is impossible without political holiness.[118] The church's social doctrine should seek to overcome the causes of injustice, not just minimize its effects. Jesus calls the church not just to feed the hungry but to confront the systemic

---

113. А. Денисенко, *Теологія визволення. Ідеї. Критика. Перспективи* [A. Denysenko, Liberation Theology. Ideas. Critique. Perspectives] (Київ: Дух і літера, 2019), 119.

114. Gustavo Gutiérrez, "Memory and Prophecy," in *The Option for the Poor in Christian Theology*, ed. D. Groody (Notre Dame: University of Notre Dame Press, 2007), 17, 22.

115. Jon Sobrino, *The True Church and the Poor* (London: SCM Press), 49.

116. Gustavo Gutiérrez, *A Theology of Liberation: History, Politics and Salvation* (Maryknoll: Orbis, 1974), 228.

117. J. H. Ellens, "Liberation Theology," in *Baker Encyclopedia of Psychology & Counseling*, ed. David G. Benner and Peter C. Hill, Baker Reference Library (Grand Rapids: Baker Books, 1999), 686–87.

118. J. Sobrino, *Spirituality of Liberation: Toward Political Holiness* (Maryknoll: Orbis Books, 2015), 86.

sins that make people hungry. This confrontation consists of embodying an alternative, calling for the necessary radical change, and condemning and punishing the offender.[119]

Gutierrez argued that where there is no justice, there is neither knowledge of God nor God himself. To know Yahweh in biblical language means to love him and to establish just relationships between people.[120] To hunger for righteousness means to be eager to see the appearance of God's kingdom and its justice in society here and now. The church cannot wait silently, with folded hands, for the coming of the kingdom, for to be a community of the kingdom means to embody its values now. In Latin America, an example of this is the "base communities" or *Comunidades Eclesiales de Base*. These are small Bible study communities that have been actively engaged in the integration of personal righteousness and social justice, worship, and social transformation.

The phrase "they shall be filled" is understood as a divine promise of liberation. It can be seen as both a future eschatological hope and an encouragement to work for justice today, trusting in God's provision. Thus, liberation theology sees this beatitude as a profound affirmation of God's commitment to justice and an invitation to join him in working to create a more just world. Although liberation theology has been heavily criticized, its contribution to understanding the integrity of righteousness and salvation, as well as the role of the church in society, is important.[121]

New Righteousness as a Marker of Church Identity in the Midst of War

The fourth beatitude has significant relevance in Ukraine. In the Ukrainian consciousness, the metaphor of hunger evokes painful allusions to the Holodomor, the famines perpetrated by the Soviet authorities in the 1930s. Approximately four million Ukrainians were starved to death by this artificial famine. Against the backdrop of this genocide, Russia's war against Ukraine takes on even greater poignancy. It sharpens the relevance of the pursuit of righteousness and justice. The Holodomor also ominously illustrates what the absence of truth and justice leads to.

---

119. Nickoloff, *Gustavo Gutiérrez: Essential Writings*, 162.

120. Gutiérrez, *A Theology of Liberation*, 195.

121. Денисенко, *Теологія визволення. Ідеї. Критика. Перспективи* [Denysenko, *Liberation Theology. Ideas. Critique. Perspectives*], 141–43.

Amidst unprovoked aggression, which is the antithesis of righteousness and justice, discussions about the Beatitudes and righteousness seem irrelevant. However, it is precisely in dark times that the call to embody God's will is most necessary. Matthew reminds us of fundamental truths. Life according to the gospel of the kingdom is impossible if its values do not become a person's worldview. The Beatitudes are a high goal that cannot be pursued unless they become part of one's consciousness. Just as it is impossible for a bad tree to bear good fruit, so evil does not come from a good heart (Matt 7:17–18; 12:35). The human heart, its identity, is of fundamental importance (Matt 15:18–19). When the Beatitudes are part of a person's consciousness, then the pursuit of the Beatitudes is a matter of desire not coercion, love not duty.

Righteousness is embodying God's will. Its other name is holiness. Matthew indicates that it is necessary to seek all righteousness, and that righteousness is an umbrella for all the Beatitudes. Therefore, the mark of Jesus's disciples is the constant pursuit of all the Beatitudes. Difficult circumstances, such as persecution or even war, do not negate the need to embody righteousness, but rather increase its necessity.

One dimension of righteousness is mercy. In the midst of suffering caused by war, we are called to manifest righteousness through obedience to God's commandments, love, mercy, and care for our neighbors, especially those who suffer. The call to seek righteousness reminds us that even in a world full of injustice, we have no right to become unrighteous. We cannot allow injustice to turn us into the unjust, and the fight against evil should not make us evil. The new righteousness calls us to remain human in all circumstances and to see the human in every neighbor, especially in suffering. War has expanded the meaning of many words: Now every person who needs help is a neighbor.

Righteousness, manifested in holiness and mercy, can become a guide for society, support for the suffering, and a testimony against the aggressor. War is the darkest night. But the church, which embodies righteousness even in these conditions, becomes a light in the darkness, a beacon for society, and thus a community of hope.

Righteousness, Justice and Truth Go Hand in Hand

Personal righteousness and social righteousness go hand in hand. They originate from the same source – God's righteousness. They cannot be separated because one without the other is incomplete. This aspect of righteousness is extremely important in the context of war as the epicenter of injustice. One of the most common problems in the reception of the text of the fourth beatitude and the general understanding of righteousness in the Ukrainian context is the reduction of righteousness to personal spirituality. Such a "spiritualization" of righteousness makes the authentic mission of the church in society impossible. It is important not to forget the significant socio-political meaning of the kingdom. The kingdom of God is a religious and socio-political term. For some reason, Jesus did not use metaphors of family, community, friends, or servants of God as often as he used the metaphor of the kingdom.[122] The title of Jesus as the Son of God and the proclamation "Jesus is Lord" had a tangible political meaning in the Roman context. That is why Herod was worried when he heard from a foreign delegation about the birth of a king. Similarly, Jesus's sentence, written on a tablet, also had a political motive. The same goes for the definition of the church as *ecclesia*. Jesus could have chosen another term instead of the socio-political "ecclesia." In Greek, there were alternatives such as *heranos* and *thiasos*, which described a private religious association that offered personal salvation through teachings and religious actions.[123] The empire granted freedom to such movements because they did not encroach on its public doctrine. However, Jesus chose a word that speaks of publicity, not privacy. The church that desires the righteousness of the kingdom is a visible and public community. Such a church seeks righteousness not only in personal life but also in public life. It is always in the midst of the world and desires its true well-being. Its righteousness has a direct relationship to how the surrounding world is arranged. The church tries to be not only an embodied example of righteousness but also a voice against lawlessness and injustice, oppression and exploitation, corruption and extortion. It is not only the hands that help the disadvantaged but also the voice that condemns all causes and means of disadvantaging. This also applies to war. A community that seeks justice not only applies a tourniquet to the arm of the wounded but also takes all appropriate measures to condemn the aggressor and fight evil.[124]

Righteousness and justice are impossible without truth, which is their integral part. In the context of war, truth takes on special significance, because, as is known, the first victim of war is precisely it. Truth is the ability and courage to call things by their names, refusing euphemisms that hide reality and

---

122. M. Borg and J. D. Crossan, *The Last Week of Jesus: A day-by-day account of Jesus's final week in Jerusalem* (New York: Harper Collins, 2006), 25.

123. L. Newbigin, *A Word In Season: Perspectives On Christian World Missions* (Grand Rapids: Eerdmans, 1994), 51. Kittel, Friedrich, and Bromiley, *Theological Dictionary of the New Testament*, 339.

124. R. Soloviy, "The Church Amidst the War of Attrition: Ukrainian Evangelical Community in Search of a New Mission Paradigm," *Religions* 15, no. 9 (2024): 14.

distort its perception. War has clearly demonstrated how words can camouflage evil. Instead of a clear recognition of the state of affairs, euphemisms such as "situation," "conflict," or "crisis" are used that blur reality and substitute the essence of events. Such expressions are often accompanied by passive sentence constructions that depersonalize the aggressor. For example, instead of the direct statement that Russia started the war, the neutral "the war started" is used. Righteousness speaks the language of truth clearly and uncompromisingly. It exposes ideologies and structures of lies, reveals deception, and is not afraid to point to its source. Righteousness passionately seeks truth, recognizes it, defends it, and opposes propaganda. One of the biggest disappointments in communicating with Russian Christians was their unwillingness to get to the truth, to question propaganda narratives, in particular that "not everything is so clear-cut," even regarding the massacre of Ukrainians and prisoners of war in Bucha. Truth is a key element of righteousness that cannot be replaced by mercy. After the start of the full-scale war, a Moscow pastor told how they helped Ukrainians by providing them with bread and shelter when the Ukrainians found themselves in their territory. I asked him: Did he think about why these people need such help? After all, their suffering has an obvious cause – Russia's aggression against Ukraine. True mercy begins with the courage to tell the truth. And this truth consists in a frank appeal to the tyrant: "Stop and repent." The biblical concept of truth includes judgment.[125] In the Old Testament, *sedaqa* is often used alongside *mišpāṭ*, which means justice. These concepts are inextricably linked, because righteousness is based on truth, justice, and fairness. Righteousness is impossible without a fair trial. If injustice is the antonym of the kingdom of God, and distorted justice contradicts the image of God as a righteous judge, then the church cannot ignore these issues. Ivan Franko vividly illustrates the essence of the fourth beatitude. He polemicizes with Psalm 1:1 about the non-participation of the blessed in the council of the wicked and, with the help of allusions to the Beatitudes, offers an alternative.

> Blessèd the man who stands before the wrong,
> And boldly lifts his voice to speak what's true;
> Who stirs their dulled discernment with a song,
> Though scoffers mock, and silence is their cue.
>
> Blessèd the man who, in decay's deep tide,
> When even keenest conscience falls asleep,
> Still rouses crowds with cries none can deride,
> Unveiling truth as if from caverns deep.

---

125. Goldingay, *An Introduction to the Old Testament*, 232.

Blessèd the man who, through the storm and blare,
Stands like an oak amid the thunder's might,
Who will not take a traitor's hand in care,
Preferring breakage to a crooked rite.

Blessèd the man whom curses still pursue,
Whom crowds condemn, and stones are hurled with hate;
Yet they themselves prepare his triumph too –
Their judgment seals their own corrupted fate.

Blessèd are they who, striving without cease,
For justice bled, though lost to memory's stream;
Their blood shall fertilize the roots of peace,
And crown mankind with an ennobled dream.[126]

Ivan Franko's thought resonates with Matthew's holistic understanding of righteousness. The author speaks the language of active engagement, emphasizing the importance of resisting evil and uncompromisingly defending the truth, even at the cost of one's life.

For a long time, mission was synonymous with preaching. Recently, there has been growing awareness of mission as holistic, combining the proclamation of the gospel with acts of mercy directed primarily toward supporting the vulnerable. Yet, the Sermon on the Mount poses a critical question: Should not the embodiment of justice also be an inseparable component of the church's mission? Just as the church encourages virtues and condemns sins in personal life, it must likewise advocate for justice and actively oppose corruption. These tasks should become priorities both in words and actions. The success of the church's mission is determined not by eloquent sermons or magnificent church buildings, but by tangible impacts on establishing fair judicial practices and reducing corruption. Distorted justice, corruption, and bribery serve as a verdict against the church in a society where the majority identifies as Christian. If this state continues, it signals a failure of the church's mission, which consists not only in proclaiming the Word but also in building a righteous society. For the Lord loves justice (Isa 61:8), and therefore his call is clear: "Justice, and only justice, you shall pursue" (Deut 16:20 NASB).

Franko emphasizes a truth from the Beatitudes: Righteousness and persecution walk side by side, because striving for righteousness is incompatible with conformism or evasion masked behind phrases such as "not everything

---

126. І. Франко, *Зібрання творів у 50-и томах*, том 3 [I. Franko, *A Collection of Works in 50 volumes*, vol. 3] (Київ: Наукова думка, 1972), 278.

is so clear-cut." The call to holistic righteousness raises the question of willingness to vulnerability. Significantly, the Beatitudes culminate in words about persecution for righteousness' sake. In other words, the Beatitudes not only acknowledge persecution but also lead to it and help to endure it. The willingness to pay the price for one's convictions is a demonstration of seeking righteousness. Paraphrasing Dietrich Bonhoeffer, we might say that righteousness that does not embrace justice and justice that is not ready for vulnerability and loss is cheap righteousness. He pointed out that there might be thousands of interpretations of the Beatitudes, yet Jesus recognizes only one – obedience.[127]

Conclusions

> But let justice roll on like a river,
> righteousness like a never-failing stream! (Amos 5:24)

The Beatitudes were first read by early Christians who found themselves in the midst of numerous challenges, standing as though at an existential crossroad. For them, the Beatitudes became reminders of foundational truths – markers of the kingdom community's identity. Today, in Ukraine, the Beatitudes resonate against the backdrop of deadly danger. They remind us again of the markers of the kingdom community's identity, one of which is a new righteousness. This new righteousness consists of both personal and social justice. It is impossible without love and mercy, truth and judgment. Such righteousness is the bread and water for the community of faith. It leads toward the most desirable outcome – "The fruit of that righteousness will be peace; its effect will be quietness and confidence forever" (Isa 32:17).

The Beatitudes are not a simple roadmap but rather a long, arduous, and sometimes perilous journey toward embodying the values of the kingdom. The new righteousness is possible precisely because the call to it is wrapped in grace. The Beatitudes invite us to trust in a great paradox, but behind it stands Christ.

---

127. Bonhoeffer, *The Cost of Discipleship* (New York: Collier Books, 1963), 118.

5

"Blessed are the merciful, for they will be shown mercy"

(Matthew 5:7)

Vitalii Stankevych

Introduction

Mercy is an essential characteristic of the church, and most churches in Ukraine recognize this from both theological and practical perspectives. Before the full-scale Russian-Ukrainian war, nearly all church communities developed various mercy-related projects: serving orphans, widows, large families, the homeless, and others. However, with the massive displacement and homelessness caused by the current conflict,[1] the scale of need now exceeds our capacity. This situation presents unique challenges for evangelicals in wartime.

First is "aid fatigue." Many people, including Christians, are less enthusiastic about engaging in works of mercy than they once were. They recognize their limitations and the overwhelming nature of the needs. In these circumstances, church leaders must remind their congregations that they have embarked on a marathon, not a sprint. It is crucial to distribute efforts effectively and consistently renew their motivation. The apostle Paul encourages perseverance in acts of mercy: "Let us not become weary in doing good, for at the proper time we will reap a harvest if we do not give up" (Gal 6:9).

---

1. According to the Ministry of Social Policy, 4.9 million people have become internally displaced as a result of the full-scale invasion of the Russian Federation. According to the UN High Commissioner for Refugees, 6.6 million people have fled the country.

Second, war inflicts trauma – both physical and spiritual. Sadly, not all Christian communities become havens of support; some have the opposite effect. There are instances where individuals, grappling with loss, find church attendance difficult because the assistance offered feels insufficient, exacerbating their pain. Simply put, some Christians struggle to empathize and "weep with those who weep." Empathy and active listening skills are underdeveloped in certain individuals, posing a significant challenge for practical theology. We must equip people to demonstrate compassion in healthy ways – to understand the needs of others and find appropriate means of meeting those needs.

Third, both aid fatigue and the awareness of widespread trauma necessitate a specific character trait to navigate these challenges and overcome the natural inclination toward isolation. Christ's words remain pertinent: "But go and learn what this means: 'I desire mercy, not sacrifice'" (Matt 9:13). People typically seek to learn what they don't understand or lack the skills to perform. The Russian-Ukrainian war has prompted a reexamination of many seemingly straightforward biblical passages including the Sermon on the Mount, a foundational ethical text in the New Testament. Every verse addressing our attitude towards others resonates deeply with those who stand in solidarity with the Ukrainian people amidst this conflict.

The passage in Matthew 5:3–12 is commonly known as the Beatitudes or makarisms. This article focuses on the fifth beatitude: "Blessed are the merciful, for they will be shown mercy" (Matt 5:7). We will begin by defining mercy, then explore its manifestations in the Old Testament, and finally examine how Matthew employs this concept in his Gospel. We will consider mercy as a defining characteristic of Christ's followers and conclude by reflecting on how this beatitude is interpreted in the context of the Russian-Ukrainian war.

The purpose of this article is: (1) to show how the theme of mercy is revealed in the pages of the Bible and in the history of interpretation, and (2) how to be merciful in the context of war. I hope that this reading of the Scriptures will encourage readers to do further research on their own (there are many biblical passages that speak of mercy, I have chosen those that I consider the most important) and help readers realize that mercy should be one of the main features of Christian life. It is about all the components of life, not just some occasional manifestations of "charity."

Blessedness, Beatitudes and Mercy

The word *makarios* used in Matthew 5:3–12, is often translated as "happy" or "blessed." This word was prevalent in the language of the time, appearing in both religious and philosophical discourse. However, New Testament writers sometimes imbued words with new meanings. Therefore, it is essential to discern the author's intended meaning when using the word "blessed." Does it signify the goal attained by believers who fulfill the precepts of the Sermon on the Mount? Or does it represent the state of being that motivates the actions Matthew describes (hungering for righteousness, being merciful, pure in heart, etc.)?

Likely, the Beatitudes are not rewards for religious efforts but rather manifestations of God's grace in the lives of believers. They are not acknowledgments of moral or spiritual achievements but should be viewed as the result of sinners being enveloped by the forgiveness offered through Christ's redemptive work. Matthew's Beatitudes are applicable to all Christians. Keener suggests that the Beatitudes are connected to the gifts of the kingdom.[2]

Matthew 5:7 contains two words sharing the same root: the adjective *eleēmōn* (gracious, merciful, compassionate) and the verb *eleeō* (to have compassion, pity, show mercy). The concepts of grace and mercy are closely linked to compassion. Mercy is compassion in action. The Hebrew word *hesed*, equivalent to the Greek *eleos*, can be translated as "mercy" or "kindness." Thus, mercy is assistance offered to someone unfortunate or needy, particularly those in debt or lacking social support. Mercy is an emotion evoked by encountering misfortune. In some instances within the Greek tradition, mercy is viewed as the antithesis of envy. This response to tragedy contributes to purification. The verb form of mercy signifies sympathizing, pitying, and being merciful.[3]

Considering these lexical nuances associated with grace and mercy, we can propose the following definition: "Mercy is a benevolent and selfless disposition toward those who, generally or in specific situations, do not deserve it." However, in this context, mercy will be examined not as an abstract idea but as the embodiment of a concrete requirement in specific circumstances.

The Mercy of Yahweh and His people

Mercy (*hesed*) is a manifestation of unselfish kindness from the Lord toward the people he has chosen for a relationship. From the very early chapters of the Bible, we can see either the direct use of the words "mercy" and *hesed* or subtle hints of its manifestation.

---

2. Keener, *The IVP Bible Background Commentary: New Testament*, 56.

3. H. H. Esser, "Mercy, Compassion," in *New International Dictionary of New Testament Theology*, edited by Colin Brown (Grand Rapids: Zondervan Publishing House, 1986), 2:594.

To properly understand mercy, we must begin by examining it not as a human trait, but as a divine attribute. God created the universe and the planet we now call Earth, filling it with his divine beauty. He created the first humans in his image and likeness. While we do not know how long this ideal world existed, we know that humanity, given one or two commands, chose to disobey and committed the first sin, which separated humanity from God. How did God respond? He showed his mercy – he did not destroy Adam and Eve. He demonstrated a benevolent and unselfish attitude toward those who deserved immediate punishment. His mercy covered them, delayed their punishment, and allowed them to continue living on Earth with an opportunity to make things right in Christ.

One of the key texts revealing the nature of God is found in Exodus, where the Lord commands Moses to carve new tablets and then appears to him. The first words the Lord speaks are: "The LORD, the LORD, the compassionate and gracious [LXX: *eleēmōn*, often translated "mercy"], God slow to anger, abounding in love and faithfulness" (Exod 34:6). Mercy is the driving force behind God's covenant with his people. He is the One who "shows mercy to a thousand generations of those who love me and keep my commandments" (Exod 20:6). This mercy is inexhaustible, yet it is not a sign of weakness or sentimentality. Systematic disobedience and a rejection of mercy, as well as the abuse of God's love and compassion, may eventually lead to God withholding it, resulting in his judgment and wrath.

Mercy and its demonstration are present throughout the Bible. From the creation of the first heaven and earth to the new heaven and earth, the entire history of salvation is infused with God's mercy. While not every instance uses the word "mercy," its manifestation is evident throughout Scripture.

Mercy is such an essential attribute of God's character that it is impossible to imagine the prayer life and spiritual heritage of God's people without it. The Psalms are full of reflections on God's mercy toward individuals, the nation, and all of creation. David, for example, cannot think of God apart from his mercy. He writes, the LORD "redeems your life from the pit and crowns you with love and compassion . . . The LORD is compassionate and gracious, slow to anger, abounding in love . . . from everlasting to everlasting the LORD's love is with those who fear him and his righteousness with their children's children" (Ps 103:4, 8, 17). David expresses his hope that "goodness and love will follow me all the days of my life" (Ps 23:6). He is confident that God's mercy will outlast his wrath: "For his anger lasts only a moment, but his favor lasts a lifetime" (Ps 30:5). These words echo God's own words in Exodus 20:6.

David turns to God when he acknowledges his wrongdoing: "Have mercy on me, O God, according to your unfailing love; according to your great compassion blot out my transgressions" (Ps 51:1). This attribute of God's nature is of the highest value to David: "Because your love is better than life, my lips will glorify you" (Ps 63:3).

Other psalmists also praise God's mercy (Pss 89, 106, and 136).[4] Ethan the Ezrahite reflects on the Lord's mercy as expressed in his covenant relationship with David: "I will sing of the Lord's great love forever; with my mouth I will make your faithfulness known through all generations. I will declare that your love stands firm forever, that you have established your faithfulness in heaven itself... Once you spoke in a vision, to your faithful people you said: 'I have bestowed strength on a warrior; I have raised up a young man from among the people, I have found David my servant; with my sacred oil I have anointed him...' but I will not take my love from him, nor will I ever betray my faithfulness" (Ps 89:1–2, 19–20, 33). The anonymous author of Psalm 106 reflects on God's boundless mercy, recalling how God repeatedly delivered his people: "Many times he delivered them, but they were bent on rebellion and they wasted away in their sin. Yet he took note of their distress when he heard their cry; for their sake he remembered his covenant and out of his great love he relented" (Ps 106:43–45). This passage is particularly important for understanding the covenant relationship. It reveals the history of the covenant and explains why the Lord remains faithful despite his people's unfaithfulness: the reason is love and mercy.

Mercy is not solely a manifestation of God's exclusive attitude toward his people. The Law, the Prophets, and the Writings emphasize that this trait should also characterize God's people. It is frequently mentioned in connection with the righteous. In his discourse with his friends, Job recalls how he was honored by those around him because of his mercy toward the needy (Job 29:7–17). The patriarchs sought to embody mercy in their actions. Abraham and Joseph are prime examples.

In Genesis 18–19, we see evidence of Abraham's merciful attitude toward his nephew Lot. Lot had chosen his dwelling place based on the beauty and economic advantages of the land, as the Ukrainian proverb says, "The eyes of the beholder have seen what they have chosen." However, Abraham repeatedly demonstrated care for Lot, risking his own life and the lives of his servants. Abraham's concern and intercession before God, appealing to divine mercy,

---

4. The uniqueness of Ps 136 is that in each verse God's mercy is sung with the addition that it endures forever.

saved the lives of Lot and his daughters. While it is uncertain whether Lot fully embraced Abraham's theology, he undoubtedly learned the theology of mercy. By showing hospitality to the men who turned out to be angels, Lot saved his own life: "When he hesitated, the men grasped his hand and the hands of his wife and of his two daughters and led them safely out of the city, for the Lord was merciful to them" (Gen 19:16). Lot recognized that his deliverance was not a consequence of his own kindness but a manifestation of God's mercy, and he appealed to this: "Your servant has found favor in your eyes, and you have shown great kindness to me in sparing my life" (Gen 19:19a). Understanding God as merciful influences how we show mercy to others, God's mercy is a fundamental biblical, theological, and ethical principle.

The story of Joseph (Gen 37–50) provides another example of showing mercy. He had ample reason to resent his brothers, but his father's favoritism, his prophetic dreams, his ability to perceive God's benevolent hand in everyday life, and his unwavering faith ultimately prevailed. Joseph's story teaches us to extend kindness to those who may not deserve it, even those whose lives are in our hands.

There are many other examples in the texts of Moses.[5] But from this brief overview, it is clear that God's mercy influenced not only the worldview of believers, but also their ethical choices in difficult life circumstances.

Among the Old Testament figures, king David stands out for his embodiment of mercy. David, a man after God's own heart, whose son would be called the Messiah, served as a model for the kings of Judah and Israel. Despite his triumphs and failures, David not only eloquently praised God's mercy in the Psalms but also demonstrated it in his own life. Twice, he spared Saul's life, even when presented with opportunities to kill him, refusing to raise his hand against the Lord's anointed. David was also willing to forgive his rebellious sons. The story of his selfless kindness to Mephibosheth (2 Sam 9) further illustrates his merciful nature. While sparing Saul can be attributed to the king's status as God's anointed, and forgiving his sons might be considered natural parental affection, pardoning Mephibosheth, the son of his former enemy, reveals the depth of David's compassion. David's example demonstrates that mercy often flows from those who have themselves experienced undeserved kindness.

The book of Nehemiah recounts the renewal of the Israelite people. A crucial aspect of this renewal was repentance during the public reading of the Law. The focus of the people's reflection was not primarily on their sins

---

5. The life of Moses itself is also an example of mercy.

but on God's mercy.⁶ In the Old Testament, mercy is often centered on God, but in its practical application, it is extended within the community of God's people. Even when dealing with enemies, they were typically considered part of this community.⁷

The prophets emphasize that God's mercy will be fully revealed in the last days (Hos 2:21, 25).⁸ However, mercy was not viewed as something distant or unattainable but as an inherent characteristic of Yahweh's people and every believer.⁹ The book of Jonah highlights the tension between God's expansive mercy and the Israelites' limited view toward their enemies. As noted, mercy was generally practiced within the community of faith. The situation was different regarding other nations. In the Law, God commands the destruction of certain peoples, forbids interaction with others, and permits relationships with some (as seen between the northern and southern kingdoms after their division). These varying approaches fall within the framework of interethnic relations, often framed within the context of familial ties.

The story of Jonah presents a challenge: The prophet receives a direct command from the Lord to preach to the enemy city of Nineveh. Jonah refuses, knowing that God's intention is to extend mercy to them, an act unacceptable to Jonah due to his nationalistic perspective. He takes actions directly opposed to the Lord's command, a scenario that resonates with many evangelical believers today.¹⁰ Jonah's reluctance stems from the suffering his people have endured

---

6. "They refused to listen and failed to remember the miracles you performed among them. They became stiff-necked and in their rebellion appointed a leader in order to return to their slavery. But you are a forgiving God, gracious and compassionate, slow to anger and abounding in love. Therefore you did not desert them, even when they cast for themselves an image of a calf and said, 'This is your god, who brought you up out of Egypt,' or when they committed awful blasphemies. "Because of your great compassion you did not abandon them in the wilderness. By day the pillar of cloud did not fail to guide them on their path, nor the pillar of fire by night to shine on the way they were to take. You gave your good Spirit to instruct them. You did not withhold your manna from their mouths, and you gave them water for their thirst (Neh 9:17–20).

7. For example the desire of a captive girl who showed mercy to her master (2 Kgs 5).

8. Of course, in the book of Hosea, mercy is perceived not only in an eschatological sense. The prophet's life was tragic. The uniqueness of the book lies in the fact that the prophet's attitude toward his wife reflects God's mercy (Hos 1:6, 7; 2:23; 4:1; 6:6; 10:12; 12:6).

9. "O man, he has told you what is good and what the LORD expects of you, namely: That you should do justice, love to show mercy, and walk humbly with your God" (Mic 6:8).

10. What does God expect from Ukrainian Christians who have lost their homes, property, and their churches because the Russian Federation destroyed them with missiles, bombs, or kamikaze drones? What does God expect from Ukrainian believers about Russian Christians who support the full-scale invasion of Ukraine? Jonah had similar difficult questions. There were hardly any influential Jewish communities in Nineveh, but there are Christian communities in Russia, and they either remain silent or support military aggression.

at the hands of the Ninevites. Despite his experience, he acknowledges God's character: "Isn't this what I said, Lord, when I was still at home? That is what I tried to forestall by fleeing to Tarshish. I knew that you are a gracious and compassionate God, slow to anger and abounding in love, a God who relents from sending calamity" (Jonah 4:2). The book of Jonah leaves the reader with questions that demand answers. Perhaps the Gospel of Matthew offers guidance on how to relate to enemies within the context of mercy.

God demonstrates mercy to Israel and humanity because it is inherent in his divine nature. Yet, people often disregard these manifestations. They fail to express gratitude and struggle to extend mercy in their own lives. This contrast persists and is even amplified in the New Testament.

The Beatitude of the Merciful

The Gospel of Matthew is a testament to God's mercy. Each passage is imbued with divine empathy for humanity. The God Emmanuel provides an example for readers to embrace and embody in their practical discipleship (Matt 28:20). The conversion of Matthew, one of the twelve disciples and the author of the first Gospel, is described in Matthew 9:9–13. During a visit to Capernaum,[11] Jesus noticed a tax collector named Matthew (whose name means "gift of Yahweh") and called him to follow him. This was in stark contrast to the typical disciples chosen by the rabbis of the time. Christ called as his apostle a Jew despised by society and religious leaders. It is plausible that Matthew himself needed healing and restoration, made possible through the Lord's mercy.

The author, having personally experienced mercy, writes this Gospel to those in difficult circumstances. Matthew's community was suffering and in need of God's intervention. The conflict troubling the Gospel's readers arose from the tension between the followers of Christ and the synagogue, between religious Jews and other followers of Christ.[12] This places the Gospel not only within a context of trauma but also within a context of healing through acceptance, forgiveness, and kindness – what we might call mercy.

David Turner suggests that the beatitude concerning the merciful initiates the second group of beatitudes, which highlight the signs of God's approval toward people.[13] Compared to the other beatitudes, mercy appears to be the

---

11. France, *The Gospel of Matthew*, 351.

12. F. Raychynets, "The Gospel of Matthew," in *Slavic Bible Commentary* (Russian Edition) (Kyiv: Summit Books, 2022), 1151.

13. France, *The Gospel of Matthew*, 152.

most straightforward. However, the experience of the Russian-Ukrainian war has revealed that it is not always clear to whom and how to show mercy. The word "mercy" encompasses a broad range of meanings. The nuances of this concept are evident throughout the Sermon on the Mount and in other passages in Matthew's Gospel. But how does Matthew himself understand mercy?

In some beatitudes, Matthew employs the principle of cause and effect, a rhetorical device present not only in the Beatitudes and the Sermon on the Mount (Matt 7:12) but throughout the Gospel. It is vital to emphasize that showing mercy to others is not the basis for receiving mercy from them;[14] rather, the cause-and-effect relationship is realized in God. This, on the one hand, guarantees God's approval, and on the other, affirms that God has already approved those who show mercy. After all, those who have experienced God's mercy are empowered to extend it to others, ensuring their pardon on the last day.[15] Grant Osborne echoes this perspective, noting that the capacity for mercy is itself a reward, manifested in the present, with the full reward realized in eternity.[16]

The fifth beatitude, as Donald Hagner observes, marks a shift in emphasis within the Beatitudes. While the first four focus on inner state, the fifth emphasizes outward behavior.[17] This beatitude also embodies the positive principle of reciprocity. Although those who show mercy are the ones who receive pardon, this act of mercy also lays the foundation for further mercy.[18] The capacity to show mercy is a test of faith (Matt 18:21–35), and mercy is often intertwined with forgiveness.[19]

It is worth noting the close relationship between mercy and justice (Matt 5:6). As Turner argues, Matthew demonstrates that these qualities do not contradict but rather complement each other.[20] Sometimes, true justice is manifested through acts of mercy.

Jesus identifies a lack of mercy in the Pharisees.[21] For them, adherence to the Law took precedence over helping those who were suffering (Matt 12:15). Jesus demonstrates that mercy, along with its associated qualities (kindness,

---

14. France, *The Gospel of Matthew*, 168.
15. Turner, *Matthew*, 152.
16. Osborne, *Matthew*, 168.
17. Hagner, *Matthew 1–13*, 93.
18. Osborne, *Matthew*, 168.
19. France, *The Gospel of Matthew*, 168.
20. Turner, *Matthew*, 152.
21. Turner, *Matthew*, 152.

compassion, empathy), holds greater significance than even fundamental observances like the Sabbath. He illustrates this by stating that if a sheep is lost on the Sabbath, one does not wait until the next day to retrieve it.

The word "mercy" appears twice in Matthew 6:1–4, which addresses the public display of charitable acts. Elsewhere, the word is not explicitly used, but there is an allusion to mercy in the discussion of attitudes toward enemies (Matt 5:43–48). Matthew 6:1–4 is relatively clear. Jesus cautions against performing acts of kindness for public recognition rather than genuine empathy for those in need. He warns against seeking earthly rewards for acts of mercy, emphasizing that true blessings come from acting secretly, motivated by compassion and gratitude for God's mercy. The reward for such actions is the ability to be merciful itself.

Matthew 5:38–42 addresses how to respond to those who cause harm (for example, hitting someone or taking possessions). This passage must be understood within the context of both Roman laws and personal relationships of that time. Matthew presents a nuanced understanding of enemies: personal enemies (Matt 5:38–40), political enemies (Matt 5:41–42), those within one's household (Matt 10:36), the devil (Matt 13:39), and even enemies of the Lord (Matt 22:44). The call to love one's enemies is not absolute; it primarily refers to personal enemies. Showing mercy to a personal enemy is a significant challenge for believers. However, this principle does not necessarily extend to political enemies, especially in the context of resisting military aggression. Other biblical principles apply in such situations.

Matthew highlights mercy throughout his Gospel.[22] One of the central themes is the merciful nature of the Messiah. The Messiah's kingdom is founded on a merciful disposition toward one another. This is exemplified in Matthew 8:1–4, where Jesus heals a leper. This act, occurring immediately after the Sermon on the Mount, emphasizes not only Jesus's power and ability to perform miracles but also his deep compassion and willingness to heal.[23] Significantly, Jesus shows mercy not only to the leper and his family but also to the priests who should have recognized this healing as an act of God. He heals those who approach him and those brought to him. Jesus performs this healing on the Sabbath, demonstrating his authority and highlighting that mercy transcends the Law and the temple (Matt 12:1–8).

---

22. Matt 9:13, 27, 36; 12:7; 14:14; 15:22; 16:22; 17:15; 18:27, 33; 20:30–31, 34; 23:23.

23. It is fair to say that all the sections in the Gospel are connected with Christ's mercy and his compassion, care, and pity.

While Matthew emphasizes mercy, it is also present in Mark's and Luke's Gospels, though framed within the context of Christ's ministry. Luke includes a version of the Sermon on the Mount (Luke 6:17–49) but does not explicitly mention mercy in his beatitudes. He does, however, address mercy in Luke 6:36, where he calls for believers to be merciful, reflecting the Father's mercy. Like Matthew, Luke connects mercy with the treatment of enemies, though he does so explicitly, while Matthew's approach is more implicit.

The New Testament frequently refers to grace and mercy, though "grace" appears more often. In the Synoptic Gospels, "mercy" and "compassion" are more frequent than "grace." Matthew and Mark do not use "grace" at all, unlike Luke, likely due to Luke's later writing and connection to Pauline traditions. John uses both terms. While related, grace and mercy have distinct meanings. Mercy is something believers receive and then extend to others. Grace is solely received, a gift from God. Grace is the ultimate expression of mercy in Christ, belonging uniquely to him (John 1:16).

Jesus consistently emphasizes the importance of mercy to God. In contrast, the Pharisees not only fail to show mercy but actively obstruct others from doing so, even Jesus himself (for example, by criticizing him for healing on the Sabbath). Matthew also addresses hypocritical displays of mercy – charity for show – which contradict Jesus's teachings. Mercy is a virtue that may require sacrifice. For Jesus, the cost of mercy was high, as demonstrated by his willingness to risk his life by healing on the Sabbath. This underscores the profound significance of mercy. The beatitude about mercy has an eschatological dimension, but it also has implications for the present. Living in a community characterized by mercy is far superior to living in a legalistic environment. In Matthew's Gospel, mercy is a freely chosen act of discipleship, reflecting Christ's example and demonstrating profound empathy for those who may not deserve it.

Historical and Contemporary Reception of the Beatitude

The fifth beatitude has held significant importance throughout the history of the Church, particularly in the realms of ethics and moral theology. It has been central to discussions on forgiveness, good works, and social responsibility. According to Ulrich Lutz, the interpretation of this beatitude has always been shaped by the Church's circumstances and theological identity.[24] Therefore, it

---

24. Luz, *Matthew 1–7*, 177.

is helpful to explore several key interpretations of the Beatitudes across different historical periods.

We should begin with the church fathers. Some of them believed that mercy is the shortest path to faith, asserting that one cannot receive God's mercy unless they are merciful themselves.[25] St. Chromatius of Aquileia (330s – ca. 406-407) understood mercy as something that can help a person gain God's favor. For the modern reader, this concept might seem inconsistent, since favor cannot be earned – it must be requested or pleaded for, though the latter could be part of the former.

John Chrysostom (344–407) offered a different perspective on charity. For him, charity is a broad category, encompassing more than almsgiving – it includes all good deeds. Chrysostom also contended that people are not pardoned because they show mercy, but rather they show mercy because they have already been pardoned. He emphasized the profound distinction between human and divine mercy.[26]

Augustine (354–430) developed an ethical model based on this very principle, which is expressed in the Sermon on the Mount as the "Golden Rule" (Matt 7:12). He explicitly taught that what we do for others will be done for us. If we ask to be pardoned, we must also pardon others. He further stressed that the way we treat others will determine how the Lord treats us.[27] An anonymous author from the time also reflects this idea, suggesting that true mercy is not merely helping those in need, but showing kindness to one's personal enemy. According to this perspective, such a virtue mirrors the character of the Lord himself.[28] Gregory of Nyssa (335–395) also wrote about mercy, considering it a virtue that signifies closeness and likeness to the Lord.[29]

However, the evangelical interpretation of biblical texts was more profoundly influenced by the Reformers. One of the most influential Bible interpreters of the Reformation, John Calvin, viewed the blessing of being merciful as a paradox that directly challenges the worldview of ordinary people. He noted that such people do not experience true happiness because they do not care about the suffering of others. According to Calvin, those who are truly happy are those willing not only to endure their own suffering but also to

---

25. Manlio Simonetti, ed., *Matthew 1-13*, Ancient Christian commentary on Scripture (Downers Grove: InterVarsity Press 2001), 85.

26. Simonetti, *Matthew*, 85.

27. Simonetti, *Matthew*, 85-86.

28. Simonetti, *Matthew*, 86.

29. See Hubertus Drobner and Albert Viciano, eds., *Gregory of Nyssa: Homilies on the Beatitudes*, Supplements to Vigiliae Christianae, 52 (Leiden: Brill, 2000), 165-75.

participate in the suffering of others. Those who show mercy, Calvin argued, not only receive mercy from God but also from people. Calvin warned that the world does not always appreciate this stance,[30] yet he affirmed that the reward for undeserved kindness is indeed blessedness. Calvin's understanding is particularly relevant in the context in which Ukrainian evangelical believers find themselves today.

An equally important component of interpreting the Beatitudes is their resonance within Ukrainian literary thought. The theme of mercy is prevalent in Ukrainian literature. Virtually every work features a hero who embodies noble qualities and demonstrates compassion toward others. However, authors often emphasize social aspects, exploring the injustices of societal structures. Consequently, those who extend mercy frequently do not receive it in return. From a purely social perspective, the law of causality appears inoperative. Yet, when viewed psychologically or spiritually, the impetus for the fictional hero's mercy and kindness resides deep within their soul, understood as a reflection of God. They simply cannot act otherwise. Thus, "they will be shown mercy" acquires a significance that transcends the social realm.

The theme of mercy is vividly portrayed in Hryhor Tyutyunyk's "Klymko," Volodymyr Vynnychenko's "Fedko Halamydnyk," Mykhailo Kotsiubynskyi's "Kharyta," and Panas Myrnyi's "Do Oxen Roar When the Manger Is Full?" (the character of Hryts). Interestingly, Ukrainian writers often employ child characters and ordinary individuals to depict pure emotions. In portraying the complex figure of the Ukrainian leader Ivan Mazepa, Bohdan Lepkyi (in "Motrya," "Do Not Kill," "Baturyn," "Poltava," and "From Poltava to Bender") demonstrates that mercy is an essential attribute of a worthy and successful leader.

Natalia Koroleva explores the gospel's concept of mercy in her story "Drachma." The writer intertwines two gospel motifs: the lost drachma and the widow's offering in the temple. The impoverished widow shelters an orphan, and her life gradually improves through the mercy of others. The woman herself recognizes God's hand in this provision. Even when she loses her entire fortune of nine drachmas, upon finding the tenth, she is comforted and offers it to God, recognizing him as the source of mercy.

This suggests that Ukrainians possess a natural inclination toward empathy, engagement in the lives of others, and caring. Despite enduring social, political, and cultural suffering for centuries (often with their charity unreciprocated),

---

30. John Calvin, *Commentary. Harmony of the Evangelists, Matthew, Mark, and Luke* (Grand Rapids: Baker, 1981), 263–64.

they have not lost this vital characteristic. This trait, coupled with the desire for freedom and other enduring aspects of the Ukrainian character, has likely enabled Ukrainians to survive despite the injustices they have faced throughout history. The ability to endure and create life might be termed "shall be shown mercy." What is sown at the personal level – in everyday life, social interactions, economic endeavors, and family relationships – develops into the social and national consequences of Ukrainian resilience.[31]

Mercy and the Challenges of the Russian-Ukrainian war

The current challenges associated with Russia's full-scale invasion have compelled a reassessment of Gospel texts. In the Ukrainian context, Oleksandr Heichenko's article, "Psalms of Imprecation: Pastoral Application in the Context of the War Against Ukraine," published in *Bogomysliye*, is indicative.[32] Heichenko argues that texts previously overlooked in peacetime have become central to Ukrainian Christian prayer during wartime. This concept applies equally to Gospel passages, including the Sermon on the Mount and the Beatitudes.

Considering the introductory questions surrounding the author's difficult circumstances and the challenging situation faced by the Gospel of Matthew's initial listeners and subsequent readers, notable similarities, though not complete identities, exist between these contexts and the situation in Ukraine. Reading Gospel texts with attention to both the historical background of the first readers[33] and the situation of the contemporary Ukrainian reader[34] is crucial. This requires understanding the context within which Gospel theology developed.

---

31. These thoughts are taken from a correspondence with Lina Borodynska.

32. See О. Гейченко, "Псалми прокляття: пасторське застосування в умовах війни проти України" [O. Geychenko, "Imprecatory Psalms: A Pastoral Application in the Context of the War Against Ukraine"], *Bogomysliye* 32 (2022): 8–26.

33. N. T. Wright's observation is relevant here: "For too long we have looked at Scripture as nineteenth-century people and asked ourselves sixteenth-century questions. It is time to see it through the eyes of the first Christians and ask questions relevant to our time" (*Justification: God's Plan and Paul's Vision* [Downers Grove: InterVarsity Press 2016], 37).

34. It is important to note that the Ukrainian experience of reading the texts of Matthew's Gospel through the prism of war is not an innovative approach (see, for example Isaac K. Mbabazi, "Listening to the Voice of St. Matthew in the midst and Civil War in the Democratic Republic of the Congo," in *Tackling Trauma: Global, Biblical, and Pastoral Perspectives*, ed. Paul R. Barker [Carlisle: Langham Global Library, 2019], 103). But it is valuable for understanding theological thought and its changes during the decade-long experience of war.

Ukrainian researchers have identified the influence of the Russian evangelical theological tradition, as the successor to the Soviet Union, on Ukrainian theological thought.[35] The call to mercy was accepted unquestioningly in all aspects of life. While this presents no issue in everyday relationships, the same cannot be said for situations of war and national defense. It is important to note that this interpretation was and remains central to the "Russian world" ideology, serving to justify military aggression, both historically and presently.

By 24 February 2022, the Ukrainian evangelical community had become somewhat accustomed to the Russian military aggression that began in 2014. The war was hybrid and localized, with major combat operations confined to two Ukrainian regions (Luhansk and Donetsk). From 2019 to 2022, a peacekeeping political stance was advocated. It later became apparent that this was a prelude to a larger war. However, diplomatic ties between Russia and Ukraine remained intact. A similar situation existed in relations between Ukrainian and Russian evangelical believers, including theological educational institutions, which were members of the same accreditation association (EAAA). Everything changed after the full-scale invasion. The majority of Russian believers did not condemn the military aggression; rather, they strongly supported Putin's so-called "special military operation," which was, in essence, a war. The final break in relations occurred after the liberation of cities such as Bucha, Irpin, and Izyum, among dozens of other settlements, where Russian atrocities were revealed: looting, rape (of children, women, the elderly, and men), torture, and the brutal murder of civilians. All communication with Russian believers ceased as they parroted Russian propaganda narratives, claiming it was all fabricated and that Ukrainian Christians were feigning victimhood.

This situation has prompted theological reflection on New Testament moral and ethical norms, including forgiveness, reconciliation, peacemaking, attitudes toward enemies, mercy, and persecution for righteousness.[36] Significantly, many of the norms requiring re-evaluation are found within the Sermon on the Mount.

Mercy's manifestation is a crucial aspect in wartime. The New Testament offers no explicit instructions. War serves as a test of mercy. Setting aside the political dimension, Ukrainians witness the Russian army's mercilessness: the

---

35. This is especially evident in the articles in *Bogosmysliye* 15.

36. Very in-depth research in this area was done by the faculty of the Ukrainian Evangelical Theological Seminary, which was published in two war issues of the journal *Christian Thought*, as well as by the faculty of Odessa Theological Seminary, the results of which can be found in the relevant issues of the *Bogomylie*.

killing of civilians, the abduction of thousands of children (for which Putin has been issued a warrant of arrest in March 2023 by the International Criminal Court), the shelling of residential areas, religious buildings, critical infrastructure, children's hospitals, and maternity wards. The well-documented abuse of prisoners by Russians confirms their profound deficit of mercy. Each prisoner exchange reveals Ukrainian defenders returning severely ill, bearing numerous injuries, and having lost 20 to 40 percent of their body weight, indicative of ruthless torture. It should be noted that Russia, as of 7 October 2024, denies access to western international organizations to monitor detention conditions.[37] Conversely, Ukraine's treatment of Russian prisoners includes state allocation of funds exceeding the minimum wage and payments for children without parental care. The Ukrainian side welcomes international inspections of all kinds.

The Ukrainian people's remarkable capacity for mass self-organization and the extraordinary growth of the volunteer movement during various cataclysms and tragedies are well-known. The full-scale war was no exception, with the nation uniting to mount a courageous defense against the enemy. Thousands volunteered to defend the country, with even more volunteering to assist in evacuating victims. Thousands of families have hosted and continue to host internally displaced persons (IDPs), while others aid rescuers in clearing debris after shelling. In showing mercy, we repeatedly experience God's mercy toward us.

The practical significance of mercy in a believer's life across various spheres, beginning with everyday interactions, is essential. A friendly and selfless attitude toward others is most often demonstrated within families and workplaces. Following Christ is impossible without showing mercy. Mercy is the primary motivation for social volunteering. Mercy, and its manifestation in forgiveness, is vital in conflict resolution. Mercy defines the boundaries of relationships with a personal enemy or a brother who has sinned against you (Matt 5:48; 18:15–17). As we have observed, showing mercy is not always necessary. For example, when there is a threat to life, when it could cause harm, when people do not need it, or when they do not ask for it.

Mercy is important in pastoral ministry because this virtue demonstrates belonging to the Messiah's kingdom. Mercy and justice are inseparable features of pastoral ministry. Therefore, showing mercy is crucial when addressing matters of church discipline. Jesus was not only merciful but also taught his disciples to be merciful. Pastoral sermons should include a homiletical call to

---

37. Or the numerous videos showing Russian soldiers shooting Ukrainians when they surrender.

charity within society, and the preacher can draw upon personal examples, while remaining mindful of the risk of hypocritical charity. During wartime, pastors who are called and possess the appropriate training should engage in chaplaincy ministry in the military.

Mercy is an integral and necessary part of the reality for believers mobilized to defend their homeland against Russian military aggression. The country, as a political and social entity, requires mercy, as defending the state is the duty of career military personnel; thus, service in the Armed Forces of Ukraine through mobilization is a manifestation of mercy. Military personnel, being in positions of power, must embrace the concept of the "second mile," which embodies a responsible and sacrificial approach to performing combat missions. Numerous testimonies exist of believers who are, or sadly were, a light in the army through good deeds and zealous, dedicated service. A merciful attitude toward the enemy on the battlefield is a separate topic requiring in-depth study. When a soldier is armed, they are God's servant (Rom 13) and should not show mercy. Of course, certain situations may arise where a soldier is guided by their conscience.[38] Mercy toward the enemy on the battlefield is demonstrated through the non-use of prohibited weapons and conducting hostilities in accordance with the rules of war.[39]

The treatment of prisoners of war is a manifestation of mercy. Chaplaincy experience demonstrates that Ukrainian soldiers adhere to international standards of conduct with prisoners of war.

The issue of forgiveness is a separate matter. Of course, we refer to forgiveness after the Russians acknowledge guilt, apologize, and pay reparations. Personal forgiveness is an expression of the will of each individual traumatized by the war. No one can be compelled to forgive. In such moments, showing mercy through forgiveness is important if it is necessary to overcome the traumatic experience.[40] At this stage of the war, preachers, theologians, or priests

---

38. During military clashes, we can assume that there may be cases when, after being wounded and unable to take prisoners, the enemy is left alive not to die in agony, but to give him a chance through mercy.

39. For example, to allow the collection of fallen soldiers, not to mine the dead or wounded, etc.

40. Each case is considered separately. At this stage, given the Ukrainian realities and communication with foreign experts on overcoming trauma, the topic of forgiving enemies has not been fully mastered by Ukrainian psychologists and counselors. There is a difference in time and circumstances. Western experts talk about combat operations as something that happened in the past. But the war in Ukraine is ongoing and it is not known when it will end. Of course, there is an understanding that the time will come for forgiveness as part of mercy in action, but at the moment this decision is at the stage of rejection.

who advocate forgiving Russians are either adherents of the "Russian world" ideology or callous and superficial individuals who do not comprehend the spirit of the Holy Scriptures.

Conclusions

Mercy is what identifies the followers of Yahweh. In both the Old and New Testaments, mercy is a sign of being like the Lord. A review of biblical texts reveals that showing selfless kindness to the undeserving is a soteriological narrow path paved by God himself. Mercy originates with the Lord and is reflected in those who draw near to him.

The beatitude of mercy lies in the believer's acquisition, through drawing closer to the Lord, of the capacity to be merciful to others. Mercy is not easily exercised. On the contrary, despite inner pain, agonizing contradictions, and a desire for justice, a person chooses to do good because God has shown undeserved mercy to them. This good will be fully realized eschatologically, but even now, the merciful experience the mystical pleasure of recognizing their unity with Yahweh.

Mercy is a voluntary act. Favorable treatment cannot be earned, though it can be requested. Just as mercy is shown by those in a better or higher position, it cannot be demanded from anyone. Forgiveness and almsgiving are two facets of mercy. Forgiveness is its most challenging component. A person suffering cannot be forced to forgive the one inflicting suffering. Nor can one demand that someone give charity to another in need. God shows mercy of his own free will. He expects it from his children but does not demand it. This is particularly relevant in wartime. Every Ukrainian who has suffered from Russian aggression must make a personal decision regarding forgiveness. Of course, the Russians can request mercy and forgiveness, but this has not yet occurred.

Mercy is a healing balm in times of suffering. The pain of loss, grief, a ruined future, a disfigured reality due to air raids and shelling in Ukraine, and hostilities that cause suffering to others can be partially overcome through acts of kindness. Compassion is the motivation for volunteering.

Mercy requires wisdom and moderation. The most difficult lesson to learn amidst suffering is that not everyone can be helped. The Gospel writer emphasizes this truth. Although God's grace can save everyone, not everyone will be saved. Christ did not heal everyone, did not resurrect everyone, and the miraculous multiplication of loaves and fishes for thousands of the destitute and hungry did not occur daily. Therefore, showing selfless kindness requires not only enthusiasm but also wisdom.

6

"Blessed are the pure in heart, for they will see God"

(Matthew 5:8)

Fyodor Raichynets

Blessed is he who knows no envy's sting,
Whose heart is pure and void of evil thing.
Who bears no stain, but cherishes the vow,
"Judge not another," even now.

Who does not envy any other man,
Nor harbors vengeance in his heart's dark plan.
Who wishes ill to none, not even foes,
Shall see God's face when life here closes.

Oleksandr Konyskyi

One Beatitude, Two Contradictory Statements

Donald Hagner, a prominent scholar of the Gospel of Matthew, aptly describes the Beatitude concerning the pure in heart as one of the "most difficult."[1] This complexity arises from the apparent contradiction between this beatitude and other biblical pronouncements and our own human experience. Firstly, the declaration of a pure human heart appears to directly contradict numerous biblical passages that emphasize the inherent corruption and depravity of

---

1. Hagner, *Matthew 1–13*, 94.

human nature (Gen 6:12; Ps 14:1; Isa 1:4; Jer 17:9–10; Matt 15:18–20; Rom 1:21; 3:10; Eph 4:18; 1 John 2:16). Secondly, the promise of beholding God in this beatitude seems to conflict with the explicit biblical statements that no human has ever seen God (Exod 19:21; 33:20; Col 1:15; 1 Tim 6:16; Heb 1:1–3). Nevertheless, this beatitude posits and promises such a divine encounter.

Considering the first statement of this Beatitude regarding the "purity in heart," we are met with a profound challenge. Dietrich Bonhoeffer, in his insightful sermon on this very beatitude, aptly captured this challenge: "A word causing the heart momentarily to skip a beat, a word prompting a bit of melancholy to come over us."[2] This statement highlights the stark contrast between our cherished aspirations for purity and the harsh reality of our own hearts.

Recognizing the complexities of our inner lives, with their inherent struggles and impulsive desires, it becomes difficult to genuinely believe that our hearts can be truly pure. We often find ourselves distancing ourselves from this ideal, projecting it onto others – individuals who, we imagine, have somehow overcome their baser impulses and achieved a state of spiritual elevation, maintaining a heart untainted by temptation. This raises a crucial question: Does this beatitude describe a genuine human possibility, or is it merely an unattainable ideal?

The second statement, concerning the (im)possibility or (in)ability of a person to see God, presents a similar dialectic within the Holy Scriptures. The apostle John articulates this in his Gospel: "No one has ever seen God, but the one and only Son, who is himself God and is in the closest relationship with the Father, has made him known" (John 1:18). Furthermore, in his first epistle, John adds: "No one has ever seen God. If we love one another, God abides in us, and his love is perfect in us . . . And we have seen and testify that the Father has sent the Son to be the Savior of the world" (1 John 4:12, 14).

John's statements reveal that we encounter the invisible God through the incarnation of Jesus Christ. Moreover, when the love we receive from Jesus is extended to others, the invisible God becomes not only perceptible but also tangible. In essence, our invisible love for God manifests visibly and tangibly when we express it towards others, particularly those who are dependent upon us, those in need, or those in vulnerable situations (1 John 4:7–11). Echoing this sentiment, Bonhoeffer states in his sermon: "To see God that means to

---

2. Dietrich Bonhoeffer, "Sermon on Matthew 5:8, Barcelona, Tenth Sunday after Trinity, August 12, 1928," in *Dietrich Bonhoeffer Works, Volume 10. Barcelona, Berlin, New York: 1928–1931* (Minneapolis: Fortress, 2008), 513.

love the Father, to look him in the eye the way we look a good friend in the eye and are blessed."[3]

Matthew presents a dialectical perspective on understanding this and other beatitudes. For him, a person of pure heart is not merely someone who discerns God and his presence in Jesus, the Messiah,[4] but also recognizes in service to needy, socially vulnerable individuals service to God himself.[5] In Matthew's view, a person of pure heart is not characterized by an impeccable and sinless heart, devoid of any negativity, but rather by a heart overflowing with mercy and compassion for the marginalized. Recognizing God in the needy and serving them constitutes true righteousness and genuine spirituality.

Beatitudes: Parameters of Possible Perception

> If your soul is not something like the eternal divine, it will never behold God[6]
>
> *Dietrich Bonhoeffer*

Biblical scholars have typically held in common that the Gospel beatitudes are a kind of literary genre that belongs to the so-called macarisms. However, there is no consensus on which biblical literary form (wisdom literature, psalmic poetry, prophetic literature) produced the macarisms as a separate genre. It depends on which history of perception (reception) one subscribes to, and which approach to their interpretation he or she tends to use.[7] The question of how best to interpret the Beatitudes (macarisms) in the Synoptic tradition remains of interest to biblical interpreters and to the authors of this volume alike.[8]

In the first perspective, the Decalogue is most commonly viewed as ten commandments that God gave through Moses to Israel, newly freed from

---

3. Bonhoeffer, "Sermon on Matthew 5:8," 515.

4. From this perspective, the title Emmanuel, which Matthew applies to Jesus, is understood better (see chapters 1, 18, and 28).

5. This helps us to better understand Matthew's favourite concept of "these little ones" (see chapters 18 and 25).

6. Bonhoeffer, "Sermon on Matthew 5:8," 513.

7. On the history of the origin and perception of the Beatitudes in Luz, *Matthew 1–7*, 177–81; Mark Moore, *The Chronological Life of Christ*, revised ed. (Joplin: College Press, 2011), 163–65; and for an exhaustive analysis of the possible origin and meaning of the beatitudes, see Betz, *The Sermon on the Mount*, 92–107; Hagner, *Matthew 1–13*, 88–91.

8. For an overview of other possible interpretations of the macarisms, see Stott, *Christian Counter-Culture*, 30–38.

slavery in Egypt (as maintained by Maimonides, Rabbi Moshe ben Maimon). These commandments form an inseparable component of the covenant, providing a basis for the remaining 613 commandments. By observing them, Israel maintained the terms of the covenant.

The second perspective interprets the Decalogue as ten divine declarations, to which the God of liberation summons the redeemed people to listen and comprehend.[9] This approach, upheld by Nahmanides (Rabbi Moshe ben Nahman) and Judah Halevi,[10] underscores God's invitation to the freed community to discern that, in contrast to Pharaoh, God's intentions serve human well-being rather than merely catering to a sovereign's whims. Obedience to these declarations arises from a free awareness of God's good purposes rather than from fear of punishment. Some, such as Rabbi Manis Friedman,[11] even suggest that the ten commandments are God's invitation to the liberated people to partner in God's purposes for humanity and creation. For such interpreters, the Decalogue acts as a marker of Israel's identity, while its genuine observance proves to be the path to authentic freedom and reflects the image and likeness of God in humanity.

Similarly, the Beatitudes (macarisms) can be interpreted along three primary lines: (1) as commandments of blessedness; (2) as eschatological proclamations; or (3) as markers of self-identification or communal identity within the new covenant. In both Greek (*makarios*) and biblical Hebrew (*ashre*), the sense can be rendered "blessed," "happy," "fortunate," "successful," or even "beloved." Translating this term with a single English word is challenging, as it does not easily capture the richness and depth inherent to it, thus leading to distinct translations and divergent interpretations.

Some interpreters argue that Matthew's Beatitudes ought to be regarded as commandments. In the Ukrainian Christian tradition they are typically referred to as "the commandments of blessedness."[12] Referring to them in

---

9. The ancient Hebrew שְׁמַע (*shma*) is a command to listen, think about what is said.

10. See more: Rabbi Joseph Telushkin, *Jewish Literacy: The Most Important Things to Know about the Jewish Religion, Its People, and Its History* (New York: William Morrow, 1991), 55–57; Rabbi Jonathan Sacks, *Essays on Ethics: A Weekly Reading of the Jewish Bible* (Jerusalem: Maggid Books, 2016), 103–108; and here: https://rabbisacks.org/covenant-conversation/yitro/structure-good-society/; https://rabbisacks.org/archive/ten-utterances/ (accessed 2 August 2024).

11. See Friedman's interpretation of the decalogue here: https://www.youtube.com/watch?v=pY4XgWEgoeM; https://www.youtube.com/watch?v=BxPl6_UJugc&t=1232s; https://www.youtube.com/watch?v=pY4XgWEgoeM&t=6s (accessed 28 July 2014).

12. See more here: Luz, *Matthew 1–7*, 185–86; F. Raychynets, "The Gospel of Matthew," in *Slavic Biblical Commentary* (Russian Language Version) (ed. S. Sannikov. Kyiv: Knigonosha, 2016), 1141.

this way shapes one's disposition toward them, treating them as directives demanding obedience. This view positions the Beatitudes as moral obligations for those who have responded to God's call to submit to the divine reign and experience God's presence as manifested in the life, mission, and teaching of Jesus Christ. Under such an interpretation, the first part of a Beatitude (for example, "Blessed are the pure in heart") becomes a human responsibility, and the second part ("for they will see God") is the divine promise in response. In other words, the second clause depends on the fulfillment of the first: Upon meeting our obligation, God enacts the promised blessing. In this perspective, it is the pure in heart who "will see God," linking moral purity to the capacity to perceive the invisible God.

Other interpreters are skeptical of this approach. To them, macarisms are not prescriptions for moral conduct; rather, they constitute declarations of a new status before God. In other words, the Beatitudes are not commandments but *eschatological proclamations* or blessings. The "blessed" are those whom God has designated as such. These statements reveal how God already sees us and what awaits us, rather than prescribing what we must do to earn a divine reward. Proponents of this position emphasize that the Beatitudes describe the manifestation of God's gracious favor, not a reward for religious zeal. While moral or spiritual achievements are not irrelevant, they are more implied than explicitly demanded. Read in this way, the Beatitudes speak to God's love, highlighting the presence of God's eschatological blessing – not only as a future promise but as a present reality for those who embrace the kingdom Christ proclaimed. Hence, the "pure in heart" are those who recognize God's reign and presence in Jesus Christ and decide to share in it, revealing God's reign and presence to the world.

A third option interprets Matthew's Beatitudes as *markers of self-identification* or *communal identity* for those who have accepted Jesus's invitation to become part of the new covenant community – the community that proclaims the reign of God. Compared to Luke's version, where the beatitudes are fewer, contrasted directly with "woes," and convey a different emphasis,[13] Matthew's beatitudes function less as a distinct literary genre (e.g., wisdom, poetry, or prophecy) and more as an integrative summary of the spiritual and ethical essence of the Tanakh as a whole. At the outset of the Sermon on the Mount, they highlight precisely what the Torah underscores.

---

13. The beatitudes in Luke's Gospel emphasize the socioeconomic relations between the poor and the rich, for comparison see 6:20–26. Also see I. Howard Marshall, *The Gospel of Luke: A Commentary on the Greek Text*, New International Greek Testament Commentary (Exeter: Paternoster, 1978), 245–57.

Matthew's beatitudes echo the prophetic reminders about Israel's distinct identity among the nations, recalling the warnings issued whenever Israel was tempted to conform to surrounding cultures rather than living out its covenant responsibilities. Thus, the final beatitude in Matthew (5:11–12) refers to suffering and persecution by the world and explicitly mentions the prophets, indicating that prophecy is not simply an independent genre but an inseparable component of the Tanakh charged with interpreting the true essence of the Torah as the covenant's stipulations.[14]

Just as the kingdom of God cannot be understood apart from the life, mission, and teaching of Jesus Christ, so the meaning of the beatitudes in Matthew cannot be fully grasped apart from these. Christ's teaching interprets them; Christ's mission embodies their true meaning; and Christ's personal example models for humanity the way to follow. His proclamation of the kingdom defines the interpretive parameters for understanding the Beatitudes. Put differently, Matthew's beatitudes illuminate the original intent of "the Law and the Prophets" in light of Christ's life, mission, and teaching about the kingdom, whereby he "fulfills" the law and the prophets (Matt 5:17). Just as the Torah was a covenantal marker for Israel, so Matthew's beatitudes in the Sermon on the Mount function as markers of self-identification for the new covenant community – fulfilled through Christ's mission and confirmed through his suffering and death, in line with what the prophets had announced (Jer 31:31–34; Ezek 36:33–36). These beatitudes set apart Christ's community from others while conforming that community to his image. Understood this way, the pure in heart are those who both recognize the inbreaking of God's reign and presence in Jesus (Matt 1:23; 28:20) and continue Christ's work by serving those in need (Matt 25:31–46). Here, purity of heart is less a static quality than an ongoing process of transformation (Pss 24:3–4; 51:10).

Possible Meaning of "Blessed are the Pure in Heart" in Matthew

> ... Become simple, clear, genuine, natural, straightforward, pure, and your hearts will reflect God's own parental heart.
>
> *Dietrich Bonhoeffer*[15]

---

14. This is how the phrase "the Law and the Prophets" should be understood, which Matthew mentions in his Gospel every time he emphasizes the integrity and essence of the Torah as an integral part of the Tanakh. See 5:17; 7:12; 22:40.

15. Bonhoeffer, "Sermon on Matthew 5:8," 514.

Biblical scholars who have studied the origins of the beatitudes in the Gospel of Matthew (both in the context of the entire Gospel, and in the context of the Sermon on the Mount) as well as their theological significance, offer varied interpretations of this text. Before proposing my own understanding of this passage, I will survey the most seminal works on the Gospel of Matthew and how they understand the saying about *the pure in heart*.

It's difficult to disagree with Donald Hagner, when he says that "[t]his beatitude is the most difficult to relate to the others." For Hagner this beatitude "is meant to indicate that even for the downtrodden and oppressed, for those to whom the good news of the kingdom comes, an inner purity is also required and is not something that can be presupposed."[16] In other words, it teaches about the need for internal transformation of people, regardless of their social position or status, and this transformation cannot be forced or imposed by anyone. It can only be a conscious and voluntary decision. Stanley Hauerwas in his theological commentary on the Gospel of Matthew proposes that Jesus has those in mind who "have been cleansed of fleshly desires"[17] in following him. This immediately raises the question of whether it is possible to achieve complete purification from all bodily desires while one is still in the body?

Many interpreters believe that with this beatitude Matthew calls for the formation of human integrity. Thus Robert Guelich, in his interpretation of the Sermon on the Mount, states that the beatitude of a pure heart "addresses a much deeper level than purity of thought or behavior. It speaks of standing with total integrity, without dissimulation, totally committed to God."[18] In their exegetical treatment of this passage Davis and Allison suggest that it speaks of "those with harmony between inward thought and outward deed,"[19] underscoring a person's integrity, which in Matthew is a hallmark of spiritual maturity, when one's words and actions agree rather than contradict one another. Mar Moor says basically the same thing, but in different words. He claims that this beatitude emphasizes "cleanness and sincerity"[20] in the life of Christ's disciples both before God, and men.

Other interpreters emphasize not so much the spiritual and ethical condition of a person or the process of forming integrity in oneself, but rather

---

16. Hagner, *Matthew 1–13*, 94.

17. Stanley Hauerwas, *Matthew*, Brazos Theological Commentary on the Bible (Grand Rapids: Brazos Press, 2006), 63.

18. Guelich, *The Sermon on the Mount*, 105.

19. W. D. Davies, and Dale C. Allison, Jr., *Matthew: A Shorter Commentary* (London & New York: T&T Clark International, 2004), 67.

20. Moore, *The Chronological Life of Christ*, 167.

the attitude of a person toward God. For example, Ulrich Lutz, in his classic interpretation of the Sermon on the Mount, states that *a pure heart* is about "undivided obedience to God without sin."[21] That is, a person of a pure heart is one who trusts God and manifests this in obedience to God. He is able to do what God commands him, not because he understands him, but because he trusts him. Craig Keener believes that pure in heart are those, "who recognize that God alone is their hope."[22] Realizing our complete dependence and trust in God in everything and relying on him fills us with hope and helps us to see God in our lives.

Some interpreters argue that it is possible to understand the meaning of this beatitude more deeply if we study it in the context of the entire Sermon on the Mount. According to John Stott, the essence of this beatitude is better understood in connection with the "single eye."[23] Stott says, "the pure heart is the single heart and prepares the way for the 'single eye' which Jesus mentions in the next chapter."[24] In other words, the human eye is a mirror or reflection of the state of the human heart. The lustful eye reveals the lustfulness of the heart. Through the expression and desire of the human eye, one can discern the desire and intention of the human heart.

Hans Dieter Betz believes that "for the Sermon on the Mount purity of the heart is a virtue of fundamental importance."[25] That is, the concept of the purity of the human heart and the promise to see God, although not mentioned further in the Sermon on the Mount, but, according to Betz, it is "given further interpretation in 7:21–23. Here it is assumed that those who enter into the kingdom of God will see God, who is the judge and before whom all must appear. It is also assumed that those who are to be rejected will not see him."[26] The pure in heart are people who not only speak on behalf of God, they are not only those who listen to his Word, but the pure in heart are also those who have the wisdom to trust what they hear and the courage to put it into practice, whether because of or in spite of the circumstances. They will see God.

I believe that the beatitude of *a pure heart* can best be understood in the context of Matthew's teaching on righteousness, which is the main theme of

---

21. Luz, *Matthew 1–7*, 196.

22. Craig Keener, *Matthew: The IVP New Testament Commentary Series* (Downers Grove: InterVarsity Press 1997), 107.

23. See Matthew 6:22.

24. Stott, *Christian Counter-Culture*, 49.

25. Betz, *The Sermon on the Mount*, 136.

26. Betz, *The Sermon on the Mount*, 137.

both the Sermon on the Mount and the entire teaching of Jesus in the Gospel. Matthew's new righteousness is first and foremost *a righteousness of the heart*. This is the essence of what is said in the central part of the Sermon on the Mount (5:17–7:12). And the ability to see God in the needy is described in the last part of the last teaching section of the Gospel (see Matt 25:31–46). The disciples of Jesus recognized Christ in the needy, and by serving them they were able to see the invisible God in this world.

The righteousness of his disciples, the community of the new covenant, must be *internal, of higher quality, above* the righteousness of the scribes and Pharisees (see Matt 5:20). It is shaped by a prophetic understanding of the Law (see Matt 5:17). The purpose of the Law, according to the prophets, is to form a holistic person who has the right attitude toward another person, not simply an external performance of religious rituals. The Law is not about controlling other people outwardly, but about one's own internal limitations. It is about forming a holistic person, in whom thought finds expression in the word, and the word becomes embodied in action. This is the process of forming a pure heart, or righteousness of the heart. Such righteousness is expressed in attitudes toward others that a person expects to be shown toward himself or herself (see Matt 7:12; 22:34–40).

The righteousness of the heart is not limited to a contemplative attitude toward another person, but it is able to see God in the needy, "one of these little ones" (see Matt 18:6, 10, 14; 25:40, 45), as Matthew likes to emphasize, and serving Christ through serving "one of these little ones." Those who *are pure in heart* learn from Christ to see the world through his eyes. To see the invisible God in the needy, defenseless, vulnerable, sick, hungry, thirsty, persecuted (see Matt 25:31–46). In this teaching, Christ is not identified with people in power who have privileges or a high status in society, but with the outcasts. People of a pure heart are able not only to see the image of God in these outcasts but are also ready to serve them as they would serve God. This is what Matthew warns the community of Christ against in chapter 18, which is entirely devoted to the doctrine of the church: "See that you do not despise one of these little ones, for I say to you that their angels in heaven continually see the face of My Father who is in heaven" (Matt 18:10 NASB). To see God in the midst of suffering, rather than denying his presence, to serve God by serving the needy, rather than ignoring them, is what purity of heart is all about in Matthew.

Cordocentrism in the Holy Scriptures and Ukrainian Philosophical Thought

> And for the pure in heart? Round them
> Let Thine angels aye attend,
> And their purity defend.
> And as for me, dear Lord, grant love
> For truth and right to the world's end,
> And grant me a sincere true friend.
>
> *Taras Shevchenko*

In the Bible, the human heart is the central anthropological concept, highlighting the integrative unity of physical, emotional, intellectual, and moral facets.[27] It is the reservoir of life and will, the center of moral and ethical decision-making, and the battleground of inner struggle.[28] In the biblical worldview, the heart is a key organ of knowing the Creator (Deut 6:5; 10:12).[29] Only God truly knows what is in the human heart, for God alone "sees the heart" (1 Sam 16:7; Prov 25:3; Jer 11:20; 1 Cor 4:5). Humans often remain partially ignorant of their hearts' contents; indeed, following one's heart is not always a rational or logical choice and can sometimes appear irrational or counterintuitive.

Hence, one's relationship to the heart demands a twofold action: on one hand, a special vigilance in guarding it; on the other, a continual *transformation*. According to the prophets and Jesus, transforming the heart is the key to genuine personal renewal, rather than feigned external changes that only mask one's unwillingness or unreadiness for true inner transformation. The prophetic and wisdom literature emphasizes this throughout (Isa 32:4; Jer 17:9–10; 20:12; Matt 15:10–20; Mark 7:14–23; Prov 4:23; Pss 7:10; 15:2).

Trials serve as a critical catalyst for such transformation. In moments of testing, humans face moral decisions that either harden the heart in bitterness – especially if trials are perceived merely as punishment – or soften the heart, producing creative and genuine renewal. Israel's forty-year sojourn in the wilderness and the Babylonian exile exemplify this dynamic. As the book of Deuteronomy concludes, the nation's long wandering in the desert was not

---

27. See more in Bruce K. Waltke, "Heart," in *The Evangelical Dictionary of Biblical Theology*, ed. by Walter Elwell (Grand Rapids: Baker, 1996), 331–59.

28. For more on the heart in Scripture, see Памфіл Д. Юркевич, *Вибрані твори: Ідея-серце-розум і досвід* [Pamphilus D. Yurkiewicz, *Selected Writings: Idea-Heart-Reason and Experience*] (Канада, Вінніпег: Колегія св. Андрія у Вінніпезі, 1984), 75–79.

29. Craig E. Evans, "Hardness of Heart," in *Dictionary of Jesus and the Gospel*, eds. Green et al. (Downers Grove: InterVarsity Press 1992), 298–99.

merely punishment but also designed for the renewal of their hearts (Deut 8:2, 5, 14, 17). Likewise, the prophets consider exile not simply a punitive measure but a furnace for refining Israel's heart (Jer 29, especially vv. 11–13). In Scripture, a pure heart is precisely that transformed heart that remains pliable and sensitive to God despite suffering, enabling the believer to perceive the world's pain through God's perspective.

Similar insights appear in the Ukrainian tradition of "philosophy of the heart," or *cordocentrism*.[30] These thinkers describe the human heart as the nexus of physical and spiritual being – a "functional center of the integral human person, the functional center of a holistic human being that is more oriented toward the irrational sphere of human reality."[31] Notable Ukrainian *cordocentrists* include N. Gogol, T. Shevchenko, P. Kulish,[32] and especially P. Yurkevych.[33]

However, it is vital to highlight the work of Hryhorii Skovoroda, often regarded as the founder of Ukrainian *philosophy of the heart*.[34] According to Nataliia Sydorenko and other scholars, the Bible was Skovoroda's primary source of inspiration, shaping his reflections on dying, transformation, birth, and the affinity for work – all tied directly to the concept of the heart.[35] For Skovoroda, the human heart is (1) a divine creation, so closely identified with

---

30. See more in Ярослав Гнатюк, "Український кордоцентризм як національна філософія" *Вісник Прикарпатського університету. Філософські і психологічні науки*, [Yaroslav Hnatiuk, "Ukrainian cordocenterism as a national philosophy," *Bulletin of the Precarpathian University: Philosophical and Psychological Sciences*] вип. 18 (2007), 39–45; Т. П. Руденко, "Кордоцентризм як головна риса української екзистенційної ментальності в українській філософії, *Гілея: науковий вісник : збірник наукових праць* [T. P. Rudenko, "Cordocentrism as the main feature of Ukrainian existential mentality in Ukrainian philosophy," *Gilea: Scientific Bulletin*], вип. 151 (№ 12). Ч. 2. Філософські науки. (2019): 116–19.

31. Гнатюк, "Український кордоцентризм" [Hnatiuk, "Ukrainian Cordocentrism"], 42.

32. See the analysis of the representatives of cordocentrism as a philosophical trend in Руденко, "Кордоцентризм як головна риса української екзистенційної ментальності в українській філософії" [Rudenko, "Cordocenterism as the main feature of Ukrainian existential mentality"].

33. Юркевич, *Вибрані твори: Ідея-серце-розум і досвід* [Yurkevych, *Selected Works: Idea-Heart-Mind and Experience*], 75–79.

34. Сковорода, *Повна академічна збірка творів* [Skovoroda, *Complete Academic Works*], 200–477; and Мирослав Попович, *Григорій Сковорода: філософія свободи* [Myroslav Popovych, *Hryhorii Skovoroda: Philosophy of Freedom*] (Київ: Майстерня Білецьких, 2008), 175–230.

35. Н. В. Сидоренко, "Ідея серця у філософії Г. Сковороди: Аспекти тлумачення" [N. V. Sydorenko, "The Idea of the Heart in the Philosophy of H. Skovoroda: Aspects of Interpretation"], *Магістеріум*, вип. 23. Історико-філософські студії (2006), 49–54; and Руденко, "Кордоцентрзм як головна риса української екзистенційної ментальності в українській філософії" [Rudenko, "Cordocenterism as the main feature of Ukrainian existential mentality"], 5.

God that he sometimes equates the two,[36] (2) the center of one's essence and connection with the world,[37] and (3) the path to knowledge (of God and of oneself), reaching divine perfection only through transformation of the heart.[38] Humanity can always turn to God, exposing the heart and welcoming the "spark of resurrection" from God. Such turning to God ensures that old, hardened hearts become new.[39] A transformed heart for Skovoroda, much like the pure heart of Scripture, is "creatively potent in love of neighbor, in understanding, and in affinity for one's calling."[40] Thus, a person's ethical conduct, self-awareness, and relationship to the world ultimately derive from the state of one's heart.

How meaningful that Ukrainian philosophical thought, particularly cordocentrism, and the biblical view of the heart so profoundly resonate. The heart has an *existential* dimension (essential to one's being), a *cognitive* dimension (eluding simple rational explanation), and an *axiological* dimension (directly influencing moral action). Our actions, prompted by the heart, often resist tidy logical explanations yet can prove profoundly right. In many instances, we act not because we already understand fully, but in order to arrive at deeper, more essential understanding.

Theological Significance of the Beatitude in the Time of War

> How do we behold God? It is as if our gaze were fixed on the things and bustle of the world, on what is dreary, gloomy, gray, ugly, as if we were no longer able to lift our eyes or look in a different direction. And yet in all this darkness we still do sense that there must be something incomparably beautiful about the light. But who will give us the eyes to see, eyes that do not immediately

---

36. Сковорода, *Повна академічна збірка творів* [Skovoroda, *Complete Academic Works*], 292–93; also in Руденко, "Кордоцентрзм як головна риса української екзистенційної ментальності в українській філософії" [Rudenko, "Cordocenterism as the main feature of Ukrainian existential mentality"], 5.

37. For more information, see Сидоренко, "Ідея серця у філософії Г. Сковороди" [Sydorenko, "The Idea of the Heart in the Philosophy of H. Skovoroda"], 53–54.

38. Сидоренко, "Ідея серця у філософії Г. Сковороди" [Sydorenko, "The Idea of the Heart in the Philosophy of H. Skovoroda"], 52.

39. Сковорода, *Повна академічна збірка творів* [Skovoroda, *Complete Academic Works*], 292–93.

40. Руденко, "Кордоцентрзм як головна риса української екзистенційної ментальності в українській філософії" [Rudenko, "Cordocenterism as the main feature of Ukrainian existential mentality"], 6.

> close the moment a ray of light falls upon them? What must we do so that we not only sense or yearn for the light, for God, but genuinely behold God?
>
> *Dietrich Bonhoeffer*[41]

Dietrich Bonhoeffer's question presses us to ask what must unfold around us so that we may not only anticipate and long for but also behold the light – behold God – in the reality of human suffering and devastation, especially in times of unprovoked and ruinous war. Why would God permit us to witness such horrors?

The seeming contradiction inherent in the beatitude about the pure in heart amounts to a kind of "prophetic paradox." Biblical prophets were not overly concerned about whether their oracles appeared consistent or comprehensible to their audiences. They were less troubled by whether God seemed logical or clearly understandable and more concerned with proclaiming precisely what God commanded, withholding nothing. If asked to elucidate a mysterious prophecy, a prophet would often simply repeat it, hoping it might prompt the hearer to view the situation from a fresh perspective. A genuine reception of prophecy demands not just intellectual effort but also spiritual discernment. Its message seldom yields to superficial significance; rather, it requires thoughtful reflection and often leads to freely chosen actions rather than forced compliance or responses borne of fear.

Jesus's public ministry stands firmly within this prophetic tradition, explaining and fulfilling the deeper intent of the Law for the people of the new covenant in their concrete historical circumstances. Announcing the Beatitudes at the outset of his public mission before the gathered crowd and the twelve disciples, Jesus similarly did not concern himself with how paradoxical or opaque these statements might seem.

Indeed, the Beatitudes contradict the commonplace assumptions of many listeners who might interpret wealth, not poverty, as evidence of God's blessing.[42] Some find it counterintuitive that hunger and thirst for righteousness rather than for power, status, or privilege would lead to success in life. Equally unsettling is Jesus's identification with the marginalized rather than with those capable of meeting the marginalized people's needs. Like the prophets, Jesus holds that authentic spirituality is gauged less by one's attitude toward

---

41. Bonhoeffer, "Sermon on Matthew 5:8," 512.

42. See the story of the rich young ruler and the disciples' confusion about this in Matthew 19:16–30.

the powerful than by how one responds to the vulnerable, the helpless, and the voiceless.

A parallel perspective appears in the works of Metropolitan Ilarion (Ivan Ohienko), particularly his sermon *To Serve the People is to Serve God*.[43] For him, this principle became a new teaching – one he espoused, lived by, and preached. He arrived at this conviction "through deep reflection on the gospel. The more [he] meditated on Scripture, the more [he] became convinced of the truth of this command as central to the gospel and flowing from its spirit."[44]

This capacity to recognize Christ precisely in suffering individuals marks, for Matthew, the ongoing process by which believers become "pure in heart" – no matter how contradictory it sounds or how nonsensical it appears to the world. This does not hinge on human ability to rationally explain the Beatitudes; it is about having the intuitive wisdom to trust them and the courage to live them out, even if there is no neat and persuasive justification for it on hand.

The Beatitudes cannot be understood apart from Jesus's public ministry and teaching, which constitute their interpretive lens par excellence. So understood, the Beatitudes function as markers of identity for the New Covenant community, called to emulate Christ's example in shaping their vision of reality, their values, and their way of life. Self-identification always carries a dual movement: One must identify with some paradigm (Christ) and differentiate from others.

Paradoxically, it often takes a crisis to purify us from all that is extraneous, to learn to see God amid affliction. War, one of the gravest upheavals, not only exposes the fragility of life but also shows how, in times of peace, we elevate secondary things into primary matters. It is precisely when life is at stake that we reevaluate our priorities. As the famous saying goes, often attributed to the German writer Erich Maria Remarque, who explored the profound and often tragic effects of war and persecution on ordinary individuals in his works, "in dark times, bright people become visible." Recasting that in the context of this beatitude, the pure in heart are most clearly recognized in dark times of unprovoked violence. They stand out by how they respond to adversity – whether cursing the darkness, fleeing from it, or, more boldly, lighting a candle and stepping into the darkness to offer illumination. The pure in heart choose this last path, the bravest and most responsible. For them, the dehumanizing nature of war does not justify brutalizing others; rather, it magnifies the call

---

43. Митрополит Іларіон, *Мої проповіді* [Metropolitan Hilarion, *My Sermons*] (Вінніпег: Товариство Волинь, 1973), 81–88.

44. Іларіон, *Мої проповіді* [Metropolitan Hilarion, *My Sermons*], 81.

to remain fully human. The darkest hour challenges us to preserve our own humanity and not to lose sight of the humanity in others.

Conclusions

The beatitude of purity in heart confronts us with a dual challenge in dark times of war: (1) the challenge of preserving our own humanity; and (2) the danger of losing the ability to recognize the image of God in those around us. To see the invisible God in the visible realm of evil, violence, and suffering – that is the essence of this beatitude. Those with a pure heart remain sensitive to God's presence in the midst of human affairs, moving alongside God even if that defies conventional religious expectations.

This beatitude presents a profound challenge to those who have experienced the atrocities of war. How can they keep their hearts pure and still behold the divine image in themselves? They need safe spaces where their pain can be expressed and genuinely heard. If articulating their trauma in a healing manner proves difficult, they should seek further professional help so that the past tragedy no longer holds them hostage. Ideally, the church can become that place of refuge, providing compassionate aid. Those who are "pure in heart" can tangibly embody God's presence in the lives of the wounded, assuring them that divine presence remains real despite suffering.

One of the most demanding aspects of this beatitude involves discerning the distorted image of God even in the face of the enemy. David's prayer is especially apt for this dilemma: "Create in me a clean heart, O God, and renew a right spirit within me" (Ps 51:10 ESV).

7

"Blessed are the peacemakers, for they will be called children of God"

(Matthew 5:9)

Taras Dyatlik

Introduction

Dealing with the beatitude "blessed are the peacemakers" in the context of war in Ukraine requires both a deep theoretical foundation and practical implementation. Following this direction, this chapter is divided into two parts. The first part (sections 1–4) lays the biblical and theological foundation by exploring the historical reception of the beatitude "Blessed are the peacemakers," analyzing its context in Matthew's community, revealing the depth of the concept of shalom and understanding the theological connection between peacemaking and divine sonship. The second part (sections 5–7) focuses more on the spiritual and practical implications of these principles by transitioning from the concept of just war to just peace, understanding the spiritual nature of peacemaking, and its eschatological perspective in the context of Russian aggression.

This two-part approach reflects the paradoxical nature of Christian peacemaking. On one hand, we recognize that peace is the highest value embedded in our nature at creation in God's image. On the other hand, in the face of unprovoked Russian aggression, we are forced to defend our land, families, and freedom. In this context, the theoretical understanding of peacemaking must find its practical implementation in concrete actions and the church's ministry.

The beatitude "blessed are the peacemakers, for they will be called children of God" (Matt 5:9) takes on particular urgency in the context of a decade of Russian aggression. How to comfort a mother whose son died in battle? How to talk about peace with those who lost their homes due to bombings? How to preserve church unity when part of the community consists of internally displaced persons? Answering these questions requires both deep theological reflection and concrete practical steps.

The purpose of this chapter is not only to theoretically explore the biblical teaching on peacemaking but also to propose specific ways to implement it in the contemporary context of the war. The church is called to be a light in the darkness and a bearer of hope for the traumatized in Ukrainian society, which requires both a solid theological foundation and practical wisdom in its application. At the same time, the author is aware of the methodological limitations and hermeneutical challenges that arise in theological reflection during an ongoing full-scale war, and does not consider the historical, philosophical, psychological, and legal aspects of peacemaking and peacebuilding, as these are subjects of separate studies.

The author dedicates this chapter to three groups of people: those who gave their lives for the freedom of Ukraine, defending it from Russian aggression, like my brother Andriy; those who continue to serve in the military, defending the territorial integrity of our state; and the clergy and believers who tirelessly work for just peace, not losing Christian hope even in the darkest times of war.[1]

Just as Christ was sent into the world as the Prince of Peace (Isa 9:6), the church is called to continue his mission: "Peace be with you! As the Father has

---

1. The author's biblical and theological reflections presented in this chapter were born out of a deeply personal experience. The fatal wounding of my brother Andriy (senior lieutenant of the medical service of the Armed Forces of Ukraine) by Russians in the Kherson region on July 6, and his passing into eternity on 21 July 2024, became the existential experience that radically deepened my understanding of biblical *shalom*. It was through personal trauma of losing my brother, who gave his life for the freedom of Ukraine, that not only a theoretical understanding but also a practical understanding of the paradoxical nature of Christian peacemaking was born in me. Completing this work in December 2024 in Kherson during a visit to local churches (together with Valentyn Syniy, rector of the Tavrian Christian Institute), I hear the explosions of Russian bombs every day. These explosions become a kind of punctuation between theoretical reflections on the nature of true peace and the practical challenges of its implementation in the context of war. My prayer for a just peace for Ukraine is intertwined with the eschatological expectation of God's final *shalom* which will become a reality only with the second coming of Christ. "Come, Lord Jesus!" (Rev 22:20) is not an escape from the reality of war, but a hope for that final resurrection where "the first heaven and the first earth had passed away" (Rev 21:1), and "a new heaven and a new earth" for eternal life awaits us.

sent me, even so I am sending you" (John 20:21). This mission requires both a deep understanding of the nature of biblical peace and the practical implementation of peacemaking ministry in the context of war and its consequences.

Historical Reception of the Beatitude "Blessed are the Peacemakers"

The history of the reception of the beatitude "blessed are the peacemakers" reflects a long evolution of the Christian understanding of peace and peacemaking – from the individual pacifism of the early church through the theological understanding of the just war concept to contemporary complex approaches.[2] For the Church in Ukraine, which today faces the challenges of a full-scale unprovoked Russian aggression, this centuries-old experience of understanding Christian peacemaking is particularly important, as it can help in finding a balance between the gospel call to peace and the need to defend justice.

In the first five centuries of the Christian period, the understanding of the beatitude was shaped by two contexts: the persecution of Christians and their attitude towards military service. The Didache (c. 100 AD) and the epistle of Clement of Rome reflect the predominantly pacifist tendencies of the early church. Origen (185–254), in his work "Against Celsus," was the first to examine the issue of peacemaking in detail, arguing that Christians are true peacemakers precisely because they refuse military service, instead waging a spiritual struggle through prayer for the emperor and the empire.[3]

A significant shift in understanding occurred after the Edict of Milan (313 AD). Augustine (354–430), in his work "City of God," developed the concept of just war. His interpretation of the Sermon on the Mount in the treatise "On the Lord's Sermon on the Mount" became the first truly systematic analysis of the Beatitudes.[4]

Medieval interpretation from the sixth to the fifteenth centuries developed the "just war" doctrine and led to the establishment of Christian political the-

---

2. See Lisa Sowle Cahill, *Blessed Are the Peacemakers: Pacifism, Just War, and Peacebuilding* (Minneapolis: Fortress, 2019); Eklund, *The Beatitudes through the Ages*; Guelich, *Sermon on the Mount*.

3. See Everett Ferguson, "Early Christian Martyrdom and Civil Disobedience," *Journal of Early Christian Studies* 1, no. 1 (March 1993): 73–83; Louis J. Swift, *The Early Fathers on War and Military Service*, 1st ed., Message of the Fathers of the Church 19 (Wilmington: Glazier, 1983).

4. See Augustine, *Concerning the City of God against the Pagans* (London: Penguin, 2003); John Mark Mattox, *Saint Augustine and the Theory of Just War*, Continuum Studies in Philosophy (London: Continuum, 2006).

ology. Thomas Aquinas (1225–1274), in the "Summa Theologica," developed Augustine's teaching, defining three necessary criteria: legitimate authority, just cause, and right intention. He considered peacemaking a special gift of grace, connecting it with the virtue of wisdom. Bonaventure (1221–1274), in his commentaries on the Gospel of Matthew, emphasized the christological dimension of peacemaking: true peacemakers imitate Christ, who reconciled humanity with God through the cross. The Eastern tradition, represented by John of Damascus (676–749), developed a more mystical understanding of peacemaking as the inner transformation of a person through the attainment of *hesychia*.[5]

The Reformation and early modern period of the sixteenth and seventeenth centuries brought new approaches to interpreting the beatitude about peacemakers, closely related to the rethinking of the relationship between church and state. For example, Martin Luther, in his work "On Secular Authority" (1523), developed the doctrine of the "two kingdoms," which significantly influenced the Protestant understanding of peacemaking. He argued that a Christian can serve in both kingdoms – spiritual and secular, acting in each according to the corresponding principles. In his commentary on the Sermon on the Mount, Luther emphasized the importance of inner peace with God as the foundation for external peacemaking. John Calvin, in the "Institutes of the Christian Religion" (1536), offered a more pragmatic approach: While recognizing the importance of peacemaking, he also justified the right of Christian authorities to use force to defend justice. The Anabaptist tradition, represented by Menno Simons (1496–1561), took a radically pacifist position, categorically rejecting any violence and military service. Anabaptists understood the beatitude about peacemakers literally, which led to the formation of historic peace churches such as the Brethren, the Friends (Quakers), and the Mennonites.[6]

The Enlightenment and modern period of the eighteenth and nineteenth centuries brought a critical approach to biblical exegesis and a new perspective on peacemaking. William Penn emphasized the ethical and moral founda-

---

5. See Gregory M. Reichberg, Henrik Syse, and Endre Begby, *Ethics of War: Classics and Contemporary Readings* (Malden: Blackwell, 2006); Bernard McGinn, *The Flowering of Mysticism: Men and Women in the New Mysticism (1200–1350), The Presence of God*, vol. 3 (New York: Crossroad, 1998); George Weigel, "Moral Clarity in a Time of War," Ethics and Public Policy Center, 2002, https://eppc.org/publication/moral-clarity-in-a-time-of-war; Gregory M. Reichberg, *Thomas Aquinas on War and Peace* (Cambridge: Cambridge University Press, 2017).

6. See Roland Herbert Bainton, *Christian Attitudes toward War and Peace: A Historical Survey and Critical Re-Evaluation*, Roland Bainton Reprint Series (Eugene: Wipf & Stock, 2008); John Howard Yoder, *The Politics of Jesus: Vicit Agnus Noster*, repr. (Grand Rapids: Eerdmans, 1987).

tions of peace, criticizing war as a means of resolving international disputes, and proposed one of the first projects of international peacemaking based on Christian principles: To create a European parliament to resolve conflicts between nations.[7] Immanuel Kant, in his treatise "Perpetual Peace," developed a philosophical justification for peace. He proposes a concept of perpetual peace based on rational principles and moral foundations that can ensure stable peace between nations and emphasizes that all peoples have the right to peace, and this right must be protected by international norms.[8] Friedrich Schleiermacher, in his lectures on Christian faith and ethics, considered peacemaking as an expression of Christian love in the socio-political context. Peace is not just the absence of war, but an active process that requires ethical effort. He emphasizes that peacebuilding is an integral part of Christian ethics and speaks of peace as a divine gift that must be sought and maintained through prayer and spiritual practice.[9]

The experience of two world wars in the twentieth century radically changed approaches to interpreting the beatitude. Dietrich Bonhoeffer in "The Cost of Discipleship," offered a new understanding of Christian responsibility in the face of totalitarianism.[10] He criticized "cheap grace," which offers forgiveness without repentance, baptism without discipline, and communion without confession. Bonhoeffer argues that peace is the result of obedience to God's commandments, emphasizing that true peace cannot be achieved without actively fulfilling God's will in the lives of believers. He embodied his theology through his own life, marked by resistance to the Nazi regime, participation in the Confessing Church, and ultimately martyrdom. Reinhold Niebuhr, in his work "Moral Man and Immoral Society," explored the conflict between individual morality and social immorality. He developed a critique of naive pacifism, emphasizing the need for a realistic approach to issues of peace and justice.[11]

Contemporary theology of peace, represented by the works of John Howard Yoder and Stanley Hauerwas, emphasizes the ecclesiological dimen-

---

7. William Penn and Peter Van Den Dungen, *An Essay towards the Present and Future Peace of Europe: By the Establishment of an European Dyet, Parliament or Estates*, repr. ed. (London, 1693; Hildesheim: Olms, 1983).

8. Immanuel Kant and Ted Humphrey, *To Perpetual Peace* (Indianapolis: Hackett, 2003).

9. Friedrich Schleiermacher and Paul T. Nimmo, *The Christian Faith*, 3rd ed. (London: Bloomsbury Academic, 2016).

10. Bonhoeffer, *The Cost of Discipleship*.

11. Reinhold Niebuhr, *Moral Man and Immoral Society: A Study in Ethics and Politics*, 2nd ed., Library of Theological Ethics (Louisville: Westminster John Knox Press, 2013).

sion of peacemaking – the Church itself must be an alternative community of peace. Yoder explores various forms of religious pacifism, including pacifism of absolute principle and pacifism of programmatic political alternatives. He emphasizes that true pacifism must include not only the rejection of violence but also the active struggle against injustice.[12] Hauerwas develops a narrative approach to Christian ethics, arguing that the moral convictions and actions of believers are formed through biblical stories and community narratives. He emphasizes the inseparability of ethics from the life of the church community and highlights non-violence as a key element of Christian ethics, which should reflect the peace and justice preached by Jesus.[13]

John Paul Lederach, in "Building Peace: Sustainable Reconciliation in Divided Societies,"[14] proposes a shift from traditional diplomacy to a more holistic approach in peacemaking. He developed an integrated framework for peacebuilding, where structure, process, resources, training, and evaluation are coordinated to transform conflict and achieve reconciliation. Lederach defines "sustainable peace" not simply as a ceasefire or a peace agreement, but as deep reconciliation, supported by a network of relationships and mechanisms that promote justice and address the root causes of enmity. His contribution has become an important step in the development of the theory and practice of peacebuilding, offering new approaches to resolving conflicts in divided societies – from the theory of "just war" to the question of "just peace."

At the turn of the millennium, theologians proposed a new approach – "peacebuilding." Johan Galtung,[15] Lisa Sowle Cahill,[16] Glen Stassen,[17] and others developed the concept of "just peacemaking." This approach goes beyond the traditional opposition between the theory of just war and pacifism, offering constructive ways to transform conflicts through nonviolent methods.

In this search for "just peace," special attention is paid to restorative justice and healing the traumas of war. "Restorative justice is a process to 'make things

---

12. John Howard Yoder, *Nevertheless: The Varieties and Shortcomings of Religious Pacifism*, rev. and expanded ed. (Scottdale: Herald Press, 1992).

13. See Stanley Hauerwas, *The Peaceable Kingdom: A Primer in Christian Ethics* (Notre Dame: University of Notre Dame Press, 1983).

14. John Paul Lederach, *Building Peace: Sustainable Reconciliation in Divided Societies* (Washington, DC: United States Institute of Peace Press, 1997).

15. "Galtung-Institut for Peace Theory and Peace Practice," accessed 13 June 2024, https://www.galtung-institut.de/en/.

16. Cahill, *Blessed Are the Peace Makers*.

17. Glen H. Stassen, *Just Peacemaking: Transformative Initiatives for Justice and Peace* (Louisville: Westminster John Knox Press, 1992).

as right as possible' which includes: attending to needs created by the offense such as safety and repair of injuries to relationships and physical damage resulting from the offense; and attending to needs related to the cause of the offense (addictions, lack of social or employment skills or resources, lack of moral or ethical base, etc.)"[18] The Church and religious communities play a special role in this process: "Restorative justice recognizes and encourages the role of community institutions, including the religious/faith community, in teaching and establishing the moral and ethical standards which build up the community."[19]

Contemporary theologians also rethink the concept of forgiveness in the context of building just peace: "Forgiveness is not undertaken for its own sake, but is rather part of a social ethic of order for the early Christian community. Such an idea of forgiveness per se must be developed within the context of a model of community building, and not be seen merely as a vehicle of restoration of relations between the penitent and their victim and, more importantly, the living God."[20]

The historical development of the interpretation of the beatitude "blessed are the peacemakers" reflects a gradual deepening of the understanding of Christian peacemaking – from personal non-violence to restorative justice and just peace in all spheres of life. The experience of Matthew's community, for which the Sermon on the Mount became a guide in the difficult circumstances of religious and political confrontation, demonstrates a similar dynamic of understanding and implementing Gospel principles.

The Beatitude of Peacemakers in the Context of the Gospel and Matthew's Community

Jesus Christ's Sermon on the Mount was delivered in the context of the Pax Romana, when Judea was under Roman occupation. Rome exercised control through local intermediaries. Although it was a time of relative stability, not open armed conflict, the main social problem was the oppression of the poor by the elites, particularly through the taxation system to support imperial power.

The immediate listeners of the sermon were a diverse audience "from Galilee and the Decapolis, and Jerusalem, and Judea and from beyond the

---

18. Michael Braswell and John Fuller, *Corrections, Peacemaking and Restorative Justice: Transforming Individuals and Institutions* (Hoboken: Taylor and Francis, 2014), 143.

19. Braswell and Fuller, *Corrections, Peacemaking and Restorative Justice*, 144.

20. Michael K. Duffey and Deborah S. Nash, eds., *Justice and Mercy Will Kiss: The Vocation of Peacemaking in a World of Many Faiths*, Marquette Studies in Theology 58 (Milwaukee: Marquette University Press, 2008), 45.

Jordan" (Matt 4:25 NASB) – representatives of a society divided by social, religious, and political conflicts. Among the listeners, Bonhoeffer emphasizes the special status of the disciples, "who had already responded to the power of his call, and it is that call which has made them poor, afflicted and hungry. He calls them blessed, not because of their privation, or the renunciation they have made, for these are not blessed in themselves. Only the call and the promise, for the sake of which they are ready to suffer poverty and renunciation, can justify the beatitudes."[21]

Matthew's community (which read his Gospel, including the Sermon on the Mount) was a unique church community, composed of Jews and Gentiles,[22] in contact with Greek culture. Having been excluded from official Judaism through persecution, it embodied the universality of Jesus's message: "Therefore go and make disciples of all nations, baptizing them in the name of the Father and of the Son and of the Holy Spirit" (Matt 28:19). This great commission reflected both the openness of God's kingdom to all nations and a rebuke to the Jewish leaders who, through their hypocrisy and refusal to accept the Messiah, themselves shut the kingdom of heaven before people (Matt 23:13).[23]

Jesus in Matthew's Gospel forms a unique community of peace, beginning with his genealogy (Matt 1:1–17). The inclusion of women and Gentiles (Tamar, Rahab, Ruth, and "Uriah's wife") in the genealogy was revolutionary for Jewish tradition, where usually only men were listed. Each of these women had a difficult history: Tamar pretended to be a prostitute, Rahab was a prostitute from Jericho, Ruth was a Moabite, and Bathsheba was the wife of a Hittite Gentile, Uriah. Their presence in the Messiah's genealogy demonstrates the universality of God's plan of salvation.

In his ministry, Jesus consistently overcomes social barriers, addressing marginalized groups in society. He touches a leper (Matt 8:2–3), breaking religious taboos; praises the faith of a Roman centurion (Matt 8:10); heals a woman with a hemorrhage (Matt 9:20–22); calls the tax collector Matthew (Matt 9:9) to the circle of disciples. His words "It is not the healthy who need a doctor, but the sick . . . for I have not come to call the righteous, but sinners to repentance" (Matt 9:12–13) reveal the essence of a new community, founded not on social status but on faith.

---

21. Bonhoeffer, *The Cost of Discipleship*, chap. 6, iBook.

22. J. D. Kingsbury, *Matthew*, Proclamation Commentaries (Philadelphia: Fortress, 1977), 101.

23. Donald Senior, *What Are They Saying about Matthew?*, rev. and expanded ed. (New York: Paulist Press, 1996), 9–10.

The culmination of the formation of the community of peace in Matthew's Gospel is the events of the crucifixion. On the way to Golgotha, Roman soldiers force Simon of Cyrene to carry Jesus's cross (Matt 27:32) – an African who becomes a symbolic representative of all nations in Christ's passion. Although in Matthew both robbers initially mock Jesus (Matt 27:44), other evangelists tell of the repentance of one of them, demonstrating that even in the last moments of life, transformation and entry into the Community of Peace are possible.

The culminating moment is the confession of the Roman centurion: "Truly this was the Son of God!" (Matt 27:54 NASB). A representative of the occupying power, a Gentile who commanded the execution, becomes a witness to Christ's divinity. This recognition, along with the torn veil of the temple, signifies the overcoming of all religious and ethnic barriers in Christ's community of peace.

After the resurrection, the great commission, "Go and make disciples of all nations" (Matt 28:19–20), finally establishes the universal character of Christ's new community. Through his death and resurrection, a community is established that overcomes all traditional divisions – racial, ethnic, social, linguistic, gender – and unites people in God's love. This universal call to all nations (Greek "εθνοι") completes the image of an inclusive community of peace, begun in Christ's genealogy and realized through his sacrificial death and resurrection.

Researchers propose different ways of structuring the Beatitudes in the Sermon on the Mount (Matt 5:3–12).[24] One approach, based on linguistic analysis, divides the eight Beatitudes into two groups of four. The first group (Matt 5:3–6) describes those who are in a state of blessedness through inner distress: poor in spirit, those who mourn, the meek, those who hunger and thirst for righteousness. The second group (Matt 5:7–10) focuses on active virtues: mercy, purity of heart, peacemaking, persecution for righteousness. Another approach considers the Beatitudes as a chiasmic structure – a literary arch where the central message is key, and the beginning and end mutually reflect each other.[25] This is confirmed by the common epithet in the first and last verses and the special use of the "divine passive" – a grammatical construction indicating God's action. Both of these approaches reveal the Beatitudes not as a simple list of moral instructions, but as a holistic spiritual picture of

---

24. Timothy D. Howell, *The Matthean Beatitudes in Their Jewish Origins: A Literary and Speech Act Analysis*, Studies in Biblical Literature 144 (New York: Peter Lang, 2011), 119.

25. David R. Bauer and Mark Allan Powell, *Treasures New and Old: Recent Contributions to Matthean Studies*, Symposium Series 1 (Atlanta: Scholars Press, 1996), 322.

life in the kingdom, where all elements are interconnected and interact with each other.

Another approach, formulated by Gregory of Nyssa in the fourth century, presents the Beatitudes as a spiritual "ladder" of growth: "Those who use a ladder to climb up high, when they step on the first rung, rise by it to the one above . . . Thus the climber by continually rising from the one he is on to the one above reaches the top of his climb. What is the meaning of this parable of mine? I think the arrangement of the Beatitudes is like a series of rungs, and it makes it possible for the mind to ascend by climbing from one to another. If someone has in his mind climbed to the first beatitude, by a sort of necessity of the logical sequence the next one awaits him, even if the saying at first seems rather odd."[26] This spiritual "ladder" unfolds as follows:

- "Blessed are the poor in spirit" (Matt 5:3) establishes the fundamental position of humility and awareness of dependence on God, without which true spirituality is impossible.
- "Blessed are those who mourn" (Matt 5:4) develops the capacity for compassion, especially important in the context of suffering.
- "Blessed are the meek" (Matt 5:5) reveals the paradoxical power of meekness as power under the control of the Spirit, like Christ, who was "gentle and humble in heart" (Matt 11:29).
- "Blessed are those who hunger and thirst for righteousness" (Matt 5:6) connects the desire for peace with justice.
- "Blessed are the merciful" (Matt 5:7) transforms justice into restorative relationships.
- "Blessed are the pure in heart" (Matt 5:8) ensures sincerity of intentions in spiritual life.
- "Blessed are the peacemakers" (Matt 5:9) becomes the culmination of this ladder, representing not just a separate virtue, but a holistic way of life that reflects God's character.

The final beatitudes about persecution (Matt 5:10–11) warn about the reality of opposition and suffering on the path of the "ladder" of spiritual growth, showing that the pursuit of peace often leads through opposition, conflict, and trials. As Mattison emphasizes, the Beatitudes are understood "It is not simply something that happens to us, or a place we find ourselves. It is something in which we participate. What qualifies those called 'happy' to receive their

---

26. Drobner and Viciano, eds., *Gregory of Nyssa*, 32.

reward is (grace-enabled) activity. Furthermore, that activity does not cease in the attainment of reward but is continuous with reward."[27]

For the church in Ukraine, the formation of the community of peace according to Matthew's Gospel carries deep hope and a clear guidance. Like the first listeners of the Sermon on the Mount "from Galilee and the Decapolis, and Jerusalem, and Judea and from beyond the Jordan" (Matt 4:25 NASB), the contemporary church is in a society divided by conflicts. Like Matthew's community, composed of Jews and Gentiles and subjected to persecution, today's Ukrainian church is called to embody the universality of God's kingdom, where all barriers are overcome.

The spiritual "ladder" of the Beatitudes, leading from humility through compassion to active peacemaking, offers a practical path for the church in times of trial. These are not just moral instructions, but a holistic program for forming the community of peace. From Christ's genealogy to the great commission, Matthew's Gospel testifies that God acts through the most unexpected people and situations, inspiring the church to be open to all, especially to those whom society rejects.

The Gospel of Matthew shows how the community of faith becomes a space where the biblical vision of peace is realized by overcoming all forms of alienation and enmity. From the inclusion of unexpected characters in Christ's genealogy to the Roman centurion's final declaration, "Truly this was the Son of God!" (Matt 27:54 NASB), this text demonstrates the gradual expansion of the borders of God's kingdom, which embraces all who respond to Christ's call. Such radical inclusiveness of Matthew's community reflects a deeper theological understanding of peace, rooted in the Old Testament concept of shalom. This term means not merely the absence of conflict, but the holistic restoration of harmony between God, people, and all creation. It is through such a comprehensive understanding of peace that the Sermon on the Mount acquires its full significance as a guide for forming a community that embodies God's plan for reconciled humanity.

---

27. William C. Mattison III, *The Sermon on the Mount and Moral Theology: A Virtue Perspective*, 1st ed. (Cambridge: Cambridge University Press, 2017), 37.

Shalom as a Key to the Biblical Concept of Peace

In Holy Scripture, the concept of peace is revealed through two key terms: the Hebrew word shalom (שָׁלוֹם) in the Old Testament and the Greek *eirene* (εἰρήνη) in the New Testament.[28]

Both of these terms are widely represented in biblical texts, with the very idea of peacemaking pervading all sacred texts, even those where the Greek word *eirenopoios* (εἰρηνοποιός) is not directly used.[29]

Over time, the concept of peace in Judaism underwent significant evolution. In late canonical Judaism, "While it [the concept of shalom] continued to be thought of as the gift of God, and as a condition that would characterize the restored Davidic kingdom of current messianic expectation, its emphasis had shifted from the total well-being of Israel to good social relationships and an absence of strife within the Jewish nation."[30] The rabbinic tradition, which best illustrates this transformation, calls a peacemaker *baal shalom*. Although this interpretation of peace is often compared to the New Testament concept of agape, it is narrower in scope and less focused on spiritual salvation.[31]

The Hebrew concept of shalom, derived from the verb *shalem* (to be whole, complete), means much more than the absence of conflict. It is a comprehensive harmony and well-being in the spiritual, physical, emotional, and social spheres – a state where everything corresponds to God's design and harmony.[32] The understanding of shalom is deepened through its synonyms: *sheket* (tranquility), *berakha* (blessing), *simha* (joy), and *tovah* (good). Its antonyms reveal additional aspects: *milhama* (war) signifies a violation of God's order, *sina* (hatred) destroys peaceful relationships, and *yare* (fear) appears as a consequence of losing trust in God,[33] as the apostle Paul states: "For you did not receive the spirit of slavery to fall back into fear, but you have received the Spirit of adoption as sons, by whom we cry, 'Abba! Father!'" (Rom 8:15 ESV).

In the Septuagint, the Hebrew שָׁלוֹם is translated by the Greek εἰρήνη (*eirene*), preserving the concept of completeness and comprehensive well-being.[34]

---

28. Eklund, *The Beatitudes through the Ages*, chap. 9, iBooks.

29. Daniel Daley, *Ideal Disciples: A Commentary on Matthew's Beatitudes* (Waco: Baylor University Press, 2024), 157.

30. H. Benedict Green, *Matthew, Poet of the Beatitudes*, The Library of New Testament Studies (Sheffield: Sheffield Academic Press, 2001), 216.

31. Green, *Matthew, Poet of the Beatitudes*, 216.

32. Daley, *Ideal Disciples*, 157–58.

33. For a deeper understanding of these terms, the reader can research them in biblical dictionaries and concordances.

34. Howell, *The Matthean Beatitudes in Their Jewish Origins*, 146.

The use of related terms is important: εἰρηνικός characterizes peace-loving people and their words, especially in Psalm 37:37, where this word describes the gentle (33:11), righteous (33:12, 17, 21, 29), and blameless (33:18, 28). In Proverbs 10:10, the verb εἰρηνοποιεῖν occurs in the context of "he who reproves boldly makes peace." Such peace requires an active stance from believers in its establishment and maintenance, as reflected in the call to "seek peace and pursue it" (Ps 34:14).

In the New Testament, the concept of *eirene* acquires particular significance. Christ introduces the unique term εἰρηνοποιός (*eirenopoios*) to denote peacemakers, which is not found elsewhere in the Septuagint or other parts of the New Testament.[35] According to Green, "It is likely that Matthew made a catchword connection between this verse and Psalm 36:37,[36] and in doing so he interpreted the weaker expression in the latter text in terms of the stronger."[37] Paul's understanding of εἰρήν emphasizes its divine dimension as "the peace of God, which surpasses all understanding" (Phil 4:7 ESV) and is a fruit of the Holy Spirit (Gal 5:22).

In John 20, the contrast between φόβος (deep fear) and εἰρήνη (peace) is revealed. The disciples, locked in a house "for fear of the Jews (διὰ τὸν φόβον τῶν Ἰουδαίων)" (John 20:19), encounter the resurrected Christ, who twice proclaims to them, "εἰρήνη ὑμῖν" (John 20:19, 21). The term φόβος here conveys not just anxiety but the deep terror of the disciples. Therefore, the demonstration of his wounds becomes not only proof of the resurrection but also an invitation to enter a new reality of peace, acquired by him through suffering.

This transition from fear to peace finds its theological interpretation in Paul, who in the letter to the Ephesians describes the transition from hostility to peace. He speaks of Christ as "our peace" (εἰρήνη), who "has made us both one" and "has broken down in his flesh the dividing wall of hostility" (Eph 2:14). On the cross, he reconciled Jews and Gentiles to God, and "put to death their hostility" (Eph 2:16). The Greek ἔχθρα acts here as an antonym to εἰρήνη, emphasizing the radical nature of the change. The cross of Christ becomes the central instrument of establishing true peace. Through it, not only external enmity between people is overcome, but also a deep alienation from God. This reconciliation through the cross becomes the culmination of the biblical narrative of shalom where divine peace overcomes both fear and hostility.

---

35. Daley, *Ideal Disciples*, 157.

36. "Consider the blameless, observe the upright; a future awaits those who seek peace" (Ps 37:37).

37. Green, *Matthew, Poet of the Beatitudes*, 216–17.

The biblical narrative of shalom begins with creation, where God establishes perfect harmony as the norm of being. In Eden, people had the fullness of life in close relationships with God and each other, reflecting his image in caring for the created world (Gen 1:26).

The fall disrupted this original shalom, manifested in Cain's fratricide (Gen 4:8) and the escalation of evil to the flood (Gen 6:5). This first murder testified to the catastrophic consequences of the broken relationship between God and humanity (vertical) and between people (horizontal), caused by sin. It demonstrated how alienation from God leads to hostility and violence, destroying God's initial design for peace and harmony.[38] Over time, humanity became very corrupt, and "every intention of the thoughts of his heart was only evil continually" (Gen 6:5 ESV), leading to its destruction by God's punishment of the flood.

However, God initiates restoration through the covenant with Noah: "Never again shall all flesh be cut off by the waters of the flood, and never again shall there be a flood to destroy the earth" (Gen 9:11 ESV) and the calling of Abraham as a bearer of blessing to all nations: ". . . In you all the families of the earth shall be blessed" (Gen 12:2–3 ESV). The Aaronic blessing, "The LORD bless you and keep you . . . the LORD turn his face toward you and give you peace" (Num 6:24–26), emphasizes the inseparable link between God's blessing and shalom, and reveals that true peace is not merely the result of human efforts but primarily a reflection of restored relationships with God.

The Old Testament prophets deepen the understanding of shalom. For example, Isaiah calls the Messiah "Prince of Peace" (Isa 9:6) and connects peace with righteousness: "The fruit of that righteousness will be peace" (Isa 32:17). Shalom is not just the absence of war but the result of a righteous life according to God's commandments. Jeremiah, addressing Israel in exile, calls them to "seek the peace and prosperity of the city" (Jer 29:7), showing that God's people are called to be peacemakers even among strangers. Yet this call to peace does not mean compromising with injustice among the people, for Jeremiah also exposes the sins of Israel and the false prophets who proclaim, "They have healed the wound of my people lightly, saying, 'Peace, peace,' when there is no peace" (Jer 6:14 ESV). Without truth, justice, and repentance, true peace is impossible.

Micah describes an eschatological vision of future peace, where nations "shall beat their swords into plowshares, and their spears into pruning hooks; nation shall not lift up sword against nation, neither shall they learn war any-

---

38. Eklund, *The Beatitudes through the Ages*, chap. 9, iBooks.

more" (Mic 4:3 ESV). Again, this peace is not just the absence of war but the result of a radical transformation of human hearts and relationships, when weapons are turned into instruments of peaceful labor. These prophetic ideas lay the foundation for understanding the peacemaking mission of Christ and his church.

The perfect embodiment of shalom is Jesus Christ, the prophesied "Prince of Peace" (Isa 9:6). He brings a unique peace: "Peace I leave with you; my peace I give to you. Not as the world gives do I give to you" (John 14:27 ESV). At the same time, this peace of Christ demands confrontation with evil: "Do not think that I have come to bring peace to the earth. I have not come to bring peace, but a sword" (Matt 10:34 ESV), showing that true shalom is impossible without inner transformation and resistance to evil. Jesus does not avoid conflicts where they are necessary to establish God's truth.

In the Gospels, Christ demonstrates the perfect example of a peacemaker, sacrificing himself to "reconcile to himself all things" (Col 1:20). Through the cross and resurrection, Christ accomplishes a threefold reconciliation – between humanity and God, between humans, and between humanity and creation. After the resurrection, he appears to the disciples with the words "Peace be with you" (John 20:19), proclaiming a new reality of reconciliation – victory over the forces of evil that destroy shalom in these three spheres of relationships. He gives them the Holy Spirit so that they can continue his mission of reconciliation in the world.

Paul develops this understanding, emphasizing that through faith we "have peace with God through our Lord Jesus Christ" (Rom 5:1). Christ not only taught about peace but is himself our peace: "For he himself is our peace, who has made us both one and has broken down in his flesh the dividing wall of hostility" (Eph 2:14 ESV). In the Body of Christ, this peace is seen as the foundation of our relationships, guiding our thoughts, words, and actions: "And the peace of God, which surpasses all understanding, will guard your hearts and your minds in Christ Jesus" (Phil 4:7 ESV). At the same time, the church must not only preserve peace but actively create it, because God "who through Christ reconciled us to himself and gave us the ministry of reconciliation" (2 Cor 5:18 ESV). As Wilkes notes, "Peacekeepers do not do the hard work of creating peace; they merely work to keep things the way they are without doing the heavy lifting of actually creating peace where there is none."[39]

---

39. C. Gene Wilkes, *A New Way of Living: Practicing the Beatitudes Every Day* (Birmingham: New Hope Publishers, 2013), chap. 9, iBooks.

The book of Revelation shows the final fulfillment of shalom, where God "will wipe away every tear from their eyes, and death shall be no more, neither shall there be mourning, nor crying, nor pain anymore, for the former things have passed away" (Rev 21:4 ESV). This eschatological vision shapes the missionary identity of the church as a witness to the future fullness of God's peace, to which the Lord leads the history of salvation. Thus, in Christ, shalom is not only a fulfilled Old Testament promise but also a reality that exists now and will be fully realized in the future kingdom of God.

The biblical concept of shalom reveals the comprehensiveness of God's peace, which touches all areas of life – from personal transformation to the cosmic renewal of creation. This peace becomes a reality through the concrete actions of God's children, who embody the character of their Father in the ministry of reconciliation. That is why Christ proclaims a special beatitude for peacemakers – they "shall be called sons of God" (Matt 5:9). This combination of peacemaking and sonship reveals the deep theological dimension of this ministry: peacemakers do not merely perform a certain function but reflect the very nature of God, who is the source of true shalom.

Sonship as the Theological Foundation of Peacemaking

Jesus's beatitude, "Blessed are the peacemakers, for they shall be called sons of God" (Matt 5:9), is deeply rooted in the understanding of God's character and his actions in the world. Peacemakers are called "sons of God," which emphasizes their special relationship with God and the reflection of his nature. In biblical tradition, sonship means not only belonging but also likeness. To be "sons of God" means to reflect the character traits of God, who is the "God of peace" (Rom 15:33; 1 Cor 14:33).

God's character such as love, mercy, justice, and peace, must be manifested in the lives of his children. The apostle John writes, "Anyone who does not love does not know God, because God is love" (1 John 4:8 ESV). As Augustine noted, "The peace of all things is the tranquility of order,"[40] emphasizing that true peace is possible only when divine relationships of love and justice are established. Thus, peacemaking is a natural consequence of our sonship, because we are called to reflect God's love and peace in the world.

Our status as "sons of God" is inseparable from Christ, the only true Son of God. In his incarnation, he not only reconciled the divine and human natures but also opened the way "so that we might receive adoption as sons" (Gal 4:4–5

---

40. Augustine, *Concerning the City of God against the Pagans*, Book XIX, chap. 13.

ESV). Through this adoption, we receive not just a new status but become "partakers of the divine nature" (2 Pet 1:4 ESV). Christ demonstrates the perfect example of sonship through his peacemaking ministry. On the cross, he "has broken down in his flesh the dividing wall of hostility" (Eph 2:14 ESV), showing that true peacemaking requires sacrificial love. His life was a constant embodiment of the principles of God's kingdom, where peace and justice are integral components.

Our entry into the reality of divine sonship occurs through participation in Christ's sufferings. "If we are children, then we are heirs – heirs of God and co-heirs with Christ, if indeed we share in his sufferings in order that we may also share in his glory" (Rom 8:17 ESV). This means that we are called to carry the cross with Christ, participating in his peacemaking mission, even if it leads to suffering, as Bonhoeffer notes, "The peacemakers will carry the cross with their Lord, for it was on the cross that peace was made. Now that they are partners in Christ's work of reconciliation, they are called the sons of God as he is the Son of God."[41] In the context of war, this participation in suffering means the willingness of God's children to carry the cross with those who suffer, showing mercy and compassion.

Divine sonship has not only a present dimension but also a future, eschatological one, and will be fully revealed in the future kingdom. When the apostle John writes, "See what kind of love the Father has given to us, that we should be called children of God; and so we are . . . Beloved, we are God's children now, and what we will be has not yet appeared" (1 John 3:1–2 ESV), he emphasizes the ontological reality of our sonship. This is not just a title or legal status, but a profound transformation of our being. Peacemaking becomes a natural expression of this new identity, just as the Son reflects the character of the Father: "Whoever has seen me has seen the Father" (John 14:9 ESV).

The Holy Spirit plays a key role in the realization of our sonship: "For all who are led by the Spirit of God are sons of God" (Rom 8:14 ESV). It is the Spirit who gives us the strength to manifest the divine nature of peacemaking even in the most difficult circumstances of our lives in war. The Spirit "bears witness with our spirit that we are children of God" (Rom 8:16 ESV), confirming us in this identity even when circumstances tempt us to hatred or despair. Through the work of the Holy Spirit, we are able to be peacemakers in a world that needs God's reconciliation. The apostle Paul writes, "God . . . gave us the ministry of reconciliation . . . Therefore, we are ambassadors for Christ . . . we implore you on behalf of Christ, be reconciled to God" (2 Cor 5:18, 20 ESV).

---

41. Bonhoeffer, *The Cost of Discipleship*, chap. 6, iBooks.

Our peacemaking activity is the embodiment of this ministry, helping people reconcile with God and with one another.

The beatitude about peacemakers being called sons of God is not just a theoretical theological concept – it finds its practical embodiment in the lives and ministries of those who courageously take on the work of reconciliation in the most difficult circumstances of human enmity. We are able to be peacemakers in a world that needs God's reconciliation solely through the work of the Holy Spirit. Our sonship is manifested through prayer for the repentance of enemies, while not abandoning truth and justice – just as Christ prayed for his crucifiers (Luke 23:34) but did not justify their actions.

This theological understanding of the relationship between peacemaking and divine sonship found its concrete embodiment, for example, in the work of Archbishop Desmond Tutu, who, in the context of overcoming the consequences of apartheid in South Africa, demonstrated how a deep awareness of divine sonship is embodied in concrete mechanisms of reconciliation: "In the modern world, where wars and conflicts cause suffering to millions of people, the understanding of divine sonship becomes especially important."[42] Archbishop Desmond Tutu, known for his peacemaking ministry in South Africa, writes:

> Theology reminded me that, however diabolical the act, it did not turn the perpetrator into a demon. We had to distinguish between the deed and the perpetrator, between the sinner and the sin, to hate and condemn the sin while being filled with compassion for the sinner. The point is that, if perpetrators were to be despaired of as monsters and demons, then we were thereby letting accountability go out the window because we were then declaring that they were not moral agents to be held responsible for the deeds they had committed. Much more importantly it meant that we abandoned all hope of their being able to change for the better. Theology said they still, despite the awfulness of their deeds, remained children of God with the capacity to repent, to be able to change. Otherwise we should, as a commission, have had to shut up shop, since we were operating on the premise that people could change, could recognize and acknowledge the error of their ways and so experience contrition or, at the very least,

---

42. Desmond Tutu, *No Future without Forgiveness* (New York: Doubleday, 2000), chap. 5, iBooks.

remorse and would at some point be constrained to confess their dastardly conduct and ask for forgiveness. If, however, they were dismissed as being monsters they could not by definition engage in a process that was so deeply personal as that of forgiveness and reconciliation.[43]

The theological understanding of sonship reveals the deep connection between the identity of God's children and their calling to peacemaking. This identity is realized through concrete service, where truth and mercy, justice and forgiveness, are combined in witnessing to God's peace. Therefore, the next step should be to understand how this theological truth is embodied in the practical transition from a just war to a just peace.

The previous four sections outlined the biblical-theological foundation of Christian peacemaking: from the historical reception of the beatitude through the experience of Matthew's community and the comprehensive understanding of shalom to the theological understanding of God's sonship. The following sections focus more on the spiritual-practical perspective of this ministry in the context of Russian aggression against Ukraine. They reveal concrete ways to embody Christian peacemaking through restorative justice, overcoming war trauma, and building a just peace.

From Just War to Just Peace

In the context of Russian aggression against Ukraine, the centuries-old Christian tradition of understanding the relationship between just war and just peace acquires renewed relevance. The development of Christian understanding of peacemaking has come a long way from early Christian pacifism through the theory of just war to the modern complex vision of just peace. "The disconnect between Christian texts and Christian practice is also instructive and demonstrates the fundamental shift in just peace thinking – practice, and not just theory, even when that theory is found in sacred texts, must guide efforts to transform violence into nonviolence, war into peace, conflict into justice."[44] Along this path, the church has constantly sought a balance between the gospel call to peace and the need to protect justice. For the church in Ukraine today, it is especially important to develop a theological understanding of just defense

---

43. Tutu, *No Future without Forgiveness*, chap. 5, iBooks.
44. Susan Brooks Thistlethwaite, ed., *Interfaith Just Peacemaking: Jewish, Christian, and Muslim Perspectives on the New Paradigm of Peace and War*, 1st ed. (Basingstoke: Palgrave Macmillan, 2012), chap. 4, iBooks.

that harmoniously combines Christian peacemaking with unwavering commitment to truth. This search for balance reflects a deeper theological truth: True peace is impossible without justice, and true justice must lead to reconciliation.

Truth in the biblical sense is not just correspondence to historical facts, but a deep reality of God's justice and righteousness. When the prophet Jeremiah exposes false prophets who proclaim: "They have healed the wound of my people lightly, saying, 'Peace, peace,' when there is no peace!" (Jer 6:14 ESV), he exposes not just their untruthfulness, but a deep distortion of God's truth for the sake of temporary comfort for those who support injustice.

Justice in the biblical sense includes three key elements. First, it is the restoration of truth. Second, it is compensation for damages caused. Third, it is the creation of conditions that prevent the recurrence of crimes in the future. The prophet Micah proclaims: "He has told you, O man, what is good; and what does the LORD require of you but to do justice, and to love mercy, and to walk humbly with your God?" (Mic 6:8). Therefore, "the first step in engaging this practice norm is to break through the capacity of individuals and nations to hide their worst deeds from themselves, as well as from others, and thus fail to even see the wrongs of the past, let alone acknowledge them . . . Breaking through the denial of abuse is the first step in engaging this practice norm, and it gives rise to acknowledging responsibility. People and nations have to see the wrongs of the past in order to even start to acknowledge responsibility . . . This kind of work helps model the role of truth telling in this norm."[45]

An example of true reconciliation based on justice is the story of Zacchaeus: "Behold, Lord, the half of my goods I give to the poor. And if I have defrauded anyone of anything, I restore it fourfold" (Luke 19:8 ESV). This example demonstrates that true repentance always includes concrete actions with willingness and effort to compensate for the damage caused and restore violated justice.

Restorative justice offers an alternative approach to understanding justice and reconciliation as "a process to 'make things as right as possible'"[46] A particularly important example of implementing the principles of restorative justice is the experience of the Republic of South Africa and the work of Archbishop Desmond Tutu, who was mentioned above. He emphasized that the theological understanding of human dignity requires distinguishing between

---

45. Thistlethwaite, *Interfaith Just Peacemaking*, chap. 4, iBooks.
46. Braswell and Fuller, *Corrections, Peacemaking and Restorative Justice*, 143.

crime and criminal, keeping open the possibility of repentance and change even for those who committed the most terrible atrocities.[47]

At the same time, "Restorative Justice recognizes that not all offenders will choose to be cooperative. Therefore there is a need for outside authority to make decisions for the offender who is not cooperative. The actions of the authorities and the consequences imposed should be tested by whether they are reasonable, restorative, and respective (for victim(s), offender, and community)."[48]

However, it is important to understand that "this pressure to forgive on the part of victims without repentance and change on the part of victimizers is sometimes given a religious interpretation. It is, however, not in line with this practice norm, as the result is often to help justify the violence, not end it . . . The 'spiral of violence' will not be interrupted unless the power inequalities that helped to give rise to the violence are changed."[49]

In the context of the war in Ukraine, restorative justice necessitates documenting and recognizing all war crimes, including mass killings, deportations, torture, destruction of infrastructure, attempts to destroy Ukrainian identity. "It is of little use to acknowledge responsibility for the suffering of victims, however, if nothing changes for them, their families, or the society. The next step in this practice norm is redressing the suffering of victims. Taking responsibility through concrete action to address the consequences of abuse must occur, or repentance stays on the surface and does not impact either individuals or their society . . . This is not unlike the role of repentance and forgiveness in domestic violence – battered women can be pressured to 'forgive, forgive' without real repentance and change on the part of their batterers."[50]

Reconciliation is possible only through deep repentance of the offender (and those who support Russian aggression), which requires a comprehensive transformation. First of all, this means recognizing the truth about the imperial nature of Russian aggression and categorically rejecting the concept of the "Russian world," which served as the ideological foundation for the war. An integral part of this process should be a sincere recognition of Ukraine's right to self-determination and independence, as well as unconditional recognition of the right to exist of Ukrainian culture and language distinct from Russia's. Such worldview changes must be accompanied by concrete actions to compensate

---

47. Tutu, *No Future without Forgiveness*, chap. 5, iBooks.
48. Braswell and Fuller, *Corrections, Peacemaking and Restorative Justice*, 143.
49. Thistlethwaite, *Interfaith Just Peacemaking*, chap. 4, iBooks.
50. Thistlethwaite, *Interfaith Just Peacemaking*, chap. 4, iBooks.

for the damage caused and, most importantly, create reliable mechanisms that will prevent the recurrence of aggression in the future. Without comprehensive repentance, any talk of reconciliation will remain empty declarations that do not lead to true peace.

It is important to remember that the defense of Ukraine by the Armed Forces of Ukraine is not an act of revenge or retribution. It is, first of all, a sacrificial service to protect the Ukrainian state and civilians from aggression. This act stems from obeying the Christian commandment to love one's neighbors. As the apostle Paul reminds: "Beloved, never avenge yourselves, but leave it to the wrath of God, for it is written, 'Vengeance is mine, I will repay, says the Lord'" (Rom 12:19 ESV). However, this does not absolve us of the responsibility to work for the establishment of justice now.

The biblical understanding of repentance and forgiveness presupposes a deeper transformation of consciousness and concrete actions to correct the evil done. The prophet Ezekiel speaks of the need for a new heart: "And I will give you a new heart, and a new spirit I will put within you. And I will remove the heart of stone from your flesh and give you a heart of flesh" (Ezek 36:26 ESV). "If anything, that is the thrust of the Hebrew legacy – and it is given still greater emphasis in the New Testament corpus. The sin against neighbor was nothing short of sin against God and so the need for reconciliation also involved a need to be reconciled with God by way of reconciliation with one's neighbor."[51]

Thus, the church is called to be an active participant in the peacemaking process, but not by imposing hasty "reconciliation," but by serving to establish justice as the basis of true peace through repentance. This service is revealed in several interrelated dimensions. The first dimension is prophetic ministry, which consists in exposing the lies and manipulations of Russian propaganda, witnessing the suffering of war victims, affirming the dignity of every person, and protecting fundamental rights and freedoms. The church must be a voice of truth and justice in society.

The second dimension is pastoral support, which includes accompanying war victims, helping to overcome trauma, supporting servicemen and their families, as well as constant prayer and spiritual care. It is through this direct service that the church becomes a place of healing and restoration for those affected by the war. The third dimension is social service, which is expressed in providing humanitarian aid, rehabilitating victims, supporting internally displaced persons, and restoring destroyed communities. This is a practical

---

51. Duffey and Nash, *Justice and Mercy Will Kiss*, 45.

embodiment of Christian love for neighbor, which the church in Ukraine has been actively carrying out since the first hours of the full-scale Russian invasion.

As a community of faith, the church is also called to help in understanding and overcoming violence through developing a theology of just peace, creating spaces for dialogue, forming a culture of nonviolence, and educating responsible citizens. Thus, church ministry covers both practical and spiritual-intellectual aspects of building a just peace.

The transition from the concept of just war to just peace requires a comprehensive theological understanding, where truth, justice, and reconciliation are inextricably intertwined. However, achieving true peace is impossible only through external mechanisms of restorative justice and social transformations. As the apostle Paul says, "For we do not wrestle against flesh and blood, but against the rulers, against the authorities, against the cosmic powers over this present darkness, against the spiritual forces of evil in the heavenly places" (Eph 6:12 ESV). This perspective reveals the deep spiritual nature of conflicts and peacemaking, where external confrontation is only a visible manifestation of a more fundamental spiritual struggle.

The Spiritual Nature of Peacemaking in the Context of War

To make peace means to create a new reality, to open up opportunities for life where previously only violence and death prevailed. This requires a special spiritual vision: To see the world and the Other through the eyes of Christ, who came "that they may have life and have it abundantly" (John 10:10 ESV).[52] In this context, peacemaking becomes not merely a social activity but a deeply spiritual practice, reflecting the very nature of God as the source of true shalom.

The biblical view of destructive conflicts reveals their deep spiritual nature, which goes far beyond the visible political or social confrontation. The apostle Paul clearly points to this spiritual dimension: "For we do not wrestle against flesh and blood, but against the rulers, against the authorities, against the cosmic powers over this present darkness, against the spiritual forces of evil in the heavenly places" (Eph 6:12 ESV). This understanding is key to comprehending the nature of conflicts and the ways to overcome them through the spiritual practices of the Church.

In the biblical perspective, the origins of war and violence lie not merely in human ambitions or geopolitical interests, but in a deep spiritual brokenness that resulted from the fall. The tragedy of Cain and Abel shows how quickly

---

52. Duffey and Nash, *Justice and Mercy Will Kiss*, 74.

the disruption of vertical relationships with God leads to horizontal violence between people. This spiritual brokenness in the socio-political sphere is still manifested today through imperial dehumanizing ideologies that deny the dignity of other nations and their right to exist.

Such dehumanizing ideologies as "Russian world" are a manifestation of the activity of spiritual forces of evil, about which Christ says "comes only to steal and kill and destroy" (John 10:10 ESV). These spiritual forces actively oppose God's design for the diversity of nations before his throne, which is glorified in John's vision: "After this I looked, and behold, a great multitude that no one could number, from every nation, from all tribes and peoples and languages, standing before the throne and before the Lamb" (Rev 7:9 ESV).

In this context, the role of the Holy Spirit in the work of reconciliation becomes particularly significant. The day of Pentecost demonstrates God's view of cultural and linguistic diversity: "they were bewildered, because each one was hearing them speak in his own language . . . And how is it that we hear, each of us in his own native language?" (Acts 2:6, 8 ESV). The Holy Spirit does not negate national characteristics, but sanctifies them, creating unity in diversity. This fundamentally differs from the actions of "rulers and authorities" who strive for unification through the suppression of the racial, ethnic, or linguistic identity of another.

As Miroslav Volf notes: "At Pentecost an alternative to the imperial unity of Babel is created, yet without a return to a pre-Babel state. Before Babel the whole of humanity spoke one language; in Jerusalem the new community speaks many languages. As the tongues of fire are divided and rest on each of the disciples, 'each one' of the Jews from 'every nation under heaven' representing the global community hears them 'speaking in the native language of each' (vv. 3–7). A theological (rather than simply historical) reading of the Pentecost account suggests that when the Spirit comes, all understand each other, not because one language is restored or a new all-encompassing metalanguage is designed, but because each hears his or her own language spoken. Pentecost overcomes the 'confusion' and the resulting false 'scattering,' but it does so not by reverting to the unity of cultural uniformity, but by advancing toward the harmony of cultural diversity."[53]

Therefore, in the context of Russian aggression against Ukraine, it is important to understand that any attempts or support for the existential destruction of the national identity, language, and culture of any people directly contradict

---

53. Miroslav Volf, *Exclusion and Embrace: A Theological Exploration of Identity, Otherness, and Reconciliation*, 17th repr. (Nashville: Abingdon, 2008), iBooks.

the work of the Holy Spirit. True reconciliation is possible only on the basis of recognition and respect for the God-created diversity of nations and languages. The Holy Spirit points us to reconciliation that does not silence crimes against another person or nation, but exposes them, demands repentance, and restores justice.

The eucharistic community of the church becomes a space where this unity in diversity takes concrete form. At the eucharistic table, representatives of different nations become one Body of Christ, without losing their cultural identity. This mystery of unity shows the way to true reconciliation, which respects the God-given diversity of humanity.

An important aspect of the spiritual nature of peacemaking is the understanding of the commandment to love enemies. Jesus taught: "But I say to you, love your enemies and pray for those who persecute you" (Matt 5:44). This commandment is not merely a moral instruction for personal life but has deep socio-political application. As Cahill notes: "While 'love of enemies' seems to call for a radical conversion of the personal and collective attitudes that produce attempts at domination, retaliation, and violent self-vindication, 'peacemaking' names the communal and political processes that follow from this conversion."[54]

Christ's words on the cross, "Father, forgive them, for they know not what they do" (Luke 23:34 ESV), and Stephen's prayer, "Lord, do not hold this sin against them" (Acts 7:60), reveal the depth of Christian prayer for enemies in the context of love. It is important to understand that these prayers were not a justification of crimes or a rejection of truth – they were requests to God for the transformation of the offenders. These situations of personal martyrdom cannot be mechanically transferred to the context of defensive war, state policy, or international relations.

The apostle Paul points to specific tools for conducting spiritual warfare: "Therefore take up the whole armor of God, that you may be able to withstand in the evil day, and having done all, to stand firm" (Eph 6:13 ESV). Each element of this spiritual armor – truth, righteousness, readiness to proclaim peace, faith, salvation, and the Word of God – is critically important for forming a biblical worldview and resisting ideologies of dehumanization and hatred.

The liturgical life of the church becomes a special space of spiritual warfare. Through prayer, fasting, and the Eucharist, we not only express our pain and receive God's comfort, but we also spiritually influence the course of events. Christ's promise, "For where two or three are gathered in my name, there am

---

54. Cahill, *Blessed Are the Peace Makers*, 63.

I among them" (Matt 18:20 ESV), reveals the spiritual potential of the church community as a place of God's presence and action.

Pastoral care of the military and their families, as well as those affected by the war, is also of particular importance. The church community must preserve and develop a space for healing spiritual trauma through comprehensive ministry that includes spiritual, psychological, and material support. It is also important to prevent emotional burnout of chaplains and volunteers through regular spiritual practices and mutual support.

Awareness of the spiritual nature of war gives hope, for we know that despite all the power of the forces of evil, the ultimate victory belongs to Christ, who came "to reconcile to himself all things, whether on earth or in heaven, making peace by the blood of his cross" (Col 1:20 ESV). This eschatological perspective does not lull us into passivity but inspires us to actively participate in God's mission of reconciliation by proclaiming his truth, establishing his justice, and serving his love.

Thus, the spiritual nature of peacemaking is revealed through the transforming power of the Gospel and the work of the Holy Spirit in the life of the church, through the development of a unique spiritual space in which God's shalom becomes visible and tangible, and through the lives of church communities transformed by Christ's love, so that society may see an alternative to hostility and violence – the reality of reconciliation with God, between people, and with all creation. This ministry of reconciliation is carried out in the tension between the reality of the present war and the hope for the final restoration of all creation. It is this tension between the "already" accomplished reconciliation through the cross of Christ and the "not yet" fullness of the kingdom of God that forms the eschatological horizon of Christian peacemaking. In this light, every act of peacemaking becomes not only an attempt to overcome a specific conflict but also a prophetic sign of the future kingdom, where "God may be all in all" (1 Cor 15:28).

The Eschatological Perspective of the Beatitude of Peacemaking

The tension between the "already" and the "not yet" permeates all Christian understandings of peacemaking. This tension is particularly palpable within the liturgical life of the church, where each Eucharist becomes a foretaste of the eschatological banquet of the kingdom. Jesus proclaimed this paradoxical reality: "The kingdom of God has come near" (Mark 1:15), yet simultaneously taught to pray, "Your kingdom come" (Matt 6:10). Through Christ's sacrificial act on the cross, reconciliation between God and humanity has already been accomplished (Eph 2:14). Nevertheless, the fullness of this reconciliation awaits its ultimate realization.

Christ's resurrection is not merely a historical event, but a guarantee of the eschatological restoration of all creation. "If only for this life we have hope in Christ, we are of all people most to be pitied. But Christ has indeed been raised from the dead, the firstfruits of those who have fallen asleep" (1 Cor 15:19–20). This truth holds particular significance for the families of fallen soldiers – their sacrifice is not in vain, for it is inscribed within the larger narrative of life's victory over death. The apostle Paul underscores the cosmic scope of this restoration: "We know that the whole creation has been groaning as in the pains of childbirth right up to the present time. Not only so, but we ourselves, who have the firstfruits of the Spirit, groan inwardly as we wait eagerly for our adoption to sonship, the redemption of our bodies" (Rom 8:22–23).

The Holy Spirit, given to us as a down payment of the age to come, already creates within the church a space of eschatological shalom. Through the church's sacraments, particularly baptism and the eucharist, we become participants in the new reality of the kingdom, where "There is neither Jew nor Gentile, neither slave nor free, nor is there male and female, for you are all one in Christ Jesus" (Gal 3:28).

The prophet Isaiah depicts the eschatological shalom of God in the powerful image of cosmic reconciliation: "The wolf will live with the lamb, the leopard will lie down with the goat . . . They will neither harm nor destroy on all my holy mountain, for the earth will be filled with the knowledge of the LORD as the waters cover the sea" (Isa 11:6–9). This vision is not simply a poetic metaphor, but a prophetic revelation of the nature of the future kingdom of God, which is already beginning to manifest in the life of the church.

The church is a sign of this future kingdom here and now. As Thomas Watson writes, "There is a fourfold peace that we must study and cherish . . . "There is a home peace – peace in families. It is called 'the bond of peace' (Ephesians 4:3). Without this all drops in pieces. Peace is a belt which ties together members in a family . . . There is a town peace – when there is a sweet harmony, a tuning and chiming together of affections in a town . . . There is a political peace – peace in a nation. This is the fairest flower of a prince's crown. Peace is the best blessing of a nation . . . There is an ecclesiastical peace – a church-peace, when there is unity and verity in the church of God. Never does religion flourish more, than when her children spread themselves as olive-plants round about her table."[55] Through the lives of family and church communities trans-

---

55. Thomas Watson, *The Beatitudes: An Exposition of Matthew 5:1–10* (New edition), Revised layout (Edinburgh: The Banner of Truth, 2014), chap. 8, iBooks.

formed by Christ's love, society and the state gain the opportunity to witness an alternative to enmity and violence.

In light of eschatology, even the smallest acts of peacemaking acquire eternal significance. "Therefore, my dear brothers and sisters, stand firm. Let nothing move you. Always give yourselves fully to the work of the Lord, because you know that your labor in the Lord is not in vain" (1 Cor 15:58). Every prayer for the repentance and transformation of enemies, every effort towards reconciliation and the bridging of societal divides, every act of mercy becomes a harbinger of the kingdom to come.

In the book of Revelation, we see the ultimate realization of this peace, where all aspects of shalom find their complete fulfillment: "He will wipe every tear from their eyes. There will be no more death or mourning or crying or pain, for the old order of things has passed away" (Rev 21:4). This complete restoration of shalom signifies the healing of all wounds, the restoration of all fullness of relationships, the triumph of justice, and eternal peace.

Pastoral accompaniment of those who have lost loved ones in war includes not only psychological support, but also a theological understanding of suffering in light of paschal hope. Shared prayer, mutual support within the community, and participation in the eucharist become concrete manifestations of eschatological reality amidst the pain of the present age.

In the context of Russian aggression against Ukraine, the eschatological dimension of peacemaking takes on particular urgency. Our calling to be children of God is realized through active participation in establishing God's kingdom through our attitudes and relationships with one another here and now, while recognizing that ultimate and eternal peace is possible only through the full revelation of our sonship in eschatological reality. As the apostle John writes, "Dear friends, now we are children of God, and what we will be has not yet been made known. But we know that when Christ appears, we shall be like him, for we shall see him as he is" (1 John 3:2).

Thus, Christian peacemaking always exists in the tension between the "already" reality of reconciliation through the cross of Christ and the "not yet" of the ultimate restoration of all creation. This tension does not paralyze us, but rather inspires us to active participation in God's mission of reconciliation, knowing that every act of genuine peacemaking is a sign and foretaste of the kingdom to come, where "Love and faithfulness meet together; righteousness and peace kiss each other" (Ps 85:10). The hope of the eschatological restoration of all creation gives us the strength to continue the ministry of peacemaking even in the darkest times, remembering that "the sufferings of this present time are not worth comparing with the glory that is to be revealed to us" (Rom 8:18 ESV). This does not diminish the reality of our present pain, but provides assurance that our sufferings and efforts in the cause of peace are not in vain, for they are part of the larger narrative of God's redemption of all creation. In this context, each eucharist becomes not only a remembrance of the past, but a prophetic proclamation and foretaste of the future triumph of God's kingdom, where the fullness of shalom will be ultimately realized.

Conclusions

A theological reflection on the beatitude "blessed are the peacemakers" within the context of ongoing Russian aggression reveals the profound paradox of Christian peacemaking: It is precisely when peace seems most unattainable that the call to peacemaking becomes most acutely relevant. The biblical ministry of reconciliation radically differs from a simplistic understanding of peace as the mere absence of war or conflict. The deep connection between peacemaking and divine sonship testifies that this ministry is not merely a moral imperative but a reflection of God's very nature within the life of his people.

The experience of the Matthean community demonstrates how the early church formed an alternative community of peace amidst violence and injustice. Their path of overcoming ethnic and social barriers remains a relevant guide for the contemporary church in Ukraine. In practical terms, Christian peacemaking in wartime conditions is revealed through:

- Consistent witness to the truth about the nature of Russian aggression.
- Active participation in the restoration of justice.
- Creation of spaces for healing for those traumatized by war.
- Development of specialized ministries for the afflicted.
- Formulation of a theological understanding of just defense.

The eschatological perspective provides a new dimension to every act of peacemaking. Prayer for the transformation of enemies, ministry to the afflicted, and efforts toward a just peace become signs of the presence of the future kingdom here and now, even though the fullness of shalom will be revealed only with the coming of Christ.

War has laid bare the spiritual nature of conflicts. Confronting ideologies of dehumanization requires the church not only to engage in social ministry but also to offer a prophetic voice and spiritual resistance. The church must be a space where truth is not sacrificed for the sake of hasty "pacification" and where justice leads to genuine reconciliation.

The experience of the Ukrainian church shapes a new understanding of the interconnectedness between just defense and Christian peacemaking, between the necessity to resist evil and the call to love enemies. Through the pain of loss and the experience of suffering, a deeper truth about the nature of biblical peace sprouts. Just as the wounds of the resurrected Christ became a testament to his victory over death, so the deep wounds of the Ukrainian people and the church, through the power of the gospel, can become a source of hope for the world. However, this demands a special divine wisdom from us in combining a firm stance for truth with openness to the possibility of transformation, even of those who currently perpetrate evil.

In the cemeteries of Ukraine, where the fallen soldiers are buried, amidst the fresh graves, a new understanding of Christian peacemaking is sprouting. It is born not in comfortable academic offices, but in places of the most searing pain, where death and resurrection meet, where human sacrifice opens the way for future peace. This is the paradoxical path by which the church carries the light of Christ's peace through the darkness of war, awaiting the day when "Love and faithfulness meet together; righteousness and peace kiss each other" (Ps 85:10).

"Come, Lord Jesus" (Rev 22:20).

8

"Blessed are those who are persecuted because of righteousness"

(Matthew 5:10–11)

Yevgeny Ustinovich

Blessed are those who are persecuted because of righteousness, for theirs is the kingdom of heaven. Blessed are you when people insult you, persecute you and falsely say all kinds of evil against you because of me. (Matt 5:10–11)

On 8 June 2014, in the city of Sloviansk, Donetsk region, an area temporarily occupied by Russian terrorists, the evangelical community "Transfiguration of the Lord" celebrated Trinity Sunday. During the service, armed men – representatives of the so-called Russian Orthodox Army – captured four members of this community. Two of them were parents of many children. When, a month later, Sloviansk was liberated by Ukrainian forces, their burned bodies were found with traces of torture and gunshot wounds. These were only the first of many Ukrainian Christians who fell victim to religiously motivated hatred by Russians. Illegal arrests, torture, sexual perversions, and killings in the Ukrainian territories occupied by Russia have been going on for ten years.

According to *Time* magazine, there are over thirty known cases of killings or kidnappings of leaders of religious communities in the territories of Ukraine occupied by Russia.[1] Since information about what is happening in such territories is very limited, the real figures may be much higher.

Christians have been persecuted in previous periods of Ukrainian history as well. In the last century, under Soviet rule, these persecutions took place on a colossal scale: millions of Christians were physically exterminated or sent to the Gulag. For a number of reasons (which deserve a separate analysis), the new generation of the Ukrainian evangelical community, which experienced explosive growth after the collapse of the Soviet Union, did not particularly emphasize its unity with the churches of previous periods. We tried to live in a world where the persecution of Christians was perceived as an anomaly, not as a pattern. Therefore, now that this world is disappearing, we are trying to comprehend some aspects of reality that we previously carefully avoided.

In this chapter, I will try to outline the following: (1) biblical principles that can help us understand the persecution of the righteous; (2) some trends in contemporary practical theology – primarily how the attitude of Ukrainian Christians towards biblical texts that reflect the experience of persecuted righteous people is changing. Matthew 5:10–11 is one such text; it is also a key intertextual element: when Christ promises blessedness to his persecuted followers, his promise encourages the disciples to a new (or rather renewed) perception of many other themes and images from the Holy Scriptures.

The persecution of Christians is a challenge not only for Ukrainian churches but also for the entire global Christian community. According to the Holy Scripture, the persecution of Christians requires specific steps from their co-religionists – liturgical and practical ones. If the church tries to ignore this challenge or downplay its significance, such an inadequate reaction can have devastating consequences. And vice versa: Where believers are aware of the unique status of the persecuted, the promised blessedness becomes part of their experience.

When it comes to the reaction of Christians to the persecution of the church, it is important to remember that the responsibility for an adequate position lies primarily with the leaders of the community and with the leading representatives of academic circles. It is they who determine what the approach to this problem will be among the "ordinary" believers.

Against the background of other bad news that bombards society from morning till night (and at night, if you need to spend the night in a bomb shelter), news about the persecution of Christians in the occupied territories

---

1. Peter Pomerantsev, "Russia's War Against Evangelicals," *Time* (April 20, 2024). https://time.com/6969273/russias-war-against-evangelicals/.

can increase the general feeling of sadness and despair. Surely, there is nothing surprising in the fact that many Christians decide either to completely ignore this topic or to treat it very superficially.

Such an approach may be acceptable and understandable for people who are actually struggling to survive in very harsh conditions. But a different attitude to this problem is expected from church leaders, because they have a greater responsibility. Even greater responsibility lies with those Christians who live in the relatively comfortable conditions of Western society. The persecution of the church in modern Ukraine is a challenge that requires specific actions from us (this topic will be developed in the last section of this chapter). It can also be a challenge for our theology if we have not previously paid enough attention to this topic.

In the following sections of this chapter, I will try to show the general biblical picture, which can become one of the foundations of a modern evangelical approach to the problem of persecution. Together with the reader, we will look for an answer to the question: "What does the Bible say, in general, about the persecution of the righteous? How is this theme revealed from the beginning to the end of the canon of the Holy Scripture?" Then it will be easier for the reader to see what role the beatitude of Matthew 5:10–11 plays in the integral plan of God's salvation.

Persecution of the Faithful in the Old Testament

One of the characteristic features of modern Protestant theology is its focus on conflict resolution. Representatives of peacemaking missions spare no time, money, or energy in holding conferences, seminars, round tables, the purpose of which is to reconcile the participants of various conflicts.[2] The methodology of such efforts is based on the idea of dialogue: No matter how different the views of the "opposing sides" may be, it is always possible to find something in common between them. In the end, they all share a common "humanity" – a common denominator that can be reached sooner or later, if there is only time and desire.

---

2. The founder of the organization Open Doors, Andrew van der Bijl, known to many as "Brother Andrew," in his book *Light Force* shared a vividly humorous description of the attempts (not always successful) that his organization made, trying to reconcile Palestinian Christians with Messianic Jews in Israel. It is unfortunate that currently Open Doors – an organization that was created specifically to help persecuted Christians in Eastern Europe – mostly refuses to investigate and comment on the persecution of Christians in the occupied territories of Ukraine.

This assumption about the unity of all mankind, of course, has a biblical basis and is connected with the doctrine of creation based mainly on the first two chapters of the book of Genesis. But in the light of almost all subsequent chapters of the Bible, this justification becomes problematic. Already in chapter 3 of Genesis there is talk about the division of mankind into two large families – the descendants of the serpent and the descendants of the woman. This division is a theme that is developed throughout almost the entire Holy Scripture.

We often talk about God, who frees people from enmity and causes the resolution of conflicts – and, of course, the Bible, like our history, contains many examples of how God reconciles enemies. But the Holy Scripture also mentions the enmity that is caused by God himself. Yes, it is difficult for many Christians to accept the idea that God can be the initiator of division, but we observe just such a paradox already in the description of the events in the garden of Eden. God says to the serpent: "And *I will put* enmity between you and the woman, and between your offspring and hers; he will strike you on the head, and you will strike him on the heel" (Gen 3:15; emphasis added). This antagonism between the righteous and the wicked, and ultimately between Christ and the serpent, is not a natural consequence of the fall. If God himself had not "put" this enmity between the offspring of the serpent and the offspring of the woman, then all the descendants of Adam and Eve would have been enslaved by the serpent.

The conflict between these two kinds of people is observed throughout the Bible – from Genesis to Revelation. According to God's promise, this conflict of universal scale is resolved through the victory of the righteous Offspring of the woman, who will crush the serpent's head. The culmination of the war comes during the crucifixion and resurrection of Christ, and the final victory – after his return in glory.[3]

The conflict between the righteous and the wicked begins already in the first generation of Adam's descendants: Cain kills Abel precisely because God recognized Abel's righteousness (Heb 11:4). In the following chapters of Genesis, the righteous are often persecuted by their brothers. (Against this background, the constant assertion of Russian propaganda – that Russians are supposedly "older brothers" of Ukrainians – takes on a truly sinister meaning.)

---

3. Cullman draws an analogy with the events of World War II: the resurrection of Jesus was like D-Day – a victory that changed the course of the war, and his return in glory will be like V-Day – the day of final victory (quoted from: Anthony A. Hoekema, *The Bible and the Future* (Grand Rapids: Eerdmans, 1994), e-book, no page number). Cullman's analogy has been justifiably criticized, but, considering that any historical analogy will always be inaccurate, the very logic on which Cullman based his comparison can be helpful.

In order not to repeat the fate of Abel, Jacob must become virtually a refugee (Gen 27:42–45). The hatred of the elder brothers had even worse consequences for Joseph, who became a slave in Egypt (Gen 37:36).

In the book of Exodus, the ungodly pharaoh oppresses an entire people – all the Jews became slaves in Egypt. At first, Moses and Aaron try to resolve the problem diplomatically. They engage in dialogue with Pharaoh and his priests many times, but when the persecutor "hardened" his heart (Exod 8:28), the problem of persecution is no longer solved by negotiations. It is not even solved by "sanctions" – economic and partly physical destruction of Egypt. Pharaoh will not stop oppressing Israel until he "is forced by a mighty hand" (Exod 3:19).

When Israel finally inherits the land, the nation's suffering does not end there. For their sins, God gave Israel into the hands of foreign invaders several times. But the righteous Israelites are oppressed not only by pagans: When Gideon destroys the idol, he does it secretly, at night, because the followers of the cult of Baal threaten him with death, and the threat is real (Judg 6:27–30). Samson, the betrayed hero of Israel, falls into the hands of the Philistines, and it is the "men of Judah" who hand him over to the enemy (15:10–13). Collaborators often play an important role in the persecution of believers – both in the ancient world and in the modern one.

Persecution (and betrayal) were also an important part of the experience of the future king David. Although he already had God's promise and even the holy anointing (1 Sam 16:13), the previous king, Saul, tried to kill him.[4] Saul literally hunts David (1 Sam 24:2), who hides from him in the deserts and Philistine cities. Even after David became king, he again had to experience exile (2 Sam 15–19). The subsequent history of Israel also includes many cases of persecution of the faithful. The kings who came after David were not always righteous, so the truly righteous often suffered persecution.

The prophet Elijah describes the mass killings of the confessors of the God of Israel during the time of Ahab and Jezebel: "For the people of Israel have forsaken your covenant, thrown down your altars, and killed your prophets by the sword" (1 Kgs 19:10). Persecutions were an integral part of the life of almost all the Old Testament prophets (Acts 7:52). The last of them, John the Baptist, was killed by Herod.

---

4. In his poem "Saul" (1860), Taras Shevchenko expresses regret that Saul missed and did not kill David. In this way, the poet presented a satirical "analysis" of the genesis of autocracy in order to discredit the voluntary slavery of his "poor in heart" contemporaries.

Persecution of the Faithful in the New Testament

In the Gospel of Matthew, Jesus is called the Son of David. Like his ancestor, Jesus also suffers persecution. The hatred of the Pharisees turns into a conspiracy against him (Matt 12:14), which leads to murder. Jesus warns his followers that they too will be persecuted, and that the main persecutors will often be their closest relatives (Matt 10:36).

The book of Acts describes the death of Stephen, the first of the Christian martyrs. The author emphasizes the connection, the continuity between the persecution of the prophets in the Old Testament and the persecution of Christians in the New (Acts 7:52–58). The "offspring of the serpent" continues what Cain started. The death of the apostle James (Acts 12:2), the attempted execution of the apostle Peter (Acts 12:3–11), the constant persecution that the apostle Paul endures – all these episodes show that the division of humanity into two kinds is quite real.

The borders between the two communities are not constant. They change through the conversion of persecutors (and through the apostasy of some Christians, as it is a two-way street). Perhaps, most notably, the apostle Paul himself was also a persecutor of Christianity, but through conversion he joined the persecuted. The borders between the two categories of people change primarily through the preaching of the gospel – "so that they may turn from darkness to light and from the power of Satan to God" (Acts 26:18 ESV). But the change in the social configuration of these two groups and the borders between them does not make them a single group. As long as the persecution of Christians exists, humanity will always consist of two fundamentally different groups. That is why the attempts of some religious figures to "build bridges," to arrange a dialogue between the persecuted and the persecutors are doomed to failure. In the book of Acts, the problem of persecution is solved either through the conversion of the persecutors (as it was with Saul), or through their death (as it was with Herod – Acts 12:23), but not through dialogue.

So, God chose a paradoxical approach to solving the problem of sin. He divides humanity into two categories in order to then unite them under the authority of Christ. The unity of humanity, which is shown in the final chapters of the book of Revelation, is actually the unity of those who were freed from the power of sin and death. That is why persecuted Christians can rejoice even "here and now" – persecution is a sign that they belong to the followers of Jesus. Therefore, they can count on an eschatological reward – on eternity in the presence of God, where they will celebrate victory over death and other consequences of sin. The expectation of this eternal joy is also part of the experience, so persecuted Christians can rejoice even now, "though now for a little while . . . have had to suffer grief in all kinds of trials" (1 Pet 1:6).

Persecution of the Faithful in the History of the Church

If the main thesis of the previous two sections is correct, then the persecution of Christians should have taken place during almost all periods of church history. This is exactly what we observe. The first three centuries of the church's existence in the Greco-Roman world were accompanied by waves of persecution in various provinces of the empire. Some areas were safer for Christians than others, some emperors (or representatives of local authorities) treated Christians better than others, so the church had times of relative peace, but early Christians generally realized that such periods of calm were the exception rather than the rule. If it is possible to talk about a rule, then it was formulated in the book of Acts as follows: "We must go through many hardships to enter the kingdom of God" (14:22).

The conversion of Constantine brought freedom and security to the Christians of the Roman Empire, although it paradoxically worsened the situation of their co-religionists in the Persian Empire.[5] However, as the examples of Athanasius of Alexandria or John Chrysostom, who were exiled for their faith, testify, this security was not absolute. Countless other Christians suffered from the invasions of the Goths, Vandals, Huns, and other barbarian tribes.

The expansion of Islam, which began in the seventh century, meant the end of a safe life for Christians in vast territories, which the Western Roman Empire gradually lost.[6] Cossack Ukraine,[7] located on the border of European

---

5. As Fairbairn explains, the persecution of Christians began after the recently converted Roman Emperor Constantine wrote a letter to the Persian Shah Shapur, "then only six years old," asking him to protect Christians in the Persian Empire (Donald Fairbairn, *The Global Church – The First Eight Centuries: From Pentecost Through the Rise of Islam* [Grand Rapids: Zondervan, 2021], e-book, no page number). Since then, the Persians began to view Christians as potential traitors.

6. The persecution of Christians in Islamic countries is a topic that deserves special attention. Interested readers can be recommended a number of sources, the authors of which consider both the conflicts between Islam and Christianity, and modern (including revisionist) attempts to interpret these conflicts: Christof Sauer and Richard Howell (eds.), *Suffering, Persecution and Martyrdom: Theological Reflections* (Johannesburg: AcadSA Publishing, 2010); Raymond Ibrahim, *Sword and Scimitar: Fourteen Centuries of War Between Islam and the West* (New York: De Capo, 2018); Thomas Schirrmacher, *The Persecution of Christians Concerns Us All: Towards a Theology of Martyrdom* (Bonn: Verlag für Kultur und Wissenschaft, 2018).

7. The Ruthenian kingdom perceived itself as a bastion protecting not only itself, but also all Christians in Central Europe from the Islamic threat.

Christian civilization, functioned as a huge fortress to protect Christians – both Orthodox and Catholics – from the Ottoman threat and from raids by the Crimean Khanate.

In Western Europe, with the beginning of the Reformation, Christians were also persecuted by other Christians – a situation that provoked many wars, divided several countries, and generally led to the fact that, in 1683, the Turkish army reached the gates of Vienna. The secular order, which appeared after the Reformation, positioned itself as a guarantee of the end of religious wars, but in fact the secular state became an even more severe persecutor of Christians, as can be seen in the examples of the French Revolution or the Soviet regime.

The twentieth century began with the genocide of Christian peoples of the Ottoman Empire – Armenians, Greeks, and Assyrians – and continued with the systematic destruction of the peoples of the USSR, including Ukrainians. The Soviet government killed people for ideological reasons, but if you trace some parallels between the killing of Christians in ancient Rome and the Soviet Union, you can identify a number of patterns that allow us to speak of the continuation of processes that began in the time of Cain and Abel. Such patterns are noticeable not only at the level of statistics, but also in the applied, ritual aspects.

For example, the average Lviv resident may not know when the last time crucifixion was practiced as an execution in his city. Most modern people are sure that such methods of torture are more characteristic of the ancient world or the Middle Ages. But in fact, the last case of crucifixion in Lviv was recorded relatively recently – in June 1941 in the prison of the Soviet security agency, the NKVD. The Greek Catholic priest, Fr. Zinoviy Kovalyk, was crucified on the prison wall; his body also bore traces of an occult ritual.[8] There are many other examples of how the persecution of Christians in a supposedly atheistic state was accompanied by religious – but not Christian – symbols and rites.

In the 1990s a period of relative freedom began for Ukraine, and the desire of modern Ukrainian Christians to forget about the Soviet times is understandable. But now we can no longer forget about the persecution of Christians, because it continues. This is an unpleasant topic, but the consequences of ignoring reality can be even worse. In the next section, we will consider some liturgical and practical aspects of serving God in conditions of persecution. The promise of blessedness, which Jesus gives to all those persecuted for the

---

8. The case of Fr. Zinoviy was investigated by a special commission from the Vatican that carefully examined all the witnesses. Unfortunately, many other similar cases are little known because the persecutors often cover up the traces of their crimes.

sake of truth, is a catalyst for the changes that are already taking place in the lives of some Ukrainian Christians. This promise is also a guideline that helps to understand the changes that should be sought in the future.

Liturgical Changes – David's Songs of Lament, Anger and Revenge

One of the most interesting trends that can be observed in the modern Protestant environment of Ukraine is a renewed interest in the Book of Psalms.[9] In this section, only three features of the Psalms will be considered, which in many communities were almost not brought up before the war.

War destroys many things, one of which is often a superficial, sentimental religiosity. Songs, sermons, and instructive clichés that previously seemed to be a source of great wisdom now look detached from reality. Although Protestant communities in Ukraine usually recognize that the entire Bible was written under God's inspiration, in fact almost every community (and person) has its own "canon within the canon" – texts that we turn to most often (even if this happens at the expense of other biblical texts). Among the texts that were not particularly popular before, but now attract attention, are the Psalms.

In the historical books of the Bible, we read about David – a hero who bravely endured all the trials. Persecution, constant danger, life in exile – nothing could break David. When he endures the last test, it makes him fit to reign over Israel. But in the Psalms, the inner life of the hero of faith is revealed to us, and we see a paradox: True resilience (in relation to people, especially enemies) coexists with brokenness before God. David is not ashamed to talk to God about his sadness, anger, despair, and helplessness.

This feature can even shock an unprepared reader. The shock is doubled and tripled when he realizes that these Psalms – all the Psalms, not just selected excerpts – were the "prayer book" of Jesus and the apostles. The Son of Man, who had nowhere to lay his head (Matt 8:28), emphasized the parallels between David's sufferings and his own experience, which he partially shared with his disciples. Even suffering on the cross, Jesus quoted David's lament from Psalm 22:1 (Matt 27:46).

For many evangelical Christians, the Psalms, especially the songs of lament, are terra incognita. As Eklund observes, in general, representatives

---

9. The title "Psalms of David" is used here in the broadest sense. Of course, David was not the author of all the psalms, but the entire collection has signs of unity, so it can be spoken of as a complete text. The patterns of using the Psalms of David apply to other texts that describe the brokenness of human life (Job, Lamentations of Jeremiah, etc.).

of the Western evangelical mainstream do not even know how to approach these texts and what to do with them.[10] The Dutch researcher Van Ommen believes that the main reason for this attitude to "texts of lament" is the "cult of normality,"[11] which often prevents representatives of religious communities from recognizing and accepting their own brokenness, which, accordingly, does not contribute to the development of empathy.

Such trends are characteristic of the Western world, but until recently they also prevailed in Ukraine. Today we see how they are changing. Psalms of lament are gradually becoming part of the liturgical practice of even those churches where they were almost never mentioned before. Such changes have not only a "therapeutic effect" but also lead to changes in our understanding of the theological dimension of grief. "Blessed are those who mourn, for they will be comforted" (Matt 5:4).

Lament and sorrow in the Psalms are often combined with strong expressions of anger. To a certain extent, it can be said that the songs of lament are also songs of anger. In some Christian circles, the topic of anger is almost a taboo, caused by a misconception that all manifestations of anger are sinful. The use of the Psalms (with deep, balanced interpretation) refutes this naive idea. The persecuted David constantly expressed anger and drew God's attention to the crimes of his enemies. If the church ignores the Psalms of anger, it can no longer adequately talk about the war crimes that are taking place in the occupied territories.

Research on this topic is only in its initial stages. It should probably start with the personal testimony of people who have experienced injustice in conditions of war and occupation and discovered new horizons of communication with God precisely through the "psalms of anger." If a person feels strong anger against the occupiers, but cannot express it, it can have a devastating impact on the immediate environment. And vice versa, anger expressed in the Psalms slowly ceases to control the person. Thanks to the Psalms, anger can be realized and understood – understood primarily as a normal reaction of a mentally healthy person to glaring injustice. Anger signals a violation of borders – a problem to which God takes very seriously (Deut 27:17). If anger is expressed in acceptable liturgical forms (Psalms), then the circumstances that caused

---

10. Rebekah Eklund, *Jesus Wept: The Significance of Jesus' Laments in the New Testament* (London; New York: T&T Clark, 2015).

11. Léon Van Ommen, *Autism and Worship: A Liturgical Theology* (Waco: Baylor University Press, 2023), 90.

this anger become a topic for prayer. When David (as well as his Descendant) suffered persecution, his anger often turned into a prayer for justice.

This is the third feature of the Psalms, which Ukrainian Christians are beginning to discover during the war. Psalms not only help to express pain and anger; they contain requests that are related to specific sins of the persecutors. These requests contain details that can be considered one of the biggest challenges for some Ukrainian communities that traditionally preached pacifism and non-violence.

The changes that are taking place in the liturgical practice of some churches during the war can be conditionally described as follows. In the first days after the Russian invasion (in February 2022), joint prayers "for peace and the end of the war" were heard in churches. Later, prayers appear for the needs of those who suffered, and for comfort for them. After that, prayers appear for a "just peace," then for victory and, finally, for the punishment of criminals. Some Christians still cannot join such prayers; in their opinion, the followers of Jesus have no right to ask God for specific manifestations of justice (according to their theology, believers have received grace from God, not justice, so we supposedly cannot demand justice).

Can the church use in common prayer, for example, such words:

> Do to them as you did to Midian, as to Sisera and Jabin at the river Kishon,
> Who were destroyed at Endor, who became dung for the ground. (Ps 83:9–10).

Can the church ask God to turn our enemies into dung? How should Christians understand such words:

> God is a righteous judge, a God who displays his wrath every day.
> If he does not relent, he will sharpen his sword; he will bend and string his bow.
> He has prepared his deadly weapons; he makes ready his flaming arrows. (Ps 7:11–13)

> For you are not a God who is pleased with wickedness; with you, evil people are not welcome. The arrogant cannot stand in your presence; you hate all who do wrong. (Ps 5:4–5)

When confrontation with such texts cannot be avoided, some religious figures reject them – they offer an interpretation that is close to the ideas of Marcion, who insisted on a complete break between the Old and New Testaments. According to his views, this gap was so huge that one could even speak of different gods: the "God of the Old Testament" was stern and cruel, but the "God of the New Testament" is supposedly completely different – a God of love.

The views of Marcion were condemned by the church in ancient times, but some of his ideas remain attractive in the twenty-first century (Even relatively conservative Christians can sometimes mention the "God of the Old Testament"). Some religious groups in Ukraine still emphasize the gap between the Old and New Testaments, and do not pay enough attention to the continuity between them, the unity of the Holy Scripture.

We cannot reject such texts just because they are contained in the Old Testament. And when we accept them as they are, we discover an important aspect in God's plan: God is zealously concerned about justice. The persecuted can rejoice in God also because one day they will see his justice: He will repay their persecutors (if they do not repent), and this retribution will testify to his glory, his perfect justice, as well as his love:

> [God] struck down the firstborn of Egypt, his love endures forever.
> to him who divided the Red Sea asunder, his love endures forever;
> and brought Israel through the midst of it, his love endures forever;
> but swept Pharaoh and his army into the Red Sea, his love endures forever.
> ... who struck down great kings, his love endures forever;
> and killed mighty kings, his love endures forever;
> Sihon king of the Amorites, his love endures forever;
> Og king of Bashan, his love endures forever. (Ps 136:10, 13–15, 17–20)

When God physically destroys the Egyptians, king Sihon, and king Og – these are manifestations of his love.

Persecution as Preparation for Reigning

Through the Psalms, we identify ourselves with the persecuted David (as well as Christ and his persecuted disciples). If we share their despair, rage, desire for justice, and desire to see God's glory, then we can also share their joy. Psalm 22, which was quoted by Jesus on the cross, helps us to realize the depth of the horror which Jesus (and his church) experienced. This is a song of lament and despair, but – paradoxically – also a song of joy.

During the torture on the cross, Jesus did not have the opportunity to quote this Psalm completely, but the text points to his entire ministry, death, resurrection, and the glorious consequences of this victory. This is a song of triumph – triumph through defeat and death.

When David's Psalms become the songs of our hearts, we begin to perceive our exile as a test, preparation for the kingdom. When the prophet Samuel pours consecrated oil on David's head, the shepherd boy, to a certain extent, already becomes the king of Israel. But he is, of course, not yet ready to reign; he does not yet have the maturity and wisdom needed for this incredibly difficult ministry. God creates various circumstances in which David can learn the art of power. David observes the life of the previous king, Saul, and learns from his mistakes, when he serves him as a court musician-exorcist, then as a loyal warrior and member of the royal family.

When David's popularity reaches its peak, Saul begins to see him as a threat and tries to kill him. The one who recently was the hero of all Israel, becomes – in the social dimension – no one. He loses everything.

The persecution for David was accompanied by "social death." Even his wife was given to another man – as if she was already a widow (1 Sam 25:44). Saul, in this way, emphasizes that David is no longer his son-in-law, and that for David there is no more protection or any other rights. Many Ukrainians understand what it means to lose all their property, all their former social connections and not be able to plan life even for the week ahead.

This is exactly how the life of the first followers of Jesus was described, and this pattern is visible throughout the history of the church, where periods of calm are rather the exception than the norm (although we are used to thinking otherwise). The period of persecution ends for David with complete defeat: he returns to the city where he found temporary shelter, but the city is looted and destroyed (1 Sam 30:1–3). David's people lose everything: wives, children, property, hope for a peaceful life. They also lose (at least some of them) faith in the fact that David is truly chosen by God as king. They are even ready to kill him (1 Sam 30:6). His life (or what is left of it) is again "reset." God saves David from this abyss, gives him and his followers the opportunity to return their families and property. Interestingly, such a return, such a victory becomes possible thanks to a slave who was left behind by David's enemies, but "came to life" on the third day.[12]

In certain cases, Christians who suffer persecution may later rebuild their destroyed lives. But there are many for whom the return of the loss will happen only through the resurrection of the righteous and other eschatological events. Christ's promise – "for great is your reward in heaven" – cannot be canceled even by death.

So, we have considered three changes that are happening in the liturgical practice of many Ukrainian churches. In worship, space appears for expressing (1) lament, (2) anger, and (3) the desire for justice. Simply put, Ukrainian Christians have begun to cry more, to be more angry, and to strive for justice more. These three changes (and many others) can be summarized in one phrase: Ukrainian churches have begun to discover the psalms for themselves and use them in worship – precisely the psalms, not hymnbooks, and not modern Christian songs, no matter how popular they may be. Of course, not all churches do this (some even put up fierce resistance), but the general trend is present and observing it can reveal interesting results.

Since the issue of justice is a painful question for many Ukrainian Christians, it is worth devoting a separate section to it.

Can We Expect Justice?

In the Gospel of Luke, Jesus tells a parable that is often interpreted as an example of persistence in prayer. The image of a poor widow who did not give up became a source of inspiration for many Christians who prayed for the growth of the church, the success of missionary service, the conversion of unbelievers, etc. Of course, all this semantic potential is present in the parable and God's providence has used it throughout the history of the church. But it is worth paying attention directly to the content of the poor widow's request. What exactly does she demand from the judge?

The widow demands: "Grant me justice [Ἐκδίκησόν] against my adversary!" (Luke 18:3). Apparently, her "adversary" is causing her some harm and threatens to inflict even more suffering (perhaps the adversary wants to seize her property or violate her rights). In such a situation, she, of course, expects

---

12. The apostle Paul writes that Christ "was raised on the third day according to the Scriptures" (1 Cor 15:4), but in the Old Testament it is difficult to find a text where it would be specifically foreseen that the Messiah will rise on the third day. Probably, Paul wants readers to pay attention to the "third day" as a general theme, a leitmotif that develops throughout the entire biblical narrative.

that the judge will forbid him to encroach on her property or harass her. This meaning almost entirely corresponds to the translation of "defend." But the Greek verb ἐκδικέω has other connotations that are lost in this translation. For example, in Romans 12:19: "Do not take revenge [ἐκδικοῦντες], my dear friends, but leave room for God's wrath, for it is written: 'It is mine to avenge; I will repay,' says the Lord." This verse speaks not only about preventing a possible violation of rights (sometime in the future), but about God's reaction to the evil that has already been done to us. The apostle Paul teaches that God is not indifferent to the suffering of Christians, that God carefully observes the sin that is committed against them, and that he will certainly repay the persecutors (unless they repent). That is why Christians should refrain from trying to repay their offenders on their own – not because God does not want revenge, but because God wants to avenge himself.

When John in Revelation sees in heaven the souls of martyrs, killed for their testimony, these souls cry out: "How long, Sovereign Lord, holy and true, until you judge the inhabitants of the earth and avenge [ἐκδικεῖς] our blood?" (Rev 6:10). These martyrs in heaven are completely safe; they no longer need defense, but they need justice. This need will be satisfied only when they see God's judgment upon their persecutors. God understands this need and promises to satisfy it (Rev 6:11).

Serving persecuted Christians will never be complete without recognizing this need: Christians who suffer persecution need God's justice. They need assurance not only that God will stop war crimes, but also that he will punish the criminals.

Are Ukrainian Christians ready to pray for the punishment of those who persecute believers? Most evangelical churches today are not yet ready to make such prayers part of their liturgical practice. Usually, conservative Christians recognize God's judgment over criminals as an eschatological event. Some recognize that God can manifest his judgment not only in eschatological events, but also in history. Christians who believe this are few and far between. Even fewer are those who believe and openly admit that God executes his judgment in the midst of history in response to the prayer of the faithful.[13] In Revelation

---

13. For example, in the book of Revelation, the prayers of the persecuted saints rise to heaven like incense. There, in heaven, God and his servants return this incense to the earth, but already in the form of specific (and very severe) manifestations of God's wrath. God's judgment covers the city where the Lord was crucified (Rev 11:8). These images can be interpreted as a symbolic description of the events that took place in 70 AD, when the Romans destroyed Jerusalem. But the meaning of these passages is not limited only to such an interpretation. What John sees in heaven is eschatological in nature, but it also corresponds to at least some of the manifestations of God's wrath on earth throughout history.

itself, it is not written what the content of such prayers was, but one can guess that these were not generally accepted prayer clichés about "peace throughout the world."

The punishment of criminals – both in the future life and in this one – is not a pleasant topic to which modern Christians, who were brought up on the ideas of pacifism, would willingly devote attention. But without concrete, meaningful answers to such questions, the testimony that the church is trying to manifest in modern Ukrainian society will be incomplete, because it is these questions that often come to the fore for Ukrainians. And the answers given within the framework of agnosticism – the most common worldview of modernity – are unsatisfactory. Without a God who directs history and promises to repay criminals, hope for justice remains illusory. It is such a God who is revealed in the Bible, and the theme of the persecution of the faithful, which is revealed throughout the Bible – from Genesis to Revelation – is a very important component in the biblical teaching about God's faithfulness and other attributes.

Who Can Count on this Promise?

Before moving on to the discussion of the practical aspects of God's promise for those who mourn, it is worth considering one more question that may cause some misunderstanding: to whom exactly does this promise of blessedness apply? The problem is also that some translations can create the impression that the promise is intended for a wider audience: "Blessed are those who are persecuted for righteousness, for theirs is the kingdom of heaven" (Matt 5:10). Can we, for example, call a journalist blessed because he suffered for exposing the truth about corruption in government? The answer to such questions should begin with a small exegetical study. What exactly did Matthew mean when he used the word that is translated as "righteousness"?

"Righteousness" is a translation of the Greek noun δικαιοσύνη (dikaiosýni), which in a religious context often described the correct relationship with God, compliance with his requirements. Matthew uses this word seven times, and five of them in the Sermon on the Mount. And sixteen more times he uses the cognate adjective δίκαιος ("righteous"). In most cases, the use of this word in Matthew has a somewhat paradoxical character. For example, we find δίκαιος already in the first chapter: "Joseph, her husband, since he was a righteous man and did not want to disgrace her, planned to send her away secretly" (Matt 1:19 NASB). How should a "righteous" man act in a situation where his fiancée is suspected of adultery? Should he, for example, try to fulfill this commandment: "If a man meets a virgin who is not pledged to be married and rapes her and they are caught, the man who raped her must pay her father fifty shekels of silver. He must marry the young woman, for he has violated her. Since he has violated her. He can never divorce her" (Deut 22:28–29)? But already here Joseph's righteousness has a somewhat strange manifestation: He cares primarily about reducing the shame for the girl who is suspected of adultery. Such righteousness is the complete opposite of the "righteousness" of the Pharisees, who wanted to create as much suffering and shame as possible for Jesus and others whom they suspected of violating the law.

"For I tell you that unless your righteousness far surpasses that of the scribes and Pharisees, you will not enter the kingdom of heaven" (Matt 5:20). Some commentators, for example, Stott,[14] believe that these words of Jesus were meant to shock his original audience: Were not the Pharisees champions in fulfilling God's commandments? But in reality in this Gospel we see that the Pharisees rejected God's commandments (Matt 15:3–9) and replaced them with their own rules, with the help of which they were able to impress the naive people. Matthew frees his readers from such naivety and shows the path of true righteousness.

True righteousness is impossible for people who try to achieve it by their own efforts. Righteousness can only be accepted as a gift – a gift that completely changes the life of a believing sinner, causes a new birth, gives a new identity in relationships with a new Father. The fulfillment of the commandments (even imperfect) is already a manifestation, confirmation, sign that a person has accepted the gift of God's righteousness.

But attempts to fulfill God's will in a society where the Pharisaic teaching about "righteousness" dominates, inevitably leads to persecution. Jesus's disciples are blessed not because they are persecuted, but because they have the gift of righteousness from God, who became their Father. Persecution is only a confirmation of their status, their blessedness.

Ukrainian philologist Oleksandr Levko notes that the use of concepts like "righteousness," in the works of Ukrainian writers correlates with the ideas about righteousness in the New Testament and testifies to the assimilation of New Testament views by Ukrainian literary culture.[15]

---

14. He writes, "Our Lord's statement must certainly have astonished his first hearers as it astonishes us today" (Stott, *Christian Counter-Culture*, 74).

15. Олександр Левко, "Діахронні виміри вербалізації концептів праведність і δικαιοσυνη в українській мові та грецькій мові нового завіту: точки перетину" [Oleksandr Levko, "Diachronic Dimensions of Verbalization of the Concepts of Righteousness and δικαιοσυνη in the Ukrainian Language and the Greek Language of the New Testament:

The first written law on Ukrainian lands was called "Ruska Pravda," where the word "Pravda" corresponds to the meaning of law, justice and righteousness. Its compiler, Prince Yaroslav, calls justice "the protection of God's Law," and those who administer justice – "servants of his kingdom."[16]

The idea of righteousness in biblical language is opposed to sin and evil. In the worldview of Ukrainians, society is also divided into righteous and unrighteous, and truth and falsehood are constant rivals. It must be added that Ukrainian (and more broadly Slavonic) word groups for righteousness/unrighteousness, truth/lie, are intrinsically connected both morphologically and semantically that it is virtually impossible to use one or the other without some implied connection between them.

The antagonism of the righteous and the lawless is traced in the language turns, which indicates that the concept of "righteousness" in its biblical understanding has deeply entered into the worldview of Ukrainians. For example, Ukrainian is replete with idioms like: to live according to righteousness, by all righteousness and falsehood, to confuse the righteous with the sinful, to sleep the sleep of a righteous man, after righteous labors, to return to the righteous path, to set on the righteous path and so on.[17]

Ukrainian literary critic Leonid Ushkalov says that the primary sources of all Ukrainian literature are connected with the struggle of truth and falsehood. Such a struggle was very acutely felt by the Ukrainian thinker Hryhorii Skovoroda. Ukraine, with its freedom-loving spirit, consistently destroyed by the Russian empire, appears to the writer as the last island of Truth in the sea of Falsehood: "This land was a part of that side, where Truth, which wandered among people, fleeing from the world that lies in evil, spent the last days of its stay on earth and had its last rest before flying from the lower land to the upper land."[18]

Points of Intersection"], *Studia-linguistica*, 2016, no. 9: 54–63 (in Ukrainian). https://studia-linguistica.knu.ua/diahronni-vimiri-verbalizacii-konceptiv-pravednist-i-v-ukrainskij-movi-ta-greckij-movi-novogo-zavitu-tochki-peretinu.

16. В. Яременко, пер. "Правда Руська," *Давня українська література (XI–XVIII ст.)* [V. Yaremenko, trans., *Pravda Ruska*, Ancient Ukrainian Literature (XI-XVIII centuries)] (Київ, Держ. видавництво худ. літ., 1960) (In Ukrainian). http://litopys.org.ua/oldukr2/oldukr51.htm.

17. Фразеологічний словник української мови. В. М. Білоноженко та ін. Уклад [V. M. Bilonozhenko et al., eds., *Phraseological Dictionary of the Ukrainian Language*] (Київ, Наукова думка, 1993), 686–87 (in Ukrainian).

18. Сковорода, *Повна академічна збірка творів* [Skovoroda, *Complete Academic Works*] (Kharkiv; Edmonton: 2011), 295 (in Ukrainian).

Leonid Ushkalov believes that a characteristic feature of the worldview of Skovoroda and his contemporary Ukrainian thinkers (as well as those who followed them), "is the idea of the 'persecuted Truth,' that everywhere in the world Falsehood reigns, and the victory of Truth over Falsehood, that is, of Christ over Antichrist, is possible only beyond the earthly life and human history as such."[19] According to Ushkalov, such an idea was inherent in the worldview of Ukrainians in general, especially at the end of the eighteenth century, when the folk song titled "Song about Truth and Falsehood," often attributed to Skovoroda became popular. It goes like this:

> No truth remains within this land!
> No trace of justice can be found.
> For falsehood now holds high command,
> While truth stands humbly on the ground.
>
> The truth is trampled underfoot,
> While lies are crowned and richly fed.
> Deceit is served the sweetest fruit,
> And honored where the nobles tread.

The hope for the victory of Truth the folk author sees only in Christ's victory, God's grace and strength:

> Who in this world upholds the right,
> Shall feel God's grace both day and night.
> For Truth is God, He humbles pride,
> And Falsehood crushed shall step aside.

In another version, the song ends with the words: "For now the Truth is locked away, / Its sign upon the cross does stay."[20]

Literary critic Serhiy Yefremov believed that the words from the song "There is no truth in the world, truth cannot be found" are the cry of the Ukrainian soul and the conclusion of the national worldview. Moreover, such an understanding of reality is visible not only in fiction, but also in scientific

---

19. Леонід Ушкалов, "Потебня і Сковорода: ловитва невловного птаха", Харківська обласна організація Національна спілка письменників, 17 липня, 2015 [Leonid Ushkalov. "Potebnya and Skovoroda: Catching an Elusive Bird," *Kharkiv Regional Organization of the National Union of Writers*, July 17, 2015], https://kharkiv-nspu.org.ua/archives/3853.

20. Михайло Грушевський, *Історія української літератури*: в 6 т. 9 кн. Т 4, кн. 2 [Mykhailo Hrushevsky, *History of Ukrainian Literature*, vol. 4, book 2] (Київ, 1994) http://litopys.org.ua/hrushukr/hrush422.htm (in Ukrainian).

literature and political views. It was caused by the total injustice that Ukrainians experienced first from the imperial regime, then from the Soviet regime.

The unthinkable torments that the persecutors inflicted on the people in all spheres of life, focused Ukrainian thinkers on the unjust suffering of Christ. Such parallels encourage the "humanization of Jesus" in Taras Shevchenko and the imitation of him, to which many other thinkers call. It is not without reason that Leonid Ushkalov notes: "The idea of 'co-crucifixion' rings in the words of Shevchenko's last great work – the poem 'Maria,' – with which he begs the Mother of God for all righteous people: 'Give them the strength / Of your martyred Son, / To carry the cross-fetters / To the very, very end.'"[21]

Christological themes are also developed by Ivan Franko. He focuses more on the image of the cross as a symbol of Christ's sufferings, drawing a parallel with the sufferings of Ukraine. At the same time, for the poet, the cross is also a symbol of victory.[22]

The idea of exile for truth also sounds unexpectedly in Lesya Ukrainka:

> A crown of thorns will always shine
> More bright than one of gold so fine.
> A path to Calvary will stand
> More grand than triumph's loud demand.
>
> But only sacrifice so free,
> With conscious heart, with will so true,
> Deserves the highest victory,
> Not chasing triumphs worldly knew,
> But seeking heights of grandeur new.

Understanding the idea of persecution for truth/righteousness in Ukrainian literature, one cannot ignore Ivan Bahrianyi's novel *The Garden of Gethsemane*, where the author reveals the confrontation between the totalitarian system and a person who tries to preserve his humanity. And although the person, persecuted for truth, dies, he wins, because he remains a person (he belongs to the kingdom of heaven).

---

21. Леонід Ушкалов, "Христос" у *Моя шевченківська енциелопедія* [Leonid Ushkalov, "Christ" in *My Shevchenko Encyclopedia*] (Харків; Едмонтон; Торонто: Майдан, Видавництво Канадського Інституту Українських Студій, 2014), 544–48 (in Ukrainain).

22. Ірина Кульчицька-Жигайло, "Поетична христологія Івана Франка" [Iryna Kulchytska-Zhyhaylo, "Ivan Franko's Poetic Christology"], *Парадигма*. 2008, Вип. 3: 144–51 (in Ukrainian).

The twentieth century saw the emergence of a group of Ukrainian thinkers who were forced to leave their homeland under pressure from the communist regime. Thus, the image of the persecution for the truth received an extremely sharp response in their work. The motifs of the "crucifixion of Ukraine" and "Calvary of Ukraine" developed. At the same time, diaspora thinkers continued the analogy and, looking up to the life of Christ, expressed hope that God would resurrect Ukraine as well:

> Great are You in Cross's sacred pain,
> In faith that shines on Easter's day,
> When Heaven's Lord shall praise Your name,
> Exalting You in bright array.
>
> Let us rise from sin's decay,
> From lies, from filth – arise anew!
> That Ukraine, crucified, may stay,
> Its towns and villages in view.
>
> Be worthy of the land's great woe,
> Of Christ's own blood in suffering shed,
> That through our trials we may show,
> Our faith, reborn from pain and dread.
> *Ivan Ovechko*
>
> We beg You now with humble voice,
> We cry, yet tears remain unseen;
> That Truth may rise and thus rejoice,
> And bring us Freedom long foreseen!
>
> *Ulyana Kravchenko*

Leonid Poltava writes that "Easter of my dear people, / Easter of my land!" is as inevitable as "the sprouting of grass."[23]

Truth and righteousness as a challenge faced Ukrainians when the communist veil fell from their eyes. Dmytro Pavlychko, who himself had gone through the process of realizing the truth, wrote about this in a very insightful and imaginative way:

---

23. Іван Барчук і Михайло Подворняк, упоряд., *Великодній ранок. Збірка великодніх оповідань і віршів.* [Ivan Barchuk and Michael Podvorniak, eds., *Easter Morning. A Collection of Easter Stories and Poems*] (Торонто: Дорога правди, 1957). Іван Овечко. *Не плач, Україно!* [Ivan Ovechko, *Don't Cry, Ukraine*] (Лос-Анжелес, 1965), 20–21 (in Ukrainian).

> One Golgotha since ancient days has stood,
> Where Thief and Maker hung in silent strife;
> In darkness, none could tell who ill or good,
> But we, in light, must see the truth of life:
> Where God lay slain, and there the cosmic knave
> Who, ere his death, enthralled the world so grave.[24]

In the horrors of the Russian-Ukrainian war, Ukrainians see persecution for the truth, for the right to life, freedom, and self-expression that God put in man through the act of creation. At the same time, it is in the context of such confrontation that their national identity crystallizes, making them realize the blessedness of this persecution and proclaim the hope of the "resurrection" of Ukraine.

God's righteousness as an undeserved gift was one of the main ideas of the Protestant Reformation five hundred years ago, but it remains relevant today. Righteousness through works is one of the main temptations in this world, one of the most attractive idols. If Ukrainian Christians fail to communicate the gospel doctrine of righteousness to society, society will quickly find a replacement for the Soviet idols it has recently lost. This is actually a unique opportunity for Ukrainian theology, the only question is how we will use this opportunity. In my opinion, a decisive role in this will be played by our attitude to the experience of Ukrainian Christians who were persecuted because they resisted Russian pseudo-Christian ideology.

Practical Aspects

Let us now consider the changes that are taking place (or should be taking place) on a practical level. The persecution of the church is a challenge for all its members. The relatively weak reaction of many Christians – both Ukrainian and western – to the persecution of the church in Ukraine also testifies to problems of practical ecclesiology. It is easier for many churches to perceive persecution as something that happens to some marginal group far away, in the occupied territories. We take a very important step when we begin to perceive the church as the Body of Christ, as a single organism: "If one member suffers, all suffer together; if one member is honored, all rejoice together. Now you are the body of Christ and individually members of it" (1 Cor 12:26–27 ESV).

---

24. Дмитро Павличко, "Толгофа," Бібліотека української літератури [Dmytro Pavlychko, "Golgotha," *Library of Ukrainian Literature*], https://www.ukrlib.com.ua/books/printit.php?tid=98, (in Ukrainian).

The ability to identify with the sufferings of other members of the Body of Christ is one of the signs of spiritual maturity. Such identification has various manifestations, but the main ones are prayer (the more we pray for persecuted Christians, the more often we begin to perceive reality through their eyes) and specific acts of help.

In one of his last conversations with his disciples, Jesus emphasizes the connection between our Christian identity and practical deeds, which primarily support persecuted Christians:

> Then the King will say to those on his right, "Come, you who are blessed by my Father; take your inheritance, the kingdom prepared for you since the creation of the world. For I was hungry and you gave me something to eat, I was thirsty and you gave me something to drink, I was a stranger and you invited me in, I needed clothes and you clothed me, I was sick and you looked after me, I was in prison and you came to visit me." Then the righteous will answer him, "Lord, when did we see you hungry and feed you, or thirsty and give you something to drink? When did we see you a stranger and invite you in, or needing clothes and clothe you? When did we see you sick or in prison and go to visit you?" The King will reply, "Truly I tell you, whatever you did for one of the least of these brothers and sisters of mine, you did for me." (Matt 25:34–40)

These verses echo Matthew 10:40–42:

> "Anyone who welcomes you welcomes me, and anyone who welcomes me welcomes the one who sent me. Whoever welcomes a prophet as a prophet will receive a prophet's reward, and whoever welcomes a righteous person as a righteous person will receive a righteous person's reward. And if anyone gives even a cup of cold water to one of these little ones who is my disciple, truly I tell you, that person will certainly not lose their reward."

"These little ones" are primarily the disciples of Christ. Of course, the gospel does not prohibit (and even requires) doing good to people who are not followers of Jesus, but these two passages are not just about charity. The main idea of the passage is related to whether we identify with the persecuted church or distance ourselves from it out of fear or shame. In other words, we can choose the expressions by which we describe the realities of persecution. We can say, "The Russians are persecuting them," but New Testament ecclesiology also allows us to say, "The Russians are persecuting us." The choice of pronoun depends on our theological position.

James expresses a similar idea in his epistle, which contains numerous parallels with the Sermon on the Mount: "Religion that God our Father accepts as pure and faultless is this: to look after orphans and widows in their distress and to keep oneself from being polluted by the world" (Jas 1:27). James also writes in the context of persecution, and it can be assumed that at least some of the orphans and widows lost their loved ones as a result of persecution.[25] It is in this key that the discussion about faith and works, which begins a few verses later, should be perceived. If we take these statements of James out of their literary and historical context, we can find a lot of theoretical material for mainly academic comparisons of "James's soteriology" with "Paul's soteriology," but in this case it is not about some abstract "works," but about concrete manifestations of faith – identification with the sufferings of the persecuted church. Such identification is impossible without real acts of helping orphans and widows.

Thus, on a practical level, the gospel requires us to provide prayerful and material support for those who have been persecuted for their faithfulness to Jesus. The responsibility of pastors and other religious leaders is to remind their people of how important such service is in the eyes of God.

Conclusions

The problem of the persecution of believers is not new; it existed in ancient times. The history of God's people – both in the Old Testament and in the New Testament – hardly knows periods when there were no cases of violence against the faithful in any region of the world. The peaceful existence of the church, however long it may be, is rather an exception than the norm. Persecution can be caused by many factors, but one of the main ones is the division of humanity into the "offspring of the woman" and the "offspring of the serpent" – a reality that is difficult to deny precisely in times of persecution.

---

25. If we are talking about orphans who lost their parents not because of persecution, then the problem is rather that those relatives of the deceased who had a duty to take care of them refused their responsibility for them because of a conflict related to faith in Jesus. The division he foresaw was quite real: "Do not think that I have come to bring peace to the earth. I have not come to bring peace, but a sword. For I have come to set a man against his father, and a daughter against her mother, and a daughter-in-law against her mother-in-law. And a person's enemies will be those of his own household" (Matt 10:34–36 ESV).

God helps the persecuted church, and one of the most important instruments of his help is Holy Scripture, where many texts are related specifically to the problem of the persecution of the righteous. Some Ukrainian churches are experiencing a real "renaissance" in their reacquaintance with the Psalms and other "texts of weeping and despair." The introduction (or rather the return) of the Psalms into the liturgical life of the church is, in my opinion, one of the signs of the spiritual maturation of the church: such texts help to raise difficult and painful topics of grief, justice, and revenge.

Liturgical changes go hand in hand with practical changes, the main of which should be special attention to the needs of those who have become vulnerable as a result of persecution. Serving the persecuted church is serving the persecuted Christ.

References

Гейченко, О. "Псалми прокляття: пасторське застосування в умовах війни проти України". *Богомисліє* 32 (2022) [Geychenko, O. "Imprecatory Psalms: A Pastoral Application in the Context of the War Against Ukraine," *Bogomyslie* 32 (2022)]: 8–26. (In Ukrainian).

Гнатюк, Ярослав. "Український кордоцентризм як національна філософія". *Вісник Прикарпатського університету. Філософські і психологічні науки*, 18 (2007) [Hnatiuk, Yaroslav. "Ukrainian cordocentrism as a national philosophy." *Bulletin of the Precarpathian University: Philosophical and Psychological Sciences* 18 (2007)]: 39–45. (In Ukrainian).

Горяча, М. "Блаженства як основа духовного росту християнина: духовна екзегеза Мт 5:3–8 у гоміліях Псевдо-Макарія". *Наукові записки УКУ: Богослов'я*, 2 (2015) [Horyacha, M. "Beatitudes as the Foundation of Spiritual Growth of a Christian: A Spiritual Exegesis of Matthew 5:3–8 in the Homilies of Pseudo-Macarius," *Scientific Proceedings of UCU: Theology* 2 (2015)]: 145–63. (In Ukrainian).

Денисенко, А. *Теологія визволення. Ідеї. Критика. Перспективи.* Сучасна протестанська теологія. Київ: Дух і літера, 2019 [Denysenko, A. *Liberation Theology. Ideas. Critique. Perspectives.* Kyiv: Dukh i Litera, 2019]. (In Ukrainian).

Митрополит Іларіон, *Мої проповіді*. Вінніпег, Канада: Товариство Волинь, 1973 [Hilarion, Metropolitan. *My Sermons* (Winnipeg: Fellowship "Volyn," 1973]. (In Ukrainian).

Попович, М. *Григорій Сковорода: філософія свободи*. Київ: Майстерня Білецьких, 2008 [Popovych, Myroslav. *Hryhorii Skovoroda: Philosophy of Freedom*. Kyiv: The Biletski Workshop, 2008]. (In Ukrainian).

Райчинец, Ф. "Евангелие от Матфея". В *Славянский библейский комментарий* Ред. С. Санников, 1131–1219. К.: Книгоноша, 2016 [Raychynets, F. "The Gospel of Matthew," in *Slavic Biblical Commentary*, 1131–219. Ed. S. Sannikov. Kyiv: Knigonosha, 2016].

Райчинец, Ф. "Евангелие от Матфея". В *Славянский библейский комментарий*, 2-е вид., 1147–240. Київ: Саммит-книга, 2022 [Raychynets, F. "The Gospel of Matthew." In *Slavic Bible Commentary*, 1147–240. Ed. S. Sannikov. Kyiv: Summit Books, 2022].

Сковорода, Григорій. *Повна академічна збірка творів*. Під ред. Леоніда Ушкалова. Харків: Майдан, 2011 [Skovoroda, Hryhory. *Complete Academic Works*. Leonid Ushkalov, ed. (Kharkiv: Maidan, 2001]. (In Ukrainian).

Ушкалов, Леонід. "Бідність як кінічний жест: українська версія". В *Сковорода, Шевченко, фемінізм . . . : Статті 2010–2013 років*, 259–69. Харків: Майдан,

2014 [Ushkalov, Leonid. "Poverty as a Cynic Gesture: A Ukrainian Version." In *Skovoroda, Shevchenko, Feminism . . .: Articles of the years of 2010–2013*, 259–69. Kharkiv: Maidan, 2014]. (In Ukrainian).

Ушкалов, Леонід. "Багатство". В *Моя шевченківська енциклопедія із досвіду самопізнання*, 38–40. Харків: Майдан, 2014 [Ushkalov, Leonid. "Wealth." In *My Shevchenko Encyclopaedia on the Experience of Self-Discovery*, 38–40. Kharkiv: Maidan, 2014]. (In Ukrainian).

Франко, І. *Зібрання творів у 50-и томах*. Т. 3, Київ: Наукова думка, 1972 [Franko, I. *A Collection of Works in 50 volumes*. Vol. 3. Kyiv: Naukova dumka, 1972]. (In Ukrainian).

Шевченко, Тарас. "Подражаніє 11 псалму". В *Зібрання творів*: у 6 т. Т. 2: *Поезія 1847–1861*. Київ, 2003 [Shevchenko, Taras. "Imitating Psalm 11." In *Collection of Works*, in 6 vols. Vol. 2: Poetry 1847–1861. Kyiv, 2003]. (In Ukrainian).

Юркевич, Д. П. *Вибрані твори: Ідея-серце-розум і досвід*. Вінніпеґ, Канада: Колегія св. Андрія у Вінніпезі, 1984 [Yurkiewicz, P. D. *Selected Writings: Idea-Heart-Reason and Experience*. Winnipeg: Collegium of St Andrew in Winnipeg, 1984]. (In Ukrainian).

Allison, Dale C., Jr. *The Sermon on the Mount: Inspiring the Moral Imagination*. New York: Crossroad, 1999.

Allison, Dale C., Jr. *Studies in Matthew. Interpretation Past and Present*. Grand Rapids: Baker Academics, 2005.

Allison, Dale C., Jr. *The New Moses: A Matthean Typology*. Eugene: Wipf & Stock, 2013.

Ålöw, Tobias. *The Meaning and Uses of βασιλεία in the Gospel of Matthew: Semantic Monosemy and Pragmatic Modulation*. Leiden: Brill, 2024.

Ambrose of Milan. *Commentary of Saint Ambrose on the Gospel According to Luke*. Dublin: Elo Press, 2001.

Aquinas, Thomas. *Commentary on the Gospel of St. Matthew*. Translated by P. Kimball. Dolorosa Press, 2012.

Aquinas, Thomas. *Summa Theologica*. Translated by Fathers of the English Dominican Province. Oates & Washbourne. Vol. 9, London, n.d.

Augustine of Hippo. *Commentary on the Lord's Sermon on the Mount with Seventeen Related Sermons*. Translated by Denis J. Kavanagh. The Fathers of the Church, 11. Washington, DC: Catholic University of America Press, 2001.

Augustine of Hippo. *Concerning the City of God against the Pagans*. London: Penguin, 2003.

Baasland, Ernst. *Radical Philosophy of Life: Studies on the Sermon on the Mount*. Tübingen: Mohr Siebeck, 2021.

Bainton, Roland Herbert. *Christian Attitudes toward War and Peace: A Historical Survey and Critical Re-Evaluation*. Roland Bainton Reprint Series. Eugene: Wipf and Stock, 2008.

Bauer, David R., and Mark Allan Powell. *Treasures New and Old: Recent Contributions to Matthean Studies*. Symposium Series, 1. Atlanta: Scholars Press, 1996.

Becker, U. "Μακάριος." In *The New International Dictionary of New Testament Theology*, vol. 4 ed. C. Brown. Grand Rapids: Zondervan, 1986.

Beetham, Christopher A. *The Concise New International Dictionary of New Testament Theology and Exegesis*. Grand Rapids: HarperCollins, 2021.

Betz, Hans Dieter. *The Sermon on the Mount: A Commentary on the Sermon on the Mount, Including the Sermon on the Plain (Matthew 5:3–7:27 and Luke 6:20–49)*. Hermeneia – A Critical and Historical Commentary on the Bible. Minneapolis: Fortress, 1995.

Billman, Kathleen D., and Daniel D. Migliore. *Rachel's Cry of Lament and Rebirth of Hope*. Cleveland: United Church Press, 1999.

Bonhoeffer, Dietrich. *The Cost of Discipleship*. New York: Collier Books, 1963.

Bonhoeffer, Dietrich. *The Cost of Discipleship*. New York: Touchstone, 1995.

Bonhoeffer, Dietrich. "Sermon on Matthew 5:8, Barcelona, Tenth Sunday after Trinity, August 12, 1928." In *Dietrich Bonhoeffer Works, Volume 10. Barcelona, Berlin, New York: 1928–1931*, 511–15. Minneapolis: Fortress, 2008.

Borg, Marcus, and J. D. Crossan. *The Last Week of Jesus: A Day-by-Day Account of Jesus's Final Week in Jerusalem*. New York: Harper Collins, 2006.

Boring, E., ed. *The Gospel of Matthew*. The New Interpreter's Bible. Nashville: Abingdon, 1995.

Boxall, Ian. *Matthew Through the Centuries*. Oxford: Wiley-Blackwell, 2018.

Braswell, Michael, and John Fuller. *Corrections, Peacemaking and Restorative Justice: Transforming Individuals and Institutions*. London: Routledge, 2014.

Brown, Francis, S. R. Driver, and Charles A. Briggs. "עָנָה." In *The Enhanced Brown-Driver-Briggs Hebrew and English Lexicon: With an Appendix Containing the Biblical Aramaic*, 1867–69. Oxford: Clarendon, 1951.

Brueggemann, Walter. *The Message of The Psalms: A Theological Commentary*. Minneapolis: Augsburg, 1984.

Bruner, Frederick Dale. *Matthew: A Commentary. Vol. 1: The Christbook. Matthew 1–12*. Grand Rapids: Eerdmans, 2004.

Brunner, Emil. *The Word and the World*. New York: SCM Press, 1931.

Cabasilas, Nicholas. *The Life in Christ*. New York: St. Vladimir's Seminary, 1982.

Cahill, Lisa Sowle. *Blessed Are the Peace Makers: Pacifism, Just War, and Peacebuilding*. Minneapolis: Fortress, 2019.

Calvin, Jean. *Commentary. Harmony of the Evangelists, Matthew, Mark, and Luke*. Grand Rapids: Baker, 1981.

Carlson, Nathaniel A. "Lament: The Biblical Language of Trauma." *Cultural Encounters* 11, no. 1 (2015): 50–68. doi:10.11630/1550-4891.11.01.50.

Carter, Warren. *Matthew and Empire: Initial Explorations*. Harrisburg: Bloomsbury Academic, 2001.

Carter, Warren. *Matthew and the Margins: A Sociopolitical and Religious Reading*. The Bible & Liberation Series. Maryknoll: Orbis, 2000.

Charlesworth, James H., ed. *The Bible and the Dead Sea Scrolls: The Scrolls and Christian Origins*. Vol. 3. Waco: Baylor University Press, 2006.

Charry, Ellen. *God and the Art of Happiness*. Grand Rapids: Eerdmans, 2010.

Cilliers, Johan. "Breaking the Syndrome of Silence: Finding Speech for Preaching in a Context of HIV and AIDS." *Scriptura* 96 (2007): 391–406. https://doi.org/10.7833/96-0-1164.

Clement of Alexandria. *Writings of Clement of Alexandria, Vol. 1*. In vol. 4 of *Ante-Nicene Christian Library*. Edited by Alexander Roberts and James Donaldson. Edinburgh: T&T Clark, 1867.

Clement of Alexandria. *Writings of Clement of Alexandria, Vol. 2*. In vol. 12 of *Ante-Nicene Christian Library*. Edited by Alexander Roberts and James Donaldson. Edinburgh: T&T Clark, 1869.

Cremer, H. *Biblico-Theological Lexicon of New Testament Greek*. Edinburgh: T&T Clark, 1895.

Crosby, Michael. *Spirituality of the Beatitudes: Matthew's Challenge for First World Christians*. Maryknoll: Orbis, 1981.

Daley, Daniel. *Ideal Disciples: A Commentary on Matthew's Beatitudes*. 1st ed. Waco: Baylor University Press, 2024.

Davies, William David. *The Sermon on the Mount*. Cambridge: Cambridge University Press, 1966.

Davies, W. D., and Dale C. Allison, Jr. *Matthew: A Shorter Commentary*. London & New York: T&T Clark, 2004.

Davies, W. D., and Dale C. Allison, Jr. *Matthew 1–7*. International Critical Commentary. 3 vols. Vol. 1. London: Bloomsbury T&T Clark, 2004.

Demarest, Bruce. *Seasons of the Soul: Stages of Spiritual Development*. Downers Grove: InterVarsity Press, 2009.

Dibelius, Martin. *The Sermon on the Mount*. New York: Charles Scribner's Sons, 1973.

Dickie, June. "The Importance of Lament in Pastoral Ministry: Biblical Basis and Some Applications." *Verbum et Ecclesia*, Volume 40, Number 1 (13 November 2019): 1–11. https://doi.org/10.4102/ve.v40i1.2002.

Donaldson, T. *Jesus on the Mountain: A Study in Matthean Theology*. Sheffield: JSOT Press, 1985.

Drobner, Hubertus, and Albert Viciano, eds. *Gregory of Nyssa: Homilies on the Beatitudes*. Supplements to Vigiliae Christianae, 52. Leiden: Brill, 2000.

Duffey, Michael K., and Deborah S. Nash, eds. *Justice and Mercy Will Kiss: The Vocation of Peacemaking in a World of Many Faiths*. Marquette Studies in Theology 58. Milwaukee: Marquette University Press, 2008.

Duhaime, Jean. "War Scroll." In *The Dead Sea Scrolls: Hebrew, Aramaic, and Greek Texts with English Translations*. Vol. 2, Damascus Document, War Scroll, and Related Documents. Edited by James H. Charlesworth and James H. Baumgarten. Princeton Theological Seminary Dead Sea Scrolls Project. Tübingen: Mohr Siebeck, 1995.

DuJardin, Troy, and M. David Eckel, eds. *Faith, Hope, and Love. Theological Virtue and Their Opposites*. Boston: Springer, 2023.

Easwaran, Eknath. *Original Goodness: A Commentary on the Beatitudes*. 2nd ed. Classics of Christian Inspiration, vol. 3. Tomales: Nilgiri Press, 1996.

Eklund, Rebekah A. "Blessed Are the Image-Bearers: Gregory of Nyssa and the Beatitudes." *Anglican Theological Review* 99, no. 4 (2017): 729–40.

Eklund, Rebekah A. *The Beatitudes Through the Ages*. Grand Rapids: Eerdmans, 2021. EPUB.

Esser, H. H. "Mercy, Compassion." In *The New International Dictionary of New Testament Theology*. Colin Brown, ed., vol. 2: G – Pre, 593–601. Grand Rapids: Zondervan; Carlisle: Paternoster, 1986.

Evans, Craig A. "Hardness of Heart." In *Dictionary of Jesus and the Gospels*, Joel B. Green, Scot McKnight, and I. Howard Marshall, eds., 298–99. Downers Grove: InterVarsity Press, 1992.

Farley, Lawrence R. *The Gospel of Matthew: Torah for the Church. The Orthodox Bible Study Companion*. Chesterton: Ancient Faith Publishing, 2009.

Feber, Ilit, and Paula Schwebel. *Lament in Jewish Thought. Philosophical, Theological, and Literary Perspectives*. Berlin: Walter de Gruyter, 2014.

Ferguson, Everett. "Early Christian Martyrdom and Civil Disobedience." *Journal of Early Christian Studies* 1, no. 1 (March 1993): 73–83. https://doi.org/10.1353/earl.0.0161.

Flusser, D. "Blessed Are the Poor in Spirit . . ." *Israel Exploration Journal*, 10, no. 1 (1960): 1–13.

France, Richard T. "The Church and Kingdom of God. Some Hermeneutical Issues." In *Biblical Interpretation and Church: Text and Context*, edited by D. A. Carson, 30–44. Exeter: Paternoster, 1984.

France, Richard T. *The Gospel of Matthew*. The New International Commentary on the New Testament. Grand Rapids: Eerdmans, 2011.

Friedlander, Gerald. *The Jewish Sources of the Sermon on the Mount*. London: Routledge, 1911.

Gaultiere, Bill, and Kristi Gaultiere. *Journey of the Soul: A Practical Guide to Emotional and Spiritual Growth*. Grand Rapids: Revell, 2021.

Goheen, Michael W. *A Light to the Nations: The Missional Church and the Biblical Story*. Grand Rapids: Baker, 2011.

Goldingay, John. *An Introduction to the Old Testament: Exploring Text, Approaches & Issues*. Downers Grove: InterVarsity Press, 2015.

Green, H. Benedict. *Matthew, Poet of the Beatitudes*. Journal for the Study of the New Testament 203. Sheffield: Sheffield Academic Press, 2001.

Green, Joel B. "Kingdom of God/Heaven." In *Dictionary of Jesus and Gospel*, edited by Joel B. Green, Jeannie K. Brown, Nicholas Perrin, 468–81. Downers Grove: IVP Academic, 2013.

Green, Joel B., Jeannie K. Brown, Nicholas Perrin, eds. *Dictionary of Jesus and the Gospels*, 2nd ed. Downers Grove: InterVarsity Press, 2013.

Green, Michael. *The Message of Matthew: The Kingdom of Heaven*. Downers Grove: InterVarsity Press, 2000.

Gregory of Nyssa. *The Lord's Prayer. The Beatitudes*. Ancient Christian Writers, vol. 18. Westminster: Newman Press, 1954.

Guelich, Robert A. "The Matthean Beatitudes: 'Entrance-Requirements' or Eschatological Blessings?" *Journal of Biblical Literature*, 95, no. 3 (1976): 415–34.

Guelich, Robert A. *The Sermon on the Mount: A Foundation for Understanding*. Dallas: Word Books, 1982.

Gundry, Robert H. *Matthew: A Commentary on His Handbook for a Mixed Church under Persecution*. Grand Rapids: Eerdmans, 1994.

Gutiérrez, Gustavo. "Memory and Prophecy." In *The Option for the Poor in Christian Theology*, edited by D. Groody, 17–38. Notre Dame: University of Notre Dame Press, 2007.

Gutiérrez, Gustavo. *A Theology of Liberation: History, Politics and Salvation*. Maryknoll: Orbis, 1974.

Gutiérrez, Gustavo. *The God of Life*. Maryknoll: Orbis, 1991.

Hagner, Donald A., and Bruce Manning Metzger. *Matthew 1–13*. Word Biblical Commentary, vol. 33A. Nashville: Thomas Nelson, 2008.

Harper, G. Geoffrey. *Finding Lost Words*. Eugene: Wipf & Stock, 2017. Kindle.

Harrower, Scott, and Sean M. McDonough, eds., *A Time for Sorrow: Recovering the Practice of Lament in the Life of the Church*. Peabody: Hendrickson, 2019. EPUB.

Hauerwas, Stanley. *Matthew*. Brazos Theological Commentary. Grand Rapids: Brazos, 2006.

Hauerwas, Stanley. *The Peaceable Kingdom: A Primer in Christian Ethics*. Notre Dame: University of Notre Dame Press, 1983.

Hays, Richard B. *The Moral Vision of the New Testament: A Contemporary Introduction to New Testament Ethics*. New York: HarperCollins, 1996.

Hilary of Poitiers. *Commentary on Matthew*. The Fathers of the Church, vol. 125, Washington, DC: Catholic University of America Press, 2012.

Howell, Timothy D. *The Matthean Beatitudes in Their Jewish Origins: A Literary and Speech Act Analysis*. Studies in Biblical Literature, vol. 144. New York: Peter Lang, 2011.

Hughes, R. Kent. *The Sermon on the Mount: The Message of the Kingdom*. Wheaton: Crossway, 2013.

James, William. *Psychology: The Briefer Course*. New York: Collier, 1962.

Jeremias, Joachim. *New Testament Theology: The Proclamation of Jesus*. New York: Charles Scribner's Sons, 1971.

Jeremias, Joachim. *The Sermon on the Mount*. Philadelphia: Fortress, 1963.

Jerome. *Commentary on Matthew*. Translated by Thomas P. Scheck. The Fathers of the Church, vol. 117. Washington, DC: Catholic University of America Press, 2008.

John Chrysostom. *Homilies on the Gospel of St. Matthew*. In volume 10 of *Nicene and Post-Nicene Fathers*, Series 1. New York: Charles Scribner's Sons, 1888.
Kant, Immanuel, and Ted Humphrey. *To Perpetual Peace: A Philosophical Sketch*. Indianapolis: Hackett, 2003.
Katongole, Emmanuel. *Born from Lament. The Theology and Politics of Hope in Africa*. Grand Rapids: Eerdmans, 2017.
Keener, Craig S. *The Gospel of Matthew: A Socio-Rhetorical Commentary*. Grand Rapids: Eerdmans, 2009.
Keener, Craig S., ed. *The IVP Bible Background Commentary: New Testament*. Second Edition. Downers Grove: InterVarsity Press, 2014.
King, Martin Luther, Jr. "Letter from Birmingham Jail." April 16, 1963, accessed 14 December 2024, https://www.thekingcenter.org.
Kingsbury, Matthew J. D. *Matthew*. Proclamation Commentaries. Philadelphia: Fortress, 1977.
Kittel, G., G. Friedrich, and G. W. Bromiley, eds. *Theological Dictionary of the New Testament*, 10 volumes. Grand Rapids: Eerdmans, 1964–76.
Kittel, G., G. Friedrich, and G. W. Bromiley. *Theological Dictionary of the New Testament: Abridged in One Volume*. Grand Rapids: Eerdmans, 1985.
Ku, Eliana Ah-Rum. *Lament-Driven Preaching: Proclaiming Hope and Suffering*. Eugene: Pickwick, 2014. EPUB.
Lachs, Samuel Tobias. *A Rabbinic Commentary on the New Testament: The Gospels of Matthew, Mark, and Luke*. Hoboken: KTAV, 1987.
Lawrence, Arren Bennet. *Comparative Characterization in the Sermon on the Mount: Characterization of the Ideal Disciple*. Eugene: Wipf & Stock, 2017.
Lederach, John Paul. *Building Peace: Sustainable Reconciliation in Divided Societies*. Washington, DC: United States Institute of Peace Press, 1997.
Lewis, C. S. *A Grief Observed*. New York: HarperCollins, 1996.
Lichtenberger, H. "Makarisms in Matthew 5:3ff. In Their Jewish Context." In *The Sermon on the Mount and Its Jewish Setting*, edited by H. J. Becker and R. Greenleaf, 40–56. Paris: Peeters, 2005.
Louw, J. P., and Eugene A. Nida. *Greek-English Lexicon of the New Testament: Based on Semantic Domains*. New York: United Bible Societies, 1996.
Lundbom, Jack R. *Jesus' Sermon on the Mount: Mandating a Better Righteousness*. Minneapolis: Fortress, 2015.
Luther, Martin. *Commentary on the Sermon on the Mount*. Translated by A. Charles and D. Hay. Philadelphia: Lutheran Publication Society, 1892.
Luz, Ulrich. *Matthew 1–7: A Commentary*. Hermeneia – A Critical and Historical Commentary on the Bible. Minneapolis: Fortress, 2007.
Luz, Ulrich. *Matthew 1–7: A Continental Commentary*. Minneapolis: Augsburg Fortress, 1992.
Luz, Ulrich. *The Theology of the Gospel of Matthew*. Cambridge: Cambridge University Press, 1995.

Mangum, D., D. Brown, R. Klippenstein, and R. Hurst. *Lexham Theological Wordbook*. Bellingham: Lexham, 2014.

Marshall, I. Howard. *The Gospel of Luke: A Commentary on the Greek Text*. The New International Greek Testament Commentary. Grand Rapids: Eerdmans, 1978.

Mattison III, William C. *The Sermon on the Mount and Moral Theology: A Virtue Perspective*. 1st ed. Cambridge: Cambridge University Press, 2017. https://doi.org/10.1017/9781316761342.

Mattox, John Mark. *Saint Augustine and the Theory of Just War*. Continuum Studies in Philosophy. London: Continuum, 2006.

McGinn, Bernard, and Bernard McGinn. *The Flowering of Mysticism: Men and Women in the New Mysticism (1200–1350)*. The Presence of God, vol. 3. New York: Crossroad, 1998.

McKnight, Scot. *Sermon on the Mount*. Grand Rapids: Zondervan, 2013.

Mertens, Christopher J. *The Beatitudes: A Pathway to Theosis*. Oosterhout: Orthodox Logos, 2020.

Moltmann, Jürgen. *The Coming of God: Christian Eschatology*. London: Fortress, 2004.

Morris, Leon. *The Gospel According to Matthew*. Pillar New Testament Commentary. Grand Rapids: Eerdmans, 1992.

Müller, Thomas, Frans Veerman, and Matthew D. Rees. "Highlighting the Dark Corners of Persecution Using the Open Doors World Watch List as a Basis," *IJRF* Vol. 12:1/2 (2019): 17–28.

Muraoka, T. "Πτωχός." In *A Greek-English Lexicon of the Septuagint*, 607. Louvain: Peeters, 2009.

Newbigin, Lesslie. *A Word in Season: Perspectives on Christian World Missions*. Grand Rapids: Eerdmans, 1994.

Newbigin, Lesslie. *The Open Secret: An Introduction to the Theology of Mission*. Grand Rapids: Eerdmans, 1995.

Neyrey, Jerome H. *Honour and Shame in the Gospel of Matthew*. Louisville: Westminster John Knox, 1998.

Neyrey, Jerome H., and Eric Clark Stewart, eds. *The Social World of the New Testament: Insights and Models*. Peabody: Hendrickson, 2008.

Nickoloff, J. B., ed. *Gustavo Gutiérrez: Essential Writings*. Minneapolis: Fortress, 1996.

Niebuhr, Reinhold. *Moral Man and Immoral Society: A Study in Ethics and Politics*, 2nd edition. Library of Theological Ethics. Louisville: Westminster John Knox, 2013.

Nolland, J. *The Gospel of Matthew: A Commentary on the Greek Text*. New International Greek Testament Commentary. Grand Rapids: Eerdmans, 2005.

Oliver, Simon, and Judith Wolfe. "A Narrative and Apocalyptic Philosophy of Prayer: Being to God." In *Biblical Narratives and Human Flourishing: Knowledge Through Narrative*, edited by Eleonore Stump and Judith Wolfe, 165–78. London: Routledge, 2024.

Osborne, Grant R. *Matthew*. Zondervan Exegetical Commentary on the New Testament. Grand Rapids: Zondervan, 2010.

Overman, J. Andrew. *Matthew's Gospel and Formative Judaism: The Social World of the Matthean Community.* Minneapolis: Fortress, 1990.

Penn, William, and Peter Van Den Dungen. *An Essay towards the Present and Future Peace of Europe: By the Establishment of an European Dyet, Parliament or Estates.* Repr. d. Ausg. London 1693. Series F, Sources on the History of International Organization / United Nations Library, Geneva 1. Hildesheim: Olms, 1983.

Pennington, Jonathan T. *The Sermon on the Mount and Human Flourishing: A Theological Commentary.* Grand Rapid: Baker Academic, 2017. EPUB.

Powell, Mark Allan. "Matthew's Beatitudes: Reversals and Rewards of the Kingdom" *The Catholic Biblical Quarterly* 58, no. 3 (July 1996): 460–79.

Przybylski, B. *Righteousness in Matthew and His World of Thought.* Cambridge: Cambridge University Press, 2004.

Reichberg, Gregory M. *Thomas Aquinas on War and Peace.* Cambridge: Cambridge University Press, 2017.

Reichberg, Gregory M., Henrik Syse, and Endre Begby. *Ethics of War: Classics and Contemporary Readings.* Malden: Blackwell, 2006.

Richards, Lawrence O. *The Teacher's Commentary.* Wheaton: Victor Books, 1987.

Robertson, A. *Word Pictures in the New Testament.* Nashville: Broadman Press, 1933.

Rutledge, Fleming. *The Crucifixion: Understanding the Death of Jesus Christ.* Grand Rapids: Eerdmans, 2015.

Rziha, John Michael. *The Christian Moral Life: Directions for the Journey to Happiness.* Notre Dame: University of Notre Dame Press, 2017.

Sacks, J. *Essays on Ethics: A Weekly Reading of the Jewish Bible.* Jerusalem: Maggid Books, 2016.

Sanders, E. P. *Jesus and Judaism.* London: SCM Press, 1985.

Schleiermacher, Friedrich, and Paul T. Nimmo. *The Christian Faith.* 3rd ed. Cornerstones (London, England). London: Bloomsbury Academic, 2016.

Schnackenburg, Rudolf. *The Gospel of Matthew.* Translated by Robert R. Barr. Grand Rapids: Eerdmans, 2002.

Schubert, Kurt. "The Sermon on the Mount and the Qumran Texts." In *The Scrolls and the New Testament*, edited by Krister Stendahl, 118–28. New York: Harper & Brothers, 1957.

Schweizer, Eduard. *The Good News According to Matthew.* Atlanta: John Knox, 1975.

Senior, Donald. *Matthew.* Abingdon New Testament Commentaries. Nashville: Abingdon, 1998.

Senior, Donald. *What Are They Saying about Matthew?* Rev. and Expanded ed. New York: Paulist Press, 1996.

Simonetti, Manlio, ed. *Matthew 1–13.* Ancient Christian Commentary on Scripture, vol. 1a. Downers Grove: InterVarsity Press, 2001.

Smith, Robert H. "'Blessed Are the Poor in (Holy) Spirit'? (Matthew 5:3)." *Word & World* 18, no. 4 (1998): 389–96.

Sobrino, Jon. *Spirituality of Liberation: Toward Political Holiness.* Maryknoll: Orbis Books, 2015.

Sobrino, Jon. *The True Church and the Poor.* London: SCM Press, 1985.

Soloviy, Roman. "The Church Amidst the War of Attrition: Ukrainian Evangelical Community in Search of a New Mission Paradigm." *Religions* 15, no. 9 (2024): 1136. https://www.mdpi.com/2077-1444/15/9/1136.

Spicq, C., and J. Ernest, eds. *Theological Lexicon of the New Testament*, 3 vols. Peabody: Hendrickson, 1994.

Stanton, G. N. "Sermon on the Mount/Plain." In *Dictionary of Jesus and the Gospels*, Joel B. Green, Scot McKnight, and I. Howard Marshall, eds., 735–44. Downers Grove: InterVarsity Press, 1992.

Stassen, Glen H. *Just Peacemaking: Transformative Initiatives for Justice and Peace.* Louisville: Westminster John Knox Press, 1992.

Stassen, Glen H., and David P. Gushee. *Kingdom Ethics: Following Jesus in Contemporary Context.* Downers Grove: InterVarsity Press, 2003.

Stott, John R. W. *Christian Counter-Culture: The Message of the Sermon on the Mount (Matthew 5–7).* The Bible Speaks Today. Downers Grove: InterVarsity Press, 1978.

Stott, John R. W. *The Message of the Sermon on the Mount.* Downers Grove: InterVarsity Press, 1985.

Strecker, Georg. *The Sermon on the Mount: An Exegetical Commentary.* Nashville: Abingdon, 1988.

Swift, Louis J. *The Early Fathers on War and Military Service.* Message of the Fathers of the Church 19. Wilmington: Glazier, 1983.

Telushkin, Joseph. *Jewish Literacy: The Most Important Things to Know about the Jewish Religion, Its People, and Its History.* New York: William Morrow, 1991.

Terry, Susanne, ed. *More Justice, More Peace: When Peacemakers Are Advocates.* Lanham: Rowman & Littlefield, 2020.

Tertullianus, Q. S. F. *The Five Books of Quintus Sept. Flor. Tertullianus against Marcion.* Translated by P. Holmes. Edited by P. Holmes. Edinburgh: T&T Clark, 1868.

Thistlethwaite, Susan Brooks, ed. *Interfaith Just Peacemaking: Jewish, Christian, and Muslim Perspectives on the New Paradigm of Peace and War.* Basingstoke: Palgrave Macmillan, 2012.

du Toit, Andrie B. "Revisiting the Sermon on the Mount. Some Major Issues." *Neotestamentica* 50, no. 3 (2016): 59–92.

Turner, David L. *Matthew.* Baker Exegetical Commentary on the New Testament. Grand Rapids: Baker Academic, 2008.

Tutu, Desmond. *No Future without Forgiveness.* New York: Doubleday, 2000.

VanGemeren, Willem A., ed. *New International Dictionary of Old Testament Theology & Exegesis*, vol. 1. Grand Rapids: Zondervan, 2009.

Verhey, Allen. *Reading the Bible in the Strange World of Medicine.* Grand Rapids: Eerdmans, 2003.

Villanueva, Federico G. *It's OK to Be Not OK: Preaching the Lament Psalms*. Carlisle: Langham Preaching Resources, 2017.

Villanueva, Federico G. *The "Uncertainty of Hearing": A Study of the Sudden Change of Mood in the Psalms of Laments*. Leiden: Brill, 2008.

Vincent, M. *Word Studies in the New Testament*. New York: Charles Scribner's Son, 1887.

Volf, Miroslav. *Exclusion and Embrace: A Theological Exploration of Identity, Otherness, and Reconciliation*. Nashville: Abingdon, 2008.

Volf, Miroslav. *For the Life of the World: Theology that Makes a Difference*. Grand Rapids: Brazos, 2019.

Wallace, Daniel B. *Greek Grammar beyond the Basics: An Exegetical Syntax of the New Testament*. Grand Rapids: Zondervan, 2012.

Waltke, Bruce K. "Heart." In *Baker's Evangelical Dictionary of Biblical Theology*. Ed. Walter A. Elwell. Baker Reference Library (Grand Rapids: Baker, 1996). https://www.biblestudytools.com/dictionaries/bakers-evangelical-dictionary/heart.html.

Watson, Thomas. *The Beatitudes: An Exposition of Matthew 5:1–10* (New edition), Revised layout. Edinburgh: The Banner of Truth, 2014.

Weigel, George. "Moral Clarity in a Time of War." *Ethics and Public Policy Center*, 2002. https://eppc.org/publication/moral-clarity-in-a-time-of-war/.

Welzen, Huub. "A Hermeneutic of Justice. Justice as Discernment in Matthew." *Acta Theologica* 2013, no. sup-7 (2013): 89–109.

Wierzbicka, Anna. *What Did Jesus Mean?: Explaining the Sermon on the Mount and the Parables in Simple and Universal Human Concepts*. Oxford: Oxford University Press, 2001.

Wilkes, C. Gene. *A New Way of Living: Practicing the Beatitudes Every Day*. Birmingham: New Hope Publishers, 2013.

Wilkins, Michael J. *Matthew*. The NIV Application Commentary. Grand Rapids: Zondervan, 2004.

Witherington III, Ben. *Matthew*. Smyth & Helwys Bible Commentary. Macon: Smyth & Helwys, 2006.

Woodley, M. *The Gospel of Matthew: God with Us*. Downers Grove: InterVarsity Press, 2011.

Yoder, John Howard. *Nevertheless: The Varieties and Shortcomings of Religious Pacifism*. Rev. and expanded ed. Scottdale: Herald Press, 1992.

Yoder, John Howard. *The Politics of Jesus: Vicit Agnus Noster*. Grand Rapids: Eerdmans, 1987.

Zerbe, Gordon M. "Economic Justice and Nonretaliation in the Dead Sea Scrolls: Implications for the New Testament Interpretation." In *The Bible and the Dead Sea Scrolls: The Scrolls and Christian Origins*, edited by James H. Charlesworth, 3:319–55. Waco: Baylor University Press, 2006.

Ziedonis, Ruth Sonia. *Healing and Wholeness Through Sharing One's Latvian Grief Story*. Riga: University of Latvia, 1997.

Contributors

Sergiy Bermas. Founding pastor of the Church of Evangelical Christians of the Holy Trinity, Odesa. Former theology and ethics lecturer at the Odesa Theological Seminary.

Eduard Borysov (Kyiv, Ukraine). Lecturer at the Kyiv Theological Seminary, director of Talbot School of Theology – Kyiv Extension, editor-in-chief of the journal *Studii*.

Taras Dyatlik (Rivne, Ukraine). VSI engagement director of Scholar Leaders in Eastern Europe, theological education consultant at Mesa Global, vice-rector for development and international partnership at Eastern European Institute of Theology.

Oleksandr Geychenko (Odesa, Ukraine). Rector and lecturer in theology at Odesa Theological Seminary.

Fyodor Raichynets (Kyiv, Ukraine). Director of Master program in transformative leadership and lecturer of courses including "Life of Jesus Christ," "Social Teaching of the Church," "Political Theology and Leadership." Pastor of Bethany Church in Bucha.

Ivan Rusyn (Bucha, Ukraine). President and professor of missions and religious studies at the Ukrainian Evangelical Theological Seminary, Kyiv. Deputy senior bishop of the Ukrainian Evangelical Church and pastor at the Temple of Christ the Savior.

Roman Soloviy (Lviv, Ukraine). Chairman of the Eastern European Institute of Theology. Regional commissioning editor for Langham Publishing, overseeing Central and Eastern Europe and Central Asia.

Vitalii Stankevych (Odesa, Ukraine). Dean of the faculty of theology, lecturer in New Testament studies and practical theology at the Odesa Theological Seminary. Pastor of Regeneration Church in Odesa.

Stanislav Stepanchenko (Lviv, Ukraine). Head of the department of biblical and theological studies at the Ukrainian Baptist Theological Seminary, lecturer in biblical disciplines.

Yevgeny Ustinovich. Senior research fellow at the Eastern European Institute of Theology. External instructor in New Testament at Evangelical Theological Faculty, Leuven, Belgium. Author of *Overcoming the World: Glory and Shame in the Gospel of John* (Langham Global Library, 2024).

Langham Literature and its imprints are a ministry of Langham Partnership.

Langham Partnership is a global fellowship working in pursuit of the vision God entrusted to its founder John Stott –

> *to facilitate the growth of the church in maturity and Christ-likeness through raising the standards of biblical preaching and teaching.*

Our vision is to see churches in the Majority World equipped for mission and growing to maturity in Christ through the ministry of pastors and leaders who believe, teach and live by the word of God.

Our mission is to strengthen the ministry of the word of God through:
- nurturing national movements for biblical preaching
- fostering the creation and distribution of evangelical literature
- enhancing evangelical theological education

especially in countries where churches are under-resourced.

Our ministry

Langham Preaching partners with national leaders to nurture indigenous biblical preaching movements for pastors and lay preachers all around the world. With the support of a team of trainers from many countries, a multi-level programme of seminars provides practical training, and is followed by a programme for training local facilitators. Local preachers' groups and national and regional networks ensure continuity and ongoing development, seeking to build vigorous movements committed to Bible exposition.

Langham Literature provides Majority World preachers, scholars and seminary libraries with evangelical books and electronic resources through publishing and distribution, grants and discounts. The programme also fosters the creation of indigenous evangelical books in many languages, through writer's grants, strengthening local evangelical publishing houses, and investment in major regional literature projects, such as one volume Bible commentaries like *The Africa Bible Commentary* and *The South Asia Bible Commentary*.

Langham Scholars provides financial support for evangelical doctoral students from the Majority World so that, when they return home, they may train pastors and other Christian leaders with sound, biblical and theological teaching. This programme equips those who equip others. Langham Scholars also works in partnership with Majority World seminaries in strengthening evangelical theological education. A growing number of Langham Scholars study in high quality doctoral programmes in the Majority World itself. As well as teaching the next generation of pastors, graduated Langham Scholars exercise significant influence through their writing and leadership.

To learn more about Langham Partnership and the work we do visit **langham.org**

www.ingramcontent.com/pod-product-compliance
Lightning Source LLC
Chambersburg PA
CBHW071739150426
43191CB00010B/1628